STAFFORDSHIRE LIBRARY AND INFORMATION SERVICES
Please return or renew by the last date shown

BURT		
11. 08.		
27. 01. 09.		
08. 10 09		
15/ 10 / 09		
5 NOV 09		
26 NOV 09		

If not required by other readers, this item may may be renewed
in person, by post or telephone, online or by email.
To renew, either the book or ticket are required

24 HOUR RENEWAL LINE 0845 33 00 740

ROY OF THE ROVERS

ROY OF THE ROVERS

THE UNAUTHORISED BIOGRAPHY

Mick Collins

Aurum

First published in 2008 by Aurum Press Limited
7 Greenland Street, London NW1 0ND
www.aurumpress.co.uk

A catalogue record for this book is available from the British Library.

ISBN 978 1 84513 361 0

1 3 5 7 9 10 8 6 4 2

2008 2010 2012 2011 2009

Typeset in Bembo by SX Composing DTP, Essex
Printed and bound in Great Britain by MPG Books, Bodmin, Cornwall

Contents

For Mum and Dad
With love and thanks

ACKNOWLEDGEMENTS

There are so many people, in so many different guises, who helped along the way that attempting to name them all is an almost impossible task. To those then who are mentioned here heartfelt thanks; to those who are not, through my own foolish oversight, identical thanks, alongside apologies for my own, useless memory.

Professionally, thanks to Barrie Tomlinson, Ian Vosper, Ray Harrison, the opinions and drawings of David Sque, the storylines of Tom Tully, the late, great Fred Baker and a host of others, as well as to Mark Towers for the wonderful www.royoftherovers.com. To Brendan Gallagher, for the fantastic *Sporting Supermen*, which everyone should own, and in particular to Peter Acton and Colin Jarman, for the hugely informative *Roy of the Rovers – The Playing Years*. Thanks also to Titan books, for reproducing some of Roy's more extraordinary adventures and also to lambiek.net, which told me more about comic artists than I ever knew there was to know.

Thank you also to Paul Linden, Steve Prettle, Tony Russell, John Gardner, Andrew Thompson, Stephen Davidson and Paul Jones for cheerfully delving into their memories and finding the time to return to childhood.

Thanks to Chris Powell, for being a good friend, a fine left back, a dignitary and now a writer of forewords. The best selection Sven ever made.

At Aurum, thanks to all for always doing things properly and with pride, and especially to Graham Coster and Natasha Martin, for being both good company and good editors. It makes their brandishing of the red pen much easier to take . . .

Elsewhere, to the respective sports desks of the *Mail on Sunday* and BBC London, and in particular Nigel Bidmead, Mark Church, Nick Godwin, Mike Lawrence, Sara Orchard, Phil Parry, Andy Rowley, Cara Sloman, Pete Stevens, Sarah Taylor and Malcolm

Vallerius, as well as all the others who offered encouragement and expressed interest. It was much appreciated.

To the friends, who kept me on my feet, and from time to time drank me off them: Charlie, Smudger, Ali, Mac, Biffa, Doc and the rest of the Far Canal. Also, Charlie, Phil, Sam, Jo, Jeanette, JVL, Wellsy, Rick and all the rest, thanks a lot.

To my family: Mum and Dad, Dan and Nets, Aidan and Ava, Mary, Joe and Pat – thanks.

But, above all, to Cas, Honor and Amy, who mean the world, and in their different ways, keep the wheels on the wagon – thank you. Oh, and not forgetting Dora the dog, who sat on my feet as I typed away. It wasn't just for the promise of a Bonio, was it?

FOREWORD

Regardless of the money that surrounds the modern game, football has always really been about two far more important things — dreams and glory. At the top end of the game, players earn huge salaries; elsewhere, down the league, much less so. But they are all united by the dream of doing something they love, and the glory that, on special days, can accompany it. Whether you play in front of thousands of fans, or in the local park, these are the two things that first make you start kicking a ball about.

Roy Race was the first football hero many of us ever had. He was always scoring the crucial goal, always bringing our dreams to life, and all of us imagined, no matter how briefly, achieving just a little of what he did.

Roy's adventures were epic stuff, week in and week out, and even today, when other descriptions fail us, if you tell someone that something was a real Roy of the Rovers moment, everyone knows exactly what you mean. This year, the PFA gave its Player of the Year award to Cristiano Ronaldo, and I'm sure he's had the phrase used about him more than once.

I made my debut on Christmas Eve 1987, and more than twenty years and 650 games later, I've still got to hang in there for as long again to match Roy's career. I'll try, but I think I might just come up short . . . Whichever team I represented, though, from Southend to Charlton to England, it was always the simple love of playing the game that made it special. Roy Race would have understood that, although he might, I admit, have scored just a few more goals along the way!

While everyone else was studying the statistics and checking the facts and figures, Mick Collins was reading comics — and very happy he seemed, too. There might have been doubters, but it wasn't a bad decision because, as I say, ultimately it's all about dreams and glory. While he might have been just a comic character to some, to those who understand those ideas, Roy of the Rovers will always hold a special place in our memories.

Chris Powell
Chairman of the Professional Footballers' Association

CHAPTER ONE

NO PLAYER IS
BIGGER THAN THE GAME

'I remember sitting there for a week, years ago, wondering how the hero was going to escape – it felt like it lasted for ever. When I finally got my hands on the next edition, it opened with the words "And with a mighty leap, he was free . . ." What a swizz! That's the thing about comics, though. Before you get a chance to feel let down, you've got involved in the next adventure.'

Pat Collins, Snr. 1981 (ish)

On 11 September 1954, with only two minutes of a goal-less local cup-tie remaining, a young, blond striker picked up the ball from midfield and made his way downfield. It was the start of, by some distance, the longest surging, swerving run in the history of football.

As he made his way towards goal, the crowd began to chat. They would have buzzed, but there weren't enough of them. In years to come they'd buzz, as well as roar, cheer, scream and surge, but for now they chatted, and as the years passed it became a trademark. Whatever else they were doing, crowds would always chat when he was playing football, and their conversations would be noted down for all of history in little speech bubbles, hanging above the stands and terraces.

There were no terraces or stands yet, though, and not much of a crowd – about fifteen according to the pictures, behind a rope, stretched around the perimeter of the pitch, presumably to stop the non-existent crowd spilling on to the playing surface. It seemed a slightly unnecessary crowd management precaution, given the attendance. These were, after all, the early days, and there was plenty of time yet to become a legend.

As for the length of the run, strictly speaking, that really depends on your perspective. If you're a reporter, it ended 40 yards later, as the young striker drove the ball beyond a despairing goalkeeper, and won the game at the death. If, however, you're inclined to step back and search for the wider view, the run lasted more than forty years. Or, to be precise, forty-four years, ten league titles, two European Cups, eight Cup Winners' Cups and nine FA Cups, alongside a smattering of additional silverware.

It was an extraordinary career, and every last minute of it was lovingly recorded for the benefit of any young comic buyer. The very first few minutes were captured more precisely than most, as the scene was set by the young Roy Race – brown leather boots over his ankles, yellow and red striped socks and shirt and navy blue shorts – seizing on the ball on the halfway line. With a flick of the right boot the ball, which, given the era, weighed the same as a modern family hatchback, was diverted away from the opposition, and headed towards goal, swiftly followed by Roy.

As the 1950s factory chimney behind the goal belched out 1950s smoke into the late afternoon, Roy bore down on the penalty area. By the time he arrived, he was still in acres of space, and a journey that had started down the right flank had brought him to the extreme left-hand edge of the area.

With the random nature of his approach run, the keeper, who had been twisting his head left and right like a tennis fan, trying to keep track of Roy, never had a chance. He opted to narrow the angle, but failed to distract his opponent, and eventually dived late and helplessly as the ball was swept home beyond him. Despite a modicum of cheering, the crowd, in keeping with their role, were keen to discuss the importance of the goal. Traditionally, this meant cramming vast amounts of conversation into improbable periods of time, and was to become an affectionately thought-of trademark of the story.

'That lad Race is too good for this kind of football. I'm going to have a word with him,' reflected one spectator, in between the ball crossing the line, and actually reaching the back of the net.

If you grew up as a young boy in Britain during the course of the last four decades, this sporting genius was probably, at some stage, delivered through your door, in printed form. For one particular trilby-wearing figure, water-coloured on to the sidelines of that September day, it was a talent too bright to miss.

The man beneath the hat was Alf Leeds, a talent scout for Melchester Rovers, pipe-smoking, moustachioed, and even amidst the excitement on the touchline, too experienced in the ways of the game to get carried away by the delight of those around him.

'He's got talent, but he'll have to work hard and take knocks to become a pro. Would he stick it?'

Alf pulled Roy aside at the end of the game; his occupation as a football scout was cunningly disguised by that hat, mac and smouldering pipe, along with the devilishly manicured moustache. If a man fitting his appearance had arrived at a schoolboy game these days, and asked for a word with the blond-haired striker before he got into the shower, the police would be called within minutes and a child protection investigation launched. Thankfully for the next forty years' worth of comic adventures, these were more innocent times, and the conversation continued, as the macintoshed stranger smoked his pipe amid a dressing room full of semi-clothed adolescents.

'You mean, you're giving me a chance to play for the Rovers?' asked Roy, as quick on the uptake as ever, after Alf had just explained to him that he was giving him a chance to play for the Rovers.

'That's right, lad,' he confirmed, doubtless hoping that the jewel he had just unearthed was quicker when it came to comprehending on-pitch situations. 'If you're interested, come and see me at the stadium at 11 o'clock on Monday.'

Turning on his heel, the trilbied silhouette of Alf was off. Sporting fiction has produced some important walk-on parts in its time, but it would be asking a lot to come up with one more crucial than the talent scout who discovered Roy Race. Alf Leeds is as important a figure in the Roy of the Rovers story as any other, and yet he was written out before the end of the very first episode. It's a funny old game, comic book football.

Needless to say, Roy made it safely to Melchester Stadium on that Monday morning, which, as obvious as it sounds, was not always the case. In years to come the simple matter of turning up to work opened up possibilities of kidnaps, crashes (helicopter and car) and a hundred other dramas, but for the time being, it was an incident-free trip. He barrelled in, almost skipping through reception with delight, before being called to attention by one of the commissionaires – Melchester, like Arsenal, was the sort of club that realised the importance of an epaulette when it came to matters of pomp.

Roy explained that Mr Leeds had asked him to come and see him, and the burly figure on the door placed a kindly hand on his shoulder, and from beneath a standard issue moustache, explained a little about the footballing hierarchy.

'Juniors aren't allowed to use this entrance, lad. Come with me – I'll put you right. So, you're another of 'em who wants to be a Rover? A lot try, but not many last the pace. If you can stick it, it's a grand life . . .'

The rest, as they say, is history.

Over the next forty years, the young striker would remain much as he had been on that September afternoon – successful, skilful and, uniquely, youthful. Alf may have expressed reservations about many players throughout the course of his talent-spotting career, but this one would never offer him further cause for doubt. This one was different. This one was Roy Race.

From his earliest days, the way in which he spoke to the commissionaire and the respect he showed to Alf Leeds, Roy always had a regard for authority, and it was clear that we were being shown a character who was 'well brought up'. We shouldn't get too carried away with that idea, though, because while he looks like a very polite and deferential footballer by modern standards, by those of the time he was perfectly normal.

When Roy Race first came to the attention of Melchester Rovers, football was (at the risk of sounding old and po-faced) a more civilised world. Players were just another part of the community, albeit an occasionally celebrated part. They didn't live in gated enclaves and escape in their Baby Bentley just to dive behind the purple rope of the VIP section of a nightclub. They didn't, in essence, think they were any better as people than those who paid to come and watch them – they were just better footballers.

Players lived in the communities around the clubs they played for, got the bus to training and were still, when Roy first appeared, seven years away from seeing the minimum wage introduced. The character of Roy Race was polite and well-mannered, but we shouldn't let our modern preconceptions of footballers lead us into the trap of believing that this was done to make him stand out. By the standards of the time, it was more likely to help him to fit in, as were so many aspects of his character. Whether it was solely the intention or not, from the moment Roy was first put on to the page, it was hard to find a potential source of attraction to the character that the writers hadn't covered – every box was ticked.

A year after Roy burst on to the scene in British comics, Elvis Presley first appeared on American television. Presley caused a huge storm – younger people loved him, older people thought the end of the world was arriving and camera operators stayed pointing firmly above his waist, for fear of what would happen to the world's young women should the lens sink lower. It summed up the difficulties of the era; too restrained, and a new hero was just like the generation before and so destined to be ignored, but too exciting, and he would have to be censored for the good of the wider community and its morals. In Roy, a character had been created who managed to create cartooned excitement, yet balanced that with an unswerving adherence to a very old-fashioned way of conducting himself. In marketing terms, he was a triumph even before he reached his peak on the pitch.

If he was a great acquisition for Melchester Rovers, he was an even better one for IPC magazines. *Roy of the Rovers* ran as a weekly comic, from that debut in September 1954, until 1993 and thereafter appeared in a variety of formats, having scaled heights to which no other fictional footballer ever came close. At the peak of the comic's success, it sold in the region of 450,000 copies each week, and helped its hero become a household name. That first surging run out of midfield featured in the pages of *Tiger*, but after an apprenticeship of merely twenty-two years and two weeks, Roy was deemed ready to be promoted to a title of his own.

Ever since, the name of Roy of the Rovers has entered the lexicon, as an invaluable descriptive tool for journalists stuck for a way to describe a moment of unexpected footballing drama, genius or excitement. When in doubt as to the size of a sporting happening, describing it as a 'Roy of the Rovers moment' leaves no one in any doubt as to the scale of the event being covered.

In its first edition as a standalone title, there was a letter from the

Duke of Edinburgh, wishing Roy good luck, while in its early days in *Tiger*, its star columnist was Sir Bobby Charlton, who, to football fans, is even more royal than the Duke. Gary Lineker was a columnist for a number of years, as Roy continued his habit of only aligning himself with the very best in the business.

Over the course of the torrent of goals he scored and the myriad dramas he endured, Roy Race entered British comic royalty, alongside *The Beano*, *The Dandy*, *Eagle*, *Tiger* and perhaps a handful of others. Of the dozens of football-based comic strips that have been aimed at Britain's youth, he rose to the top of the pile, and has never seriously been threatened.

Part of the considerable charm of the character of Roy is that we so readily and happily forget that he was just that – a character. Long before the ball hit the back of the net, his adventures were scripted, his progress planned and his goals thumbnail sketched. And that illusion, without apology or further explanation, is one that deserves to continue. The point of Roy was the glory, not the process by which it reached the page. In due course, that process will be considered with those who partook in it, but for the time being, cynicism and realism, just as they were when many thousands of other readers first lived through Roy's adventures, should be suspended. He was, as far as we, the readers, were concerned, a real person.

It hardly gives too much away, even at this early stage, to run through a brief summary of quite how Roy was to set about dispelling Alf Leeds's doubts. His four decades at the very summit of the beautiful game brought him trophies and adventures in equally prodigious amounts. By the time his playing career came to a close, he was turning 50, and still as square of jaw as he had been when his first goal was captured in pen, ink and paint.

He had scored and triumphed, been kicked and kidnapped, married and widowed and entered the lexicon. Along the way, Roy, his team-mates and escapades, acted as the caricatured backdrop to millions of adolescent (and many supposedly more mature) lives. No matter how flawed your real life side proved to be, Roy of the Rovers provided equalisers and late winners galore, routinely snatched victory from the jaws of defeat and populated a world bursting at the seams with goals and glory. Through all of this, he maintained a self-effacing and highly moral view on the game, mixing a Corinthian outlook with a predator's instinct.

'No player,' he said, seemingly on a weekly basis, 'is bigger than the game.'

He was wrong. If you followed the game in the late 1970s, when I first did, and when Roy was given his own comic, football was grim. Unless you supported a tiny, select few clubs, it meant Saturday afternoons in a huge, dilapidated ground, occupied by about a tenth of the number of fans who had once packed in. It meant a bumpy pitch and woeful facilities, and a communal toilet block that posed a considerable biological threat. The moments of glory were few and relative, and the disappointments many and varied. For all but a fortunate few fans, only the thickest of rose-tinted lenses could obscure the unremitting greyness of the whole experience.

And this reality had to compete with the extraordinary events that had arrived through the letterbox that morning, in the form of *Roy of the Rovers*. Between front and back cover, chances were missed in order only that the winning goal, as it always did, arrived even later and laden with more drama. The pitch was an extended, grassy billiard table, the passing crisp and precise, and the crowd as good-hearted and encouraging as you might expect from a group of fans who never tasted boredom, let alone defeat.

Roy of the Rovers captured the attention of its readers for many different reasons, but prime among them was that it provided a respite from what was, for so many fans, particularly the younger ones, the sheer drudgery of 'real' football. When he graduated from being a comic strip within another comic – *Tiger* – and gained his own publication in 1976, the national game was not in the greatest health. There were great sides – Liverpool's assault on European trophies was about to begin – but scratching beneath the surface revealed that world of shabby grounds, in which fans were treated like cattle and entertainment was a long way down the list of priorities. He might not have been bigger than the version of the game *he* played, with its constant excitement, perfect pitches and flawless passing, but like it or not, to an eight-year-old child he was a lot bigger than the ugly reality so many people trekked along to see each Saturday afternoon.

Roy served two purposes. For the youngster who went to football and failed to fully understand what all the romance and affection for the game was supposed to be about, he filled that gap in weekly instalments. Melchester Rovers were your second team, the one you didn't have to disclose, and who never appeared on Final Score, but equally, the one that delivered the dash and flair that your 'real' side somehow failed to serve up.

For the slightly older reader, Roy's launch was a chance to see an expanded version of his adventures, set free from the shackles of a two-page spread in *Tiger*. There are those of a curmudgeonly outlook who will dispute this, of course, arguing that grown-ups never really read the magazine. It is an argument that fails on two fronts. First, at its peak, Roy sold almost half a million comics every week, and they weren't all to children. Second, his name was well-enough known to be used in newspaper reports written for many millions of adults, in order to illustrate a point. They weren't all relying on memories of years gone by.

Roy of the Rovers was a footballing phenomenon, both in terms of the achievements of the character, and the achievements of the comic that carried the tales of his glories. It took him more than twenty years from when that first, glorious outing on a school football pitch was conveyed to the readers of *Tiger*, to secure his own comic, but when he did, it was with typical panache.

If you think back to the comic book heroes of the past, they might have enjoyed top billing, but they rarely lent their name to the title itself. Dan Dare zipped around the galaxy, battling the Mekon, in *Eagle*, while Alf Tupper and co relied on the covers of *Tiger* to offer them a home. Numerous war heroes were pen and inked to triumph in the pages of *Victor*, while the combined might of Dennis the Menace and Gnasher still couldn't stop *The Beano* being called, well, *The Beano*, rather than anything more self-referencing.

Roy Race, though, was different. When he finally finished that surging, zig-zagging run forwards, and when the poor, confused opposition goalkeeper was finally put out of his misery and the ball buried somewhere behind him, he set about forging a professional career to envy.

Alf Leeds, as ever, had done his scouting work well, and

Melchester Rovers wasted no time in acquiring what would become football's most prestigious signature. From that first scrawl of the pen, a union was formed which went on to become part of the language. Always the inclusive sort, he never really wanted top billing over his team-mates, and to that end, it was never going to be Roy *and* the Rovers, because from the outset he was Roy *of* the Rovers.

His story was told in *Tiger* from 1954 through to 1976, when he was set free to fill the pages of his own title. Once he arrived, comics would never be the same again, and within a couple of decades, thanks to the vast influx of television money, neither would football. The modern era has brought about many different ways of watching the game, from actually going to the ground, using both satellite and terrestrial television, or now, even the Internet.

Obviously, for the committed, nothing will ever compare to actually going to the ground and soaking in the atmosphere, but as ticket prices rise, so the numbers of the committed, or at least the variety of the committed, diminishes. For the price of a ticket to watch one game of Premiership football, you can get a satellite television company to beam a month of it into your front room, where you can watch it on widescreen, flat-screen, split-screen, high definition, with or without commentators, deluged by statistics and blinded by luminous arrows endeavouring to explain all manner of tactical nuances.

In addition to this, you can also watch games on your iPod, on portable televisions the size of a cigarette packet, and even on a mobile phone. And yet, for all of this technology, the perfect way of watching football has remained unchanged for almost half a century. Mankind has yet to discover a more enjoyable way of studying a football season than through the weekly turning of comic book pages. For all the high definition, highly marketed action the television companies churn out, they cannot, regardless of how much they might like us to believe otherwise, guarantee excitement.

The most lavishly promoted game, with two sides of talented millionaires hurling themselves through ninety minutes of prime-time action, can still turn out to be as dull as ditchwater. Sometimes the product, as they call football now, just doesn't stand up to scrutiny. Unless, of course, the game's in a comic, because then the odds are stacked rather more firmly in favour of the spectator.

For the small sacrifice of being utterly fictitious, football becomes utterly compelling. Late chances never fail to materialise, hopeful long-range shots always find the top corner, and when someone stands on the pitch and wonders to themselves 'this can't get any worse, can it?' it's time to buy a crash helmet, because that's exactly what's about to happen.

In real life, football will, given time, find a way to break your heart. In comics, the opposite is true, as the game always leaves you uplifted and enthralled. Increasingly, in the world of real football, the powers that be find new ways to test your determination to keep turning up. Despite the supposed advances of the last couple of decades, they remain the sporting version of strip joints. They are, after all, one of the few places, outside of some of the seedier side streets of Central London, where you can be placed in quite so much discomfort for an hour and a half, while at the same time being charged quite so much money for something which never turns out to be quite as exciting or fulfilling as you'd hoped it was going to be.

Fiction has other, additional, benefits over reality, however. There is a school of thought that suggests you should never meet your heroes. Anti-climax and disappointment lie in store for anyone unfortunate enough to attempt such a rendezvous – no good, they maintain, can ever come from shaking the hand of an idol.

There is, of course, a simple solution to this, which eradicates all risk at source. Simply make as your hero a man who existed only through the inventiveness of an author and the dexterity and skill of an artist. Because there was no Roy Race to meet, nobody ever found themselves clutching an unsigned autograph book staring through teary eyes as a figure who was 'too busy right now' strode off into the distance. He never got fat, lost his hair, wore bad jumpers or appeared on *A Question of Sport*, hamming along with his team captain's false laughter. He never even played pro-celebrity golf.

Being fictional has its benefits, not the least of which is that the constraints and ravages of age apply themselves with less rigour than in real life. Once he'd stopped playing, Roy always looked after himself – he refused to become a fat ex-footballer. He was Roy Race. He had an aura to protect; a water-coloured aura, granted, but an aura nonetheless.

Every goal Roy Race scored, every team talk he gave and every piece of glory he earned, was down to the imagination, dexterity and desires of a team of writers, illustrators and editors. Because of the way in which his triumphs were arrived at, satisfaction was virtually guaranteed. Blond-haired, granite-jawed, muscular and tough, with a career stretching over four decades, Roy was like a fictitious, footballing version of Martina Navratilova, and just as successful.

His modesty and his seemingly overly-developed desire to defer to people (his tempers were rare, and the provocation which launched them was meticulously detailed) might have left him looking slightly wet, were it not for the way in which he was presented to the world.

As befitted a lead story, Roy of the Rovers occupied a coloured, double-paged berth. It was clean and precise. Mud on the knees showed evidence of an all too clear brown paintbrush being applied once Roy had already been drawn. The mud always seemed to be purely on the knees, as well. Roy's shorts and shirt were not to be messed with and remained pristine throughout. Even when it rained, as denoted by dark grey skies and a horde of neat lines running vertically across the picture, Roy's hair seemed to stay the same, as did the hang of his shirt. Like Superman, he always emerged from his adventures pristine – getting dirty didn't really fit the image.

If a pitch was supposed to be really bad, and this only seemed to happen during occasional European away games – those sneaky foreigners never could maintain a perfect playing surface – it was shown by a similar brown paintbrushed assault on a previously flat, green, perfect expanse. It was the same with blood. Roy never bled on the pitch – never so much as scratched his knee. Not due to any lack of courage, for nobody ever leaped in amongst the flying boots as readily as Roy, but because it never seemed to have crossed anyone's mind that he might fall prey to such a human tendency.

The first time Roy ever really bled was when terrorists bombed the Melchester team bus – a move which didn't so much foretell the onset of a new level of global terrorism, not in the minds of ten-year-olds anyway, but signalled the increasing departure into a world outside football which ultimately led to both the magazine's and Roy's downfall.

Roy Race was, in short, a proper comic book hero. He hit greater heights than any other character of his type, stayed there for an improbably enormous length of time, and then, seemingly falling as quickly as he rose, disappeared from sight once more. He left his mark though, and did so through the implanting of billions of individual memories, which over the years have embedded themselves deeper and deeper into the subconsciousness of millions of former readers. They say that you never know what lurks in the back of your mind, until the correct buttons are pushed to cause it to spring back to the front, where it reappears, as vividly as the day it was first put there.

Over the course of this book, we'll relive the life of a man who was, to many of us, our very first sporting hero, and a man who, whether we realised it or not, would lurk in our memories for the rest of our lives. Nobody was bigger than the game? With all due respect to the great man, the more we remember those dramatic late winners, the Johnny Dexter tackles, the Blackie Gray runs and the Paco Diaz crosses, the more we know that just isn't true . . .

And, yes, that was a quite shameless push of some of those memory buttons, right there, right at the end of the very first chapter. Will Blackie return? Is Johnny still furious? Can Paco send over one last, teasing cross? Next week's issue, thankfully, is just a chapter away . . .

CHAPTER TWO

EARLIEST DAYS

'I had a team with my school friends, up in Hull, and we played in Melchester colours. Everyone wanted to be Roy, but I didn't have blond hair, so I had no chance.'

Phil Sandilands

So who was Roy Race? And, for that matter, who were Melchester Rovers, and where did they come from? We can ask such questions now, safe in the knowledge that we have never asked them before. As children, neither of them mattered. Roy was Roy – he didn't have to be based on anyone, and to think that he was would be to surrender a little bit of his personality to the serious, boring grown-up world from which we escaped whenever we opened the comic. Roy of the Rovers was about glory, drama and, maybe above all, escapism. Searching for hidden meanings wasn't what it was all about.

Besides, both Roy and Melchester were, from the start, deliberately kept vague as far as connections with the real world were concerned. In chapters to come, several claims to be the 'real Roy' are made, and one by one, they are all knocked down. He was, probably by design, kept as generic as possible, while retaining an image slightly distinct from anyone else football had to offer; the great players of the era from which Roy first appeared, for example, were black-haired and Brylcreemed. Football had only just left the age of Tommy Lawton and Len Shackleton, while the World Cup squad that travelled to Switzerland in 1954 just before the comic was born, featured Tom Finney and Stanley Matthews – dapper, short, dark-haired to a man. There was no obviously tall, blond-haired striker anyone could point a finger at and claim that he was the inspiration behind Roy.

Similarly, his club was equally hard to pin down. In the years running up to Roy's arrival, the league title had been won by Tottenham, Manchester United, Wolves, Arsenal and then Chelsea. The FA Cup was collected by Newcastle on three occasions, which perhaps suggests a Geordie influence, but it was also won by West Brom, Blackpool and Arsenal. The simple fact is that there was no one side at the time putting themselves forward as a credible template for Melchester Rovers.

The reigning Footballer of the Year when Roy first reached the printing presses was Don Revie, who would go on to court more controversy than possibly any other English national manager in history, but Roy picked up few, if any, identifiable traits from that direction. Similarly the league's top goalscorer, Ronnie Allen of West Brom, was an unlikely blueprint, standing at a shade over 5 feet 8 inches tall, and weighing about 11 stone. Even as a schoolboy, Roy was a bigger, burlier centre forward than Allen, regardless of the Albion striker's prodigious scoring record.

On the face of it, all the examples may look like an unsuccessful search for evidence to support a theory, but in fact, the absence of candidates simply underlines one of the reasons the character and his team lasted so long. Roy was a little bit of your side's hero, with perhaps a degree of another player you'd always admired, but your club would never sign. That was the point – Roy was whoever you wanted him to be; a blank canvas for the footballing dreams of millions of young boys. To have aligned him with one side, or to have likened him to one player, would have alienated everyone who held a different allegiance. Who you thought Roy might be depended on who you supported. It was a simple yet brilliant idea.

Similarly, Melchester were any team you wanted them to be, with scarcely an identifying trait to stop them being able to take on all manner of identities. The same can be said of any of their domestic opponents, so as not to offer any hints to their roots through comparison. Melchester never went 'up' to sides in the North, nor headed 'down' South, they could have been in the Midlands, but they might just as well have been anywhere else you care to name. There was a river running through the middle of it, complete with a ferry, drumming up images of Liverpool perhaps, but nothing that could seriously be suggested as a clue.

The Rovers' kit, for example, was unlike anything worn by real-life football teams. Who could look at its red base, super-imposed with yellow, vertical stripes, running along opposite sides of shirt and shorts, and honestly claim it was just like theirs?

Watford fans might be able to claim allegiance with the colours, but the design is different, and with all due respect, in 1954, a new comic strip football team was hardly going to base its kit on what was then such lowly fare.

Just as Roy was a blank canvas for the dreams of the reader, so his side were available for 'day-dreaming' hire. Without feeling like we were being disloyal to our 'real' sides, we adopted the Rovers, with their talismanic striker, who didn't seem quite like any other team we could think of – or at least, not enough like any other team to make us feel guilty. It was a brilliant plot device, made more so by the fact that, despite its simplicity, it worked. We screamed on Roy and his Rovers in their colourful, exciting world, without ever having to desert our local team, in their frequently dull, often slightly dreary one. No wonder we look back on them as happy days.

While we look back now, as we waited anxiously to see if the young footballer got the big break his talents seemed to deserve, in hindsight we were worrying about nothing. Every good comic story always ends on a cliffhanger, but expecting an audience to wait, genuinely concerned, to see whether Roy would take up the offer from Alf Leeds and Melchester would be stretching credibility a little far. Of course he would, and, in any event, there was an inevitability about his career choice.

His grandfather, Billy Race, had captained Melchester, thus ensuring the Race family were made aware of the traditions and history of the club. They also lived in the area, in a modest house, so the Rovers were Roy's local team. He went to Melchester Grammar School, having initially been educated elsewhere.

We know snippets of the history of both the town of Melchester and Melchester Rovers themselves, as they were dropped into various stories over the years. The town stands on the River Mel, and when the Rovers were founded, back in 1885, they played at a ground in Crib Lane. And as we start to cast our minds back, wondering what the ground looked like, it's worth remembering that the ground was never there, just as the river isn't and Crib Lane never existed.

As readers, we want to thank Jonathan Drake, who founded the club way back then, and we can imagine the heavy pitches and hefty challenges of 1905, when Billy Race captained them through the second division of the Southern League. We can almost see the celebrations as the 1907 FA Cup was captured (with apologies to Sheffield Wednesday, whose 2–1 victory over Everton in the same season, despite being real, seems far less authentic by comparison) and the glory days of the 1930s under the management of George Armstrong are those by which all future triumphs would be judged.

These details are now available to us as a result of the comic filling in the small gaps in his history, while at the same time squeezing a little bit more out of the legend of Roy, by running a strip entitled 'Roy Race's Schooldays'. Whether we needed to learn as much about the great man as we did is open to debate. The strip (comprised of little more than a string of minor details, stretched into black and white comic storylines) did, however, plainly enthuse the editorial department. Through Roy's formative adventures, a little historical flesh was added to the Race bones, with the end result that an entire childhood was created and presented.

The man responsible for first putting the character of Roy Race on to the page had the circus-ringmaster style name of Frank S. Pepper. Pepper was an established comic writer, and had already created a successful strip entitled 'Captain Condor' which ran in *Lion* magazine. Throughout a working life which travelled down all manner of avenues, Pepper also wrote comic stories under the name of Hal Wilton, in later life compiled a well-recognised and regarded dictionary of quotations, and presumably did it all in order to escape the boredom of his original source of employment as an experimental railway draughtsman, based in Derby. Few people can have offered so minimal a clue as to their future job prospects than Pepper did when he first sat down to design dull, run of the mill parts for steam engines. He did not, as it transpired, stay with Roy for long, but his input was no less crucial for its brief nature.

When *Tiger* was launched, it was intended to run alongside *Lion*, and compete with *Eagle*. *Tiger* was, at the time, published by Amalgamated Press, and represented an attempt to enter into a circulation battle with *Eagle*, which was published by Hulton. The then managing editor of *Tiger* was Reg Eves, and his brief to Pepper was to produce a footballing hero for his new comic, who was dramatic and exciting, yet realistic.

Comics today are more sophisticated than the versions that appeared in the 1950s, which were, in turn, different from their predecessors. When comics first appeared in Britain, they were known as 'penny dreadfuls' and despite the occasional 'strip' as we recognise it today, were largely intended to amuse the working classes, for whom the cost, and the education with which to read them, made books an unattractive prospect. It was a huge market – Alfred Harmsworth, the owner of Amalgamated Press, launched two comics in the 1890s, *Illustrated Chips* and *Comic Cuts*, and watched them grow to such heights he was eventually able to launch both the *Daily Mail* and the *Daily Mirror* with the profits he garnered from them.

As the standard of literacy among the working classes increased, however, the interest in comics slowly moved from adults to children, possibly as the former objected to the thought of reading such 'simplistic' fare, and also as the potential market among millions of the latter became irresistible to publishers. By the time the Second World War was imminent and Dundee-based DC Thomson brought out *The Beano* and *The Dandy*, they not only gained huge audiences throughout the bleak days of wartime, but benefited hugely from a ban on starting up new comics in order to safeguard paper stocks.

By the time hostilities concluded, the firm had such a head start over everyone else, it was the best part of a decade before anyone began to catch up. Among that chasing pack was IPC, publishers of *Tiger*, and it was a young footballer to whom they turned, in a bid to close the gap on their Scottish rivals. There were other comic book sporting heroes of the time, such as Alf Tupper, the long distance runner who thrilled the readers of *Rover* and *Victor*, regularly showing how working-class grit could overcome upper-class privilege, and Wilson, famously of *The Wizard*, whose all-round sporting prowess was unparalleled, but both of these achieved incredible feats – the enjoyment was in knowing that their achievements could never be matched. What, people mused, would be the response to a character who achieved greatness in a slightly more believable way?

It is worth taking a look at the entertainment of the time, to see where Roy and his adventures might have been expected to fit in with their prospective audience. Children's entertainment was, to say the least, limited, consisting almost entirely of comics and the occasional radio programme. If young boys weren't enjoying *The Beano* or *The Dandy*, they were probably out in the street kicking a ball about. If someone could combine those two interests – football and comics – the potential was huge. That nobody had done so before was extraordinary.

It was an interesting world into which to launch a new, distinctly British character. Elvis may still have been a year short of his career properly taking off, but people were still starting to turn across the Atlantic for their entertainment. Apart from the peculiarly British delights of *The Goon Show*, people yearned for the likes of Jack Benny, Bing Crosby, Tony Curtis and a chap called Frank Sinatra, who appeared to have great promise. In a determined bid to leave the austerity of the war years behind, people were enjoying the mystique and glamour America offered, and even when they settled for something closer to home, it was the surrealism of the Goons which guaranteed them their popularity.

For Pepper, it was an engaging challenge and he was sure that not only could he turn Reg Eves's idea into a success, but that a traditional British-style hero would still appeal to the younger generation. Schoolboys looked up to sporting idols like Billy Wright and Len Hutton, while someone like Colin Cowdrey – all Brylcreem and square-cuts – was seen as impossibly dashing. There was something reassuringly solid and trustworthy about them, and the way they unfailingly placed sportsmanship ahead of victory, yet still emerged triumphant, time after time. If a comic book hero could be presented in the right way, he could learn from their more admirable character traits.

Roy was on the front cover of that first issue of *Tiger*, which immediately made it a high profile story. There would be others, buried inside the pages, who would never achieve such prominence, but from the start this new football story seemed to be pushed forwards. Even for a veteran like Pepper it was exciting. He had long been established as a writer of boys' adventure stories, published purely in text form with no accompanying pictures, but the new era of comic strips was now taking over, and telling stories which worked alongside pictures, rather than in place of them, was the order of the day.

Coincidentally, two of his previous stories neatly combined to produce almost a perfect template for Roy of the Rovers. 'Rockfist Rogan' was a fighter pilot and boxer, and appeared in the pages of *Champion* in the years immediately post war, while football-themed 'Danny of the Dazzlers' was, in many ways, a dress rehearsal for Roy of the Rovers. Combining the drama of the first with the footballing content of the second ensured the final product.

Pepper was initially paired up with artist Joe Colquhoun (with whom he had worked previously on *Champion*) to produce the new storyline, but this time it was not destined to be a long-term partnership. Pepper was very much in demand, and evidently took on more work than he had time to deal with when he agreed to script Roy of the Rovers. That suspicion was confirmed when he left the strip after just four episodes, having been forced to prioritise by the sheer weight of work; he concluded that there wasn't space in his diary for this new title. In the world of comics, Frank S. Pepper could be viewed in the same way as Pete Best, who gave up his drums to a bloke called Ringo Starr, when it became clear that their new group would never go on to achieve anything of note.

In an intriguing move, Colquhoun took over the writing duties himself, but had to be helped by the *Tiger* staff on anything pertaining to football (which must have been something of a hindrance) due to his almost total lack of knowledge about the game. As he freely admitted, he knew 'damn all about soccer', but didn't see why, assisted by a good team around him, that should keep him from producing an entertaining strip, and so it proved.

Colquhoun certainly never allowed his lack of passion for the subject to hold him back, and wrote and drew Roy for five years, until 1959 (then again from 1965–67) all under the name of Stewart Colwyn.

It all added up to a slightly inauspicious arrival for a hero. His natural 'father' surrendered him after only four episodes, and his adoptive one feigned interest, but was ultimately happy to admit that he couldn't care less for the game Roy loved so much.

What Roy did before he moved to Melchester, nor why his family, who had strong ties with the area, ever left in the first place, we have never known. In fairness to the various authors of the strip, this is hardly a criticism. Over the years, various storylines have allowed vast chunks of Roy's history to be drip fed to the reader, and the task of filling in details has frequently been undertaken with some degree of relish. Whether he was a primary school footballing genius however, or at what age he first sat in his cot and demanded a ball, is something we'll never know.

Regardless of how he got there, we do know for sure that by the age of about 14, Roy Race was a pupil at Melchester Grammar School, even if an early school report marks him down as a student of mixed ability. Under the tutelage of his form teacher, Mr O'Shaughnessy, Roy was averagely talented in mathematics, quite promising in English Language, where he 'demonstrated the ability to eloquently transcribe his thoughts into poetry', but destined never to be a hit in the laboratory, displaying as he did a 'lack of interest in all things scientific'.

He was already, predictably, a valued member of the school football team, but had been warned by his form teacher 'not to let the sporting side of his nature exclude the more important aspects of his study'. He did, it is pleasing to read, already show 'leadership qualities'.

And therein lies one of the most fascinating parts of the whole character of Roy Race, the way in which we stop remembering him as a 'character' and start to think of him as a person. Reading through school reports, detailing the opinions of a schoolmaster who never existed, from a school which never existed, talking about a pupil who never existed, it is easier to go along with the belief that everything is perfectly real. Comics are built, after all, on the suspension of reality, and this is a perfect example. It's almost as if the person who wrote the 'report' opted to believe the story themselves, filling in the blanks in the past of a real person.

It is simple to look back on Roy's adventures and adopt an adult opinion of them; simple, but also completely self-defeating. Nobody who ever sat down to write a story in the comic ever tried to aim it at anyone other than the schoolboy reader, and therein rests its charm. Roy of the Rovers was refreshingly free of double meanings and smart arse moments. It was pitched exclusively at children, never trying to capture anyone older along the way with a subtext or a string of alternative interpretations. If we want to appreciate it to the same extent as we once did, we need to discard cynicism and recapture the childish sense of excitement Roy's adventures once caused us.

What we do know about the young Roy Race, partly as a result of these 'flashback' features, and partly due to the strips of the day (which, in any event, began when he was but a schoolboy), is that his desperately heightened sense of fair play was in evidence from our first encounter with him. While he was becoming known for playing football outstandingly well, he was also known for an exemplary attitude to the game and its rules.

Almost every team-mate he ever played with, even a few who got off to a bit of a false start (which was never Roy's fault, and normally born out of a misunderstanding), ended up respecting and looking up to him. Somehow, though, there was always one who refused to join in with the dressing room camaraderie and his schooldays were no exception. Where Vic Guthrie and others would tread later in his career, Roy's first nemesis was a fellow pupil called Bert Beston.

Bert thought that he was a better player than Roy and, indeed, the best player in the whole school. There was an obvious way of proving this – just watching them as players and reaching an opinion – but that would have been straightforward, and as such could never be countenanced. We might have been children, and we might have had a pretty good idea what the conclusion was going to be, but we wanted to reach it with a little bit of drama along the way. Underpinning all of this, of course, was the fact that, if you were opposed to Roy Race, you were by default up to no good and so were destined to fail. It really was as black and white as that, and Bert, by definition, was up to no good.

Fittingly for a comic book character, Bert set about trying to earn the mantle of Melchester Grammar's finest player through old-fashioned comic book antics. As soon as Roy claimed a place in the under-15 side, Bert attempted to sabotage matters by directing him to the wrong ground, setting up various diversions in a bid to have him miss the game altogether. It was, to be fair to Bert, a very sophisticated scheme, involving altering the directions given to Roy's father, but in the event all he achieved was to inadvertently forge one of comics' great friendships: Roy found himself in this hopeless position alongside a young midfield player by the name of Blackie Gray.

Blackie earned his nickname, with a disconcerting lack of originality, because of his shock of black hair, and remained a friend and ally of Roy's throughout his career, standing alongside him no matter what. Unfortunately, on that particular day, he was standing beside him as they headed off in the wrong direction, victims of the scheming Bert's plan, ensuring they arrived well after the kick off with the school already trailing 3-0. Aware that if he was to be considered the best player in the school he needed first to make sure he turned up for matches on time, Roy had to make amends.

Knocking in his first just before the break to ensure Melchester Grammar headed in 3-1 down at half-time, Roy twice hit the post before narrowing the margin further with a low, left-footed drive, causing consternation in the opposition defence. Their captain, showing a shrewd tactical sense, did his best to stop Roy, largely, it seems, by standing hands on hips in midfield, and calling to his back four: 'Watch that chap. Don't let him get the ball . . .'

Unfortunately, despite such Churchillian urgings, his defence were not equal to the task. Shortly afterwards, a pass threaded its way through to the lethal latecomer, described as being 'as elusive as an eel', and another left-footed rocket levelled matters.

With complete redemption just a fourth goal away, Roy, as the captions informed us, confused the defence by dropping into his own half. Lured into his plan, the opposition surrendered possession, as the panic he sent around their ranks erupted into dissent. 'Get the ball away from him!' demanded the captain, who was proving better at giving orders than making tackles.

'It's all very well for you to shout! Try it yourself,' yelled his centre half in reply, and in that moment, their fate was sealed.

Roy's fourth goal – an early example of Racey's Rocket – guaranteed Melchester a victory against all the odds. The side, with the exception of Bert Beston, were thrilled, and the episode closed with Roy's father's car driving away from the game, filled with team-mates predicting that the side would 'win plenty more with Roy playing for us'.

While, admittedly, that particular strip was a 'look back' written once Roy had already enjoyed success, it neatly encapsulates all the essential elements of a good Roy of the Rovers story. Before the recovery commences, success must seem virtually impossible, with the odds stacked absurdly against Roy. The comeback should be achieved with the minimum of personal exuberance, and the eventual triumph greeted with modesty and dignity. And obviously, if it's possible to catch a look at the face of the scheming individual who saw their plan crumble to dust, so much the better.

It also illustrates, long before we encounter the chronological issues surrounding Roy's never-ending career, the difficulties of trying to link Roy's world with the real-life outside version. Roy was an established success when, in 1970, the schoolboy strips were run, detailing what he was up to in 1952, and a lot had changed in the intervening period. Perry Como topped the charts when Bert Beston first got up to no good, and by the time the world had seen how events panned out, Jimi Hendrix was at number one. For a comic book footballer, he was managing to hang in there and span some huge cultural changes.

The nefarious plans of Bert Beston having been put to rights, and Alf Leeds having identified his target, Roy began life on the lowest rung of the Rovers' ladder. As luck would have it, his old school pal Blackie had also caught Alf's eye, and the duo soon found themselves playing in the Melchester 'A' team together. It was there, in December 1954, that Roy latched on to another through ball from Blackie, clipped a right-footed shot beyond another keeper, and claimed his first goal in Melchester colours. If they'd known what he would achieve in the future, they would have put down a plaque, there and then. From schoolboy to reserve team goalscorer in just two months – could he not pace himself a little better, for fear the story could run out of steam too soon? Thankfully, yes.

It was another eight months, at the start of the following season in August 1955, before the duo got to make their first-team debuts, against Elbury Wanderers. It is difficult to imagine that anyone could have found these scenes novel, but football stories had rarely gone into this sort of depth before, and Britain was still used to sport being conveyed in a certain way – commercial television itself wouldn't be born for another month. The crowd, as they would for the next forty years, chatted animatedly through the game, providing a constant commentary. This was a feature the artist and writers of the time enjoyed so much, they extended it to scenes from outside the ground before the kick off, where the two sets of supporters mingled.

'Good luck, Rovers!' enthused an Elbury fan, with sarcasm that ill-befitted a man only just clinging on to his dignity by wearing a black and white chequered bowler hat, above a similarly coloured scarf and rosette. To avoid doubt as to his allegiance, the Melchester fan he addresses is also wearing a scarf and rosette, this time red and yellow, having been pinned on to his lapel by the owner of a stall labelled 'Get your Favours'. 'Your lads'll need it to stop our inside right! Hedlow's the hottest shot in footer-boots!'

It was ignored with knowing looks between two other men, who assured him that, having seen them play for the reserves last year 'Roy and Blackie make a fine partnership'. Admittedly, the air of optimism is slightly punctured by a mournful chap nearby, equipped with a gravedigger's face and a deep-set frown, quick to remind everyone: 'That was with the reserves. Playing with the first team won't be so easy . . .' But then, there always is a killjoy in every football crowd, desperate to prove that the Bovril is half empty, not half full.

This particular scene also serves as a reminder of how much extra information can be conveyed by accompanying the words with pictures. In Pepper's early days, yard after yard of text was required to describe the action to a young audience, and in all likelihood, no matter how cleverly it was written, much of the impact disappeared in the process. In one panel alone, from this 1955 strip, five men in the crowd sport four rosettes, four scarves, one cap and one ridiculous top hat between them, all in team colours. Through Colquhoun's pictures, the image is conveyed in a second, causing the story to inform while moving along, rather than stopping every time description was needed. It is easy to see why comics were increasing in popularity at such a rate.

As it transpired, both the optimist and pessimist had reason to celebrate at various points through the game, as Melchester took the lead when Roy latched on to a pass from Blackie and thundered home a drive from the edge of the area for a goal on his debut. They then went two up, before Charlie King, their right winger, collapsed under a challenge, and had to go off. 'I-I'm sorry Melchester,' stuttered the Elbury left back, shocked to the point of a stammer by a footballing injury. 'It was a complete accident!'

'Fair enough, couldn't be helped,' replied skipper Andy McDonald, while poor Charlie just writhed on the ground in agony, doubtless thinking less charitable thoughts. Reduced to ten men, with substitutes still years away, Elbury's Arty Hedlow set about proving why he was the 'hottest shot in footer-boots'.

There was no disputing his first, a neat header, while his second, the equaliser, was a considered finish after a jinking run, but his third possibly offered a hint of what Arty was all about, as the referee failed to spot a sly handball. He seemed to have secured the points for Elbury, but Blackie had other ideas and a neat pass to Roy, followed by a crashing shot, saw our hero emerge with two goals on his debut and Melchester stealing a draw.

It was hard not to wonder why we had been shown the sneaky side of Arty – such details were never left in superfluously, and almost always meant that a plot twist of some kind was around the corner. By the time he wandered over to Roy as they left the field, we knew he was up to no good.

'Not a bad show, kid! But you're not quite up to this class of soccer yet. I guess you and Gray will be back in the reserves next week. Tough luck!'

Roy, being Roy, resisted the temptation to do anything more dramatic than grimace and shake his head, and the arrival of the following week's papers confirmed his wisdom. Ben Galloway, a manager who was to the world of comic football what Shankly, Busby and the like were to the real game, decided Rovers needed strengthening, and for the record fee of £10,000, Arty Hedlow was their man.

And, as we soon learned, Arty's opinions weren't just saved for the opposition. At half-time in his first game, he decided to give Roy a lecture.

'You refused to listen to my advice, Roy. You hogged the ball, and then funked it whenever you came up against that heavyweight Cobdale centre half.'

Even half a century later, it's possible to count on the fingers of one hand the occasions when Roy lost his temper. Which means his explosion against Arty was even more unexpected, but an accusation of funking is one no man can ignore. Before anyone could react, Roy was shaking Arty by the throat and shaping to hit him.

'I'm not taking that from you, Hedlow! You've been moaning at me all the first half, and making sure the others didn't hear, but nobody calls me a funk! I'd like to knock your thundering block off!'

The argument was just about defused in time for the start of the second half, but only after Arty made clear how thrilled he'd be were Roy to be dropped as a result. Our hero was furious and frustrated.

'You've got the best of it now, Hedlow, but sooner or later the others'll find out just what a rotter you are.'

Roy never quite got his wish, though. He scored plenty of goals, certainly enough to make sure he would never get dropped, which must have annoyed Arty, and he set up enough goals for his striking partner to make sure he could never be accused of being greedy. Just when you felt sure Hedlow would be exposed as the rotter he plainly was, however, injury cut his career short.

It began with an absence of a few weeks, then an operation ruled him out for the rest of the season, and then, as quickly as he arrived, Arty was gone. Off to do whatever footballers who retired early did in 1956, although first would be a (surely) brief stop to manage Dunbar City, a Southern League side.

A long line of rotters had been launched, and while there might occasionally have been a gap between each new arrival, as Roy calmed down after the shabby behaviour of the latest cad, you could always rest assured that his life of good order and exemplary behaviour would soon be threatened again by someone exhibiting less admirable values.

In the outside world, change continued everywhere. By the time Arty had gone, Elvis had arrived, as 'Heartbreak Hotel' hit the charts. Perhaps it's just a wishful reminiscence, but in the wake of this, Roy's quiff seemed to get just that little bit higher. Whether that was intentional on the part of the artist, is a matter of con-jecture. Given that the ultimate in children's entertainment offered by society up to then was Muffin the Mule, which played on the limited number of televisions which were in private ownership at the time, making Roy look a little bit more like the man who would become the biggest musical icon of the 20th century was never going to be a bad move.

If the panels featuring the crowd in the strip documenting Roy's senior debut conveyed a vast amount of information in a limited space, on a larger scale the writers had achieved a similar feat with regards to the story. A matter of months after it launched, we knew something of Roy's character, a great deal about his abilities, understood how his adventures would pan out, the pace at which they ran and the ways in which they resolved themselves. Already, the reader had a feel for the character and storylines, and saw them as being slightly different, a little more human and detailed, from anything that had gone before.

Roy claimed the Young Player of the Year prize at the end of that first season, 1956–57, which Galloway described as being full of promise, but leaving the club wanting more. The manager's answer, in yet another example of the comic being ahead of its time, was to turn to the continent, with a pre-season jaunt to France seeing him return with a charismatic winger, Pierre Dupont.

Established Melchester winger Sam Higby was furious, seeing Dupont as a threat to his place, and embarked on a deranged scheme to stop the new signing replacing him. On his way to his debut, poor Pierre found himself kidnapped, tied up, and left miles from Mel Park, while Higby grinned slightly too readily for a man who knew nothing of the plot. Even after being challenged by Roy and Blackie, Higby refused to admit any involvement in Pierre's disappearance, but offered a frank assessment of foreign footballers, asking them why he should worry about 'an untrustworthy blighter like Dupont'?

Kidnaps would become a recurring theme in Roy's world, whether happening to him, or to people close to him, and somehow we never questioned their occurrence as deeply as we might have done. This was largely because Roy's kidnaps, though motivated by malicious intentions, were generally carried out without the slightest suggestion of violence.

Ironically perhaps, for a story which generally kept itself so separate from the more depressing aspects of real life, it was a real life event which seemed to put the lid on kidnaps: following the Balcombe Street siege in 1975, when two members of the public were held hostage by a four-man IRA gang, domestic kidnaps suddenly seemed rather more laden with menace. After Balcombe Street, if Roy needed to be kidnapped, which he plainly still did on a regular basis, he was required to go abroad, as we shall see in due course.

In the meantime, though, back in the innocent days of the late 1950s, there was hostage taking to be gotten on with. If you were a good enough sport to be the victim of a kidnapping in Roy of the Rovers, you didn't do anything to threaten the story, such as trying to avoid being taken hostage in the first place; you stuck your chin out, stiffened your back, and accepted your fate with a degree of fortitude. One might think of it as a particularly English approach, were it not for the fact that the first victim was, of course, French.

Inevitably, Pierre eventually freed himself, and came crashing through the dressing room door at five to three. In case there was any doubt as to his continental origins, he was dressed in tight trousers, a bolero-style jacket, with gelled hair and (as if on an extended sightseeing trip, or just to remind us that he was, after all, foreign) a camera around his neck.

Ben Galloway listened to Pierre's explanation and in a less than whole-hearted show of support, declared it too complicated to be investigated now, but worthy of the benefit of the doubt. Higby stormed off in disgust, and Pierre set about getting changed. By the time he appeared on the pitch, doubtless having had trouble getting the trousers off, Rovers were 3-0 down.

Thankfully, nobody doubted Galloway's tactics in playing with ten men and presenting a three-goal head start, and they were rewarded by a Roy Race hat-trick, with Blackie claiming the other goal, and Pierre playing a blinder. As Roy thanked Pierre afterwards, he replied in a language that was meant to represent French, while being understood by a 1950s English-speaking audience. Outside the lamentable BBC sitcom *'Allo 'Allo*, it has probably not been heard before or since:

'Ma foi! You praise me too 'igh, Roy! You won ze game – not me!'

Roy and Blackie just nodded and smiled, presumably as bemused as everyone else. In the real world, Manchester United had fallen just an FA Cup Final defeat to Aston Villa short of collecting the double, and yet not one of Roy's younger readers would even begin to accept that their season could have been anywhere near as exciting as Melchester's, despite their lack of silverware.

By the following season, however, the side was beginning to fall into place. Sam Higby had gone the same way as Arty Hedlow, shuffling off to the former cartoon graveyard in the sky, and Andy McDonald announced it would be his final year at the club. 'I've had 12 wonderful years here,' he said, 'but as yet, I've not won a cup or a championship. I'm determined to set Rovers back on the road to glory before I go.'

All right-minded people were heading off to place their life savings with the bookies before the captain had finished his sentence. Telling people how long it had been since Rovers had won anything was a classic example of the plot device, where a piece of information is dropped, seemingly for no reason, with all the subtlety of a house brick. As a child, I loved it. As an adult, if I'm being perfectly honest, I feel exactly the same – it was what the comic was all about, and I'm not about to start mocking it now.

The season started with the press doubting McDonald's fitness, and asking whether he would last the entire season. So, from that point on, the results were never in doubt. By the time they reached the title run-in, with Melchester on a sixteen-match unbeaten run, there weren't many, ahead of their forthcoming clash, who gave Brookleigh Wanderers much of a chance.

Even when Brookleigh, who were undefeated all season, league leaders and seemingly needing only to avoid defeat to wrap up the title for themselves, headed in at half-time 3-0 up, you wouldn't honestly have made them any better than evens for the title. Blackie played Roy in for Rovers' first, just after the break, before scoring himself to make it 3-2, midway through the half. Pierre Dupont, with freedom going to his head, set up Roy to score the equaliser, and in the last minute, Andy McDonald, centre half, captain and player least likely ever to take a free kick, slotted one home to claim a 4-3 win.

Brookleigh were a broken side, and a few weeks later Rovers wrapped up the title, while the nation's bookmakers tried to hide from people carrying comics and betting slips. In contrast to the millions of pounds today's stars take from the game on retirement, Andy McDonald was presented with a scrapbook by his fellow players, and offered a job as assistant manager. Hughie Griffiths replaced McDonald, but his character obviously did something to displease the writers, as he soon succumbed to a knee injury – the Bermuda Triangle of footballing ailments, into which characters who were dispensable disappeared, never to return.

In his place Roy – who was told of the decision by a board of directors sitting in a line at a long table, looking like a fearsome interview panel – was made captain. Nobody seemed to mind that he was still only about nineteen years old, and Ben Galloway seemed unconcerned that such a decision was made by the directors and handed down, rather than being made by him directly; despite seeming the oddest aspect of the episode, given the era, it was possibly the most authentic.

The players were thrilled to be led by Roy, and nobody seemed happier than Billy the goat, the team's mascot, who for reasons nobody ever queried, used to wander around the dressing room, eating whatever was left strewn around on the floor. Billy, of course, wore a Melchester bow tie, as the idea of a goat wearing a rosette is clearly ridiculous; although, in turn, not nearly as absurd as the season the Rovers were about to go through.

The story was now a well-established one, and had run in *Tiger* for five years. It is easy now, with perspective born of hindsight, to think of it as being in its very early stages, but by comic standards of the time, Roy was already reaching a fair age. Five years was a long haul for such stories, particularly in an environment where editors thought nothing of axeing tales they felt had lost their lustre. Readers of the time could easily have thought of it as merely the story of a young footballer, and therefore destined soon to reach the end of the road.

What we did know about the story, however, was how, while influenced by the wider world, in terms of Roy's appearance or his actions, it would go out of its way not to refer directly to real life events. While Melchester were winning the league title, in a parallel universe, so were Manchester United. That this passed by without comment was of little surprise to us, because we understood by now that this was the way things worked. By the following year, February 1958, however, tragedy arrived on a frozen Munich runway, as the plane carrying the Manchester United squad, flying home from Belgrade via Germany, crashed on take off.

The British European Airways plane had carried forty-four people, of whom twenty-three died, among them many of the young stars of English football's most exciting young team. It was a disaster which grasped the public, whether United fans or not, as the desperate toll of fatalities rose ever higher, and household names lay in a distant hospital bed fighting for their lives. It was never mentioned in the storyline, and indeed it was difficult to see how it ever could have been.

It was the most tragic incident to afflict one football team in the history of the English game, and suddenly the comic format, which had so often shown its ability to carry huge amounts of information in a few pictures, was revealed as hopelessly inappropriate. For that reason alone, it remains impossible to argue with the decision of the writers not to make any reference to the events of Munich. The audience was simply too innocent to have been confronted with such details from such a source. Roy of the Rovers was an oasis, tucked out of the reach of harsh, tragic reality.

If there was a hint offered that the story's durability was about to surprise us, deciding to make Roy the club captain, as the board did at the start of that 1958–59 season, was perhaps as broad as it got. His first campaign in command saw the first appearance of a character who was to stay in both the side and the story for many years to come, as Tubby Morton took his place in goal. Originally a centre half, Tubby was simply too tubby to stay there, and so donned a green jersey and waddled backwards 20 yards.

It was never made clear what Len Dolland, Melchester's previous keeper, had done wrong, as having gone into the season as league champions, charging to the title with a nineteen-game unbeaten run, it's safe to assume he had some idea of what he was doing. As a reward for his performances, though, he was suddenly out on his ear, without mention of injury or incident, replaced by a morbidly obese defender, too slow to be trusted with his feet any more, so trying his luck instead with his hands. It could have been that Dolland issued a 'him or me' edict in relation to the goat, and Ben Galloway called his bluff, but we will probably never know.

For the first few games of the season, Tubby's performances were all you might expect from a man who could scarcely fit between the posts. Somehow he failed to get his immense frame between the ball and the goal with any regularity, but slowly, things began to improve. In the fourth round of the FA Cup against

Portdean, Roy dealt with an injury crisis by taking Tubby out of goal, playing winger Dick Stokes there instead, and watching delightedly as Tubby made one and scored another to see Melchester safely through. In keeping with the Melchester way of doing things, however, both players were returned to their normal positions the following week, assuming that either of them still remembered what their 'normal' position was meant to be.

The fifth round saw them two down to Carnbrook at half-time, and to nobody's surprise, recovering to win 3-2 with Roy, to less amazement still, claiming the winner in the last minute; a second hat-trick in two games saw Bronton City dispatched in the following round. The semi-final was another mundane, run of the mill encounter, which saw them fall a goal behind against Brampton United, before Tubby saved a penalty, and Roy scored twice to send them through to the FA Cup Final. On the way to the final Roy got kidnapped. A pattern was forming.

Roy, and those around him, got kidnapped a lot. Pre-season tours routinely meant a spell chained up in a foreign dungeon, while mercenaries haggled over a ransom. Just over two seasons since poor Pierre Dupont was snatched by a fellow player, Roy and Blackie, just to give it added dramatic impact, were snatched by a crazed fan, with the team already on the way to Wembley. Wiser men than Blackie might have declined to travel with Roy at all, after the Bert Beston affair, but sheer, habitual loyalty meant he never really had an option.

Ted Smith had been a chauffeur for Mr Mason, Melchester's chairman, before getting sacked. Swearing revenge, he eschewed such simple vengeful tactics as scratching Mason's car, or spreading a spot of gossip, in favour of kidnap. On the morning of the Cup Final, while the other players were preparing for the game, Roy and Blackie were preparing for the worst, bobbing up and down, tied up in a boat, drifting hopelessly some way outside Portsea Harbour.

To cut a long (and while entertaining, rather predictable) story short, the two friends were located, saved and delivered back to Wembley just in time to burst into the dressing room, clad in their club blazers, while Ben Galloway was delivering his pre-match team talk. Presumably this centred on how to cope with their two star players disappearing without explanation, so Galloway was delighted to dispense with it. However, with Roy and Blackie still weary from their ordeal, and sneaky Ted Smith looking on from the stands, Rovers were two down at half-time.

Mr Mason, inexplicably, was also in the dressing room at the break, to sympathise with his two recently freed stars, and when Blackie asked for a penknife to cut a loose lace from his boot, the chairman instantly recognised the knife as being from his former chauffeur. As luck would have it, Roy was able to explain that it had been dropped by the man who had kidnapped them.

Within half a dozen frames of frantic cartooning, Roy had scored a hat-trick and Melchester had won a Cup Final. As he lifted the cup, the police arrested Ted Smith, and good had recorded a notable victory over evil. While being carried on the shoulders of his team-mates, Roy was left to reflect on his day, in the way only a 1950s hero could.

'Gosh, I'm the happiest chap in Britain today! I'm proud to be the skipper of the finest bunch of lads in football!'

If it was a victorious time for Roy, it was also a fine send-off for Joe Colquhoun, who had overseen Roy's adventures so diligently. It is worth considering how Colquhoun managed to steer the story away from the realistic and, perhaps, even slightly dour slant that Reg Eves had envisaged it should have, in order to introduce some additional humour and excitement. Colquhoun's storylines remained true to life to a certain degree, with events on the pitch realistically portrayed, even if the frequency with which the various pieces of action were put together led to the overall picture being slightly absurd.

The additional tales he wove into his storylines, however, with the kidnaps and late arrivals, caricatures and novelties, were to have a lasting effect on the way Roy Race was portrayed. True to Eves's vision of him, Roy would remain dynamic and fearless; the individual goals would never arrive in a fantastical fashion, but the drama would never be curtailed for fear of things becoming far-fetched, and a last-minute winner would never be resisted.

Colquhoun was as important as anyone in shaping both the way Roy would be portrayed, and the manner in which his adventures would be communicated. Roy's occasional lectures on the 'right' way to conduct oneself as a footballer were rarely too po-faced, thanks to the extraordinary background adventures against which they were set. The straight-laced side had to counter-balance the fantastical, which ensured that Roy would forever remain the sort of man to score a hat-trick in injury time in order to win the FA Cup, only to then stop before collecting the trophy and deliver a speech on the importance of sportsmanship.

In the 1950s, where Britain was still trying to find out exactly what sort of society it was, the creators of Roy of the Rovers had stumbled across a formula for a character to appeal to all. The after-effects of the war were still all around, and bananas, the final casualty of food rationing, did not escape from the list of limited foodstuffs until the year Roy first appeared in print. There was re-building going on everywhere, from houses to factories to relationships. Six years of war had left a scar, which would take far longer to fade than the eight years which had so far elapsed.

Through a combination of luck and judgement, the writers had ended up with a cartoon footballer who was well disciplined enough to appeal to those who craved classic, clean cut heroes, yet had enough triumphs and close calls to appeal to anyone seeking an adventure hero. Joe Colquhoun may, by his own admission, have known 'damn all about soccer' when Frank S. Pepper so unexpectedly handed him control, but the sense of adventure he added created something unique. Without Colquhoun, or Stewart Colwyn, as the readers knew him, Roy and Blackie might as well have stayed bobbing about on that boat, and listened to the Cup Final on the radio.

It had, by any standards, been an impressive five years for Roy. He had been a promising member of his school side when the public's gaze first settled on him, since when he'd picked up a league title, captained a team to FA Cup Final victory, all while playing for a club who kept a goat in the dressing room.

Everyone who had ever crossed him seemed to eventually disappear from the scene, either through injury, loss of form or, in the case of Ted 'the nautical kidnapper' Smith, loss, presumably, of liberty. All in all, though, it had been a quite dramatic time, and he left the 1950s still only a few years into his career and yet already with enough memories to last a lifetime. As Roy and his Rovers looked to the future, and prepared for a new decade, it seemed unlikely that the 1960s would be any less swinging.

CHAPTER THREE

THE SWINGING SIXTIES

'I remember good old "Bomber" Reeves, playing at centre half. Broke his leg? Falling out of a plane? Did he? Blimey, I didn't remember that bit. I must have missed buying it that week!'

Pete Stevens

Forged through a combination of the storytelling instincts of Frank S. Pepper and Joe Colquhoun, Roy arrived at the start of 20th-century Britain's most carefree decade as a blond, handsome and muscular footballing superstar. In hindsight, it's a good job his personality retained the occasional hint of piety, because as annoying as his occasional sermons could be, all manner of fates could have befallen him had he followed a more hedonistic path.

There must have been those who predicted the worst for Roy – his leap to success had been too swift and too sudden for it not to all end in acrimony and tears. At the very least, injury surely beckoned for one so young, who enjoyed throwing himself head first into a crowded penalty area with such gusto? Roy was a brilliant prospect, with trophies to prove it, but like Arty Hedlow before him, injury could strike at any time, and his single-mindedness and bravery could yet prove to be his undoing.

Except that, as we entered the 1960s, it seemed more likely that Roy and Blackie would go down the road of Ted Smith and poor, deranged old Sam Higby, with the forces of law and order curtailing his career. If the brief episode of pre-Cup Final piracy had been a far-fetched tale, even for Roy of the Rovers, the way its stars left 1959 and entered the Sixties left us in no doubt that there was to be no shortage of adventures ahead. Who knew, the story might even survive for another five years?

Over the Christmas period at the end of 1959, Mel Park, and specifically the dressing room area, was engulfed by fire. Most of the ground survived, but those famous rooms, where superstars had prepared for games, and soothed away the aches and pains of battle in their large, communal baths, were reduced to ashes. During the course of the fire, Blackie got singed, and ended up in Melchester General Hospital, recovering from his injuries.

The arrival of this storyline is, in itself, an indicator of the thought process which caused many of Roy's adventures to come into being. In 1956, at the start of the season, a huge fire had swept through the West Stand at Leeds United – perhaps putting the seed of an idea in the minds of the writers. Two years later, and just before fire struck Mel Park, the pier at Southend burned down, and the events made the national news. Did they cause the writers to revisit the possibility of a story about a fire at the ground? Perhaps, but what was certain was that, as the years drew on, they cheerfully admitted to being influenced by such happenings.

For reasons that were never made entirely clear, other than that he was very close to the source of the fire (judging by his burns, rather too close) Blackie was also being waited upon by the police. Having decided that the blaze was started deliberately, they wanted to interview him as a suspect in an arson inquiry. The matter was further complicated by the rest of the Melchester squad blaming Ken Harcombe, who had replaced Blackie in the side after his injuries. Roy, in typical style, went off and sniffed around, coming to the conclusion that neither of the two men was responsible, but keeping any further discoveries or theories firmly to himself.

In the middle of all of this, European football came calling, as an Austrian side called Flaudermitz visited Mel Park for a game. Quite why they were visiting for a friendly in early January was never explained, especially to a ground recently ravaged by fire, but then the Rovers' fixture list often raised more questions than it answered. The squad, almost to a man, seemed to think that Harcombe was responsible, while nobody believed that Blackie was capable of such an act. Roy kept an enigmatic silence, which could have been mistaken for sitting, baffled, on the fence, were it not his name on top of the comic. The more Roy said nothing, the more obviously he knew something, but what?

With just minutes to go before kick off, Ben Galloway was preparing to read out his side, when the dressing room door opened, and in walked Blackie Gray. It was beginning to feel odd when someone turned up at the correct time, such was the proliferation of fires and kidnaps. Actually, to be accurate, it was the board room door, as the dressing room was being repaired after the fire, and Blackie slumped in, rather than walked, but the end result was much the same. The midfielder had discharged himself from hospital, and declared himself fit to play. Blackie failed to let his team-mates know that, as soon as they realised his hospital bed was empty, half the Melchester constabulary would be following him to the ground. It led to a storyline which made being cast adrift seem perfectly plausible.

The effectiveness of the NHS in 1960s Britain, in ensuring a full recovery, was confirmed when Blackie set up the first goal, but the sudden presence of a collection of police officers, standing in the tunnel, understandably concerned him. Even when Roy confided that he knew they had come to arrest Blackie but not to worry, as he had a cunning plan, the nerves persisted. They were not helped when Roy, the proud owner of the aforementioned cunning plan, got himself knocked out and disappeared to the dressing room on a stretcher.

The demeanour of the referee as this was done also offers a hint as to the differences between the way the game was played in 1960 and the way it proceeds today.

'Get your man off the field to attend to him, trainer. We can't hold up play while you do it here.'

This direction was delivered with the totally unconscious Roy laying at his feet, and a dismissive waving of the hand in the general direction of the touchline. What would have happened had a crowd of players all surged towards him, screaming, swearing and questioning a decision, is hard to imagine, but he wouldn't have taken a backwards step, no matter how determined the snarling. It's entirely possible that he might have produced a firearm and let loose a warning shot over their heads. Referees were a sterner breed in those days.

When Roy woke up, aided by Taff Morgan's advanced medical technique of pouring ice-cold water over him, half-time was imminent, and as he charged from the dressing room, Blackie was walking towards the tunnel, where a uniformed officer was about to apply the handcuffs. Lashing out at a ball which, conveniently, just happened to be laying about, Roy knocked the first officer over, and, yelling at Blackie, made a break back into the depths of the stand.

The caption of the next frame 'Footballers are trained to think like lightning!' seemed like a slightly optimistic take on proceedings. 'Footballers, then as now, are prone to do some really bloody stupid things when confronted by evidence of their wrongdoing' would have been a more accurate assessment. However, and as ever, Roy had a plan. As they hurtled into the building site that was the old dressing rooms, they found a man with a shovel, digging into the floor.

The players recognised him as Reg Murphy, a local builder and Melchester fan, but seeming less than thrilled to meet his two heroes, he instead tried to wrap his shovel around Roy's already battered head. This, as Reg presumably reflected in the years to come, was a mistake.

'Take that you treacherous skunk!' announced Roy, and as the next frame records 'Roy's whipcrack uppercut completely laid out the burly builder'.

Therein also lies a Roy of the Rovers moral tale that we embraced warmly as children – time-wasting and overly defensive play is bad; punching criminals is good.

The mystery was solved within a matter of frames. Roy had overheard something, put two and two together, and solved the crime. Buried under the changing rooms was a box Murphy had interred, containing the proceeds of the Melchester National Bank robbery. The hiding place was, perhaps, not the most brilliant, requiring the burning down of a football stadium and a period of heavy digging to recover the loot, but he still would have got away with it, if it hadn't been for those pesky footballers. Relieved at such a turnaround during a half-time break that usually offered only the promise of a cup of tea and an orange segment, Blackie scored in the second half to wrap up a 2-0 victory. Whether anyone apologised to the wrongly accused Ken Harcombe, we never discovered.

At most clubs, it was an incident people would discuss for decades to come. But this was Melchester – it was only the third most interesting thing to happen that season. Days after the 'incident packed' Flaudermitz game, Rovers flew to Beltigua (it's in South America, don't bother checking) for a quarter-final of the little known International Club Cup. If Roy and Blackie had previously endured misfortunes involving boats, they were about to experience something, courtesy of a plane, which made everything before seem trivial.

Somewhere over the Beltiguan jungle, rebel soldiers shot down their plane, which is always an unpromising start to a football tour. Somehow the plane made it to the ground in one piece, and having been taken prisoner by the rebels (the third kidnap Roy had experienced or witnessed in less than five years) the Rovers were marched through the jungle to a remote camp. In an unlikely twist, the rebels, rather than demand any particular ransom, seemed content just to play football against Rovers, who, faced with little option, added an unexpected extra match to their South American itinerary. In years to come, Roy of the Rovers would feature a story called Durrell's Palace (of which more later) in which a non-league side would repeatedly solve their financial woes by phoning up big clubs and begging to play lucrative friendlies. It might have seemed an unlikely plan, but it was simpler than continually abducting your next, high-profile opponents.

With the game over, the players came up with a plan to escape. Unsurprisingly, given their location, their break-out into the jungle was a temporary one, before getting recaptured by the rebels, and as a punishment, forced to play another game. As plans went, it made Reg Murphy's, the treasure-burying builder, look sophisticated. After the second game, a release was finally allowed, and rather than going home, as any sensible side might, Rovers opted to carry on to San Angino, who they had originally been scheduled to play before their jungle 'incident'.

Looking back at the events of 1960 in the real world, it is easy to see where the idea for the 'Beltigua' incident came from, and very hard to understand quite how, by modern standards, anyone thought this kind of stereotyping was in any way acceptable. The story depended on mad mercenaries, armed and dangerous, engaged in a civil war somewhere far away from British shores. They were portrayed as dark and suspicious – people not to be trusted and people who certainly didn't possess the same moral scruples as Roy and his team-mates.

'Beltigua' is a name clearly influenced by the Belgian Congo, while the mercenaries are almost certainly influenced by the actions of 'Mad' Mike Hoare, who became a macabre cult figure of the time, due to his actions in the region. Ironically, for a man who influenced characters who specialised in shooting down planes, Hoare eventually married an airline stewardess.

Given the coincidence of timing, it seems inevitable that it was events happening in the wider world that set the ball rolling as far as the Beltiguan plot was concerned. Some months earlier, Harold Macmillan, speaking in his role as British Prime Minister, made his famous 'Winds of Change' speech, firstly in Accra and then in Cape Town, expressing his desire for the British Government to grant independence to several African nations.

In the wake of Macmillan's speech, nations across Africa began to declare independence – Cameroon, Togo, Ghana, Somalia, Chad, Nigeria, Senegal and the Ivory Coast to name but a few. It was a period where the process of correcting the mistakes of history seemed to be getting underway, with all the dreams, hopes and stumbles that would inevitably incur. Against that background then, and despite setting the fictional events in South America, rather than Africa, it does seem remarkable that such a storyline was undertaken.

To take it a step further, coming just a few years after the horrors of Munich, to commence a comic storyline with a football team involved in a plane crash seems a little insensitive. When viewed through modern eyes, it is hard to argue otherwise, but it should also be remembered that, in the late 1950s, plane crashes were far more frequent than is now the case. Also, flying was something done by famous people – a very special form of travel. We were still half a century away from the EasyJet generation, when planes became little different from buses.

It does also, however, provide a timely reminder of that eternal cliché about there being nothing truly original. When people claim that the material served up for young people today is inappropriate and inflammatory, it is worth remembering this particular tale, and the world events that provided the inspiration for it. Tasteless, and some would say downright offensive, storylines were around long before some, particularly those who like to opine about things 'in my day', might choose to believe.

To return to strictly fictional football-related matters, though, the way the storyline developed appeared to leave the writers with a (self-imposed) dilemma. Even by Roy's standards, to come back and win, after his side's adventures, would not only be hard to believe, but would mean the setting-up of a bigger adventure still, for the semi-final. The problem was solved by a rare Rovers defeat.

All of which created a scenario that defined clearly the magic of the comic. Almost anywhere else, after such adventures, the season would be allowed to drift quietly to a conclusion. The idea of playing a game at anything other than flat-out was not for Roy, though, and in his eyes the league was there to be won. It was why we viewed him as such a hero. Portdean were ten points clear, but Rovers' adventures had left them with five games in hand, and despite being forced to play six times in fifteen days, they fought their way to a last-day decider at Portdean Stadium, where the home side stood to be crowned champions if they could just avoid defeat.

It doesn't take a genius to guess what happened next. With the game level at one-all going into the last minute, Roy was brought down in the area, earning Melchester a penalty, and decided to try a new style of penalty he had been working on in secret. Slashing his boot across the ball, Roy curved it, with the outside of his right foot, sent the keeper the wrong way, buried it in the opposite corner, and won Melchester the title. Easy.

One point to remember is that, in February 1960, a couple of months before the season ended, the comic had proudly unveiled Bobby Charlton as their new scriptwriter. The Charlton fingers never touched a typewriter in anger, of course, but nominally, it was Bobby who was guiding Roy and his side through their adventures. To put matters into context, football still existed under a maximum wage structure, and would do for another year, meaning that the most a player could earn a week was the meagre sum of £20. In 1961 Johnny Haynes became the first £100-a-week footballer, but for the time being, the rewards were limited in draconian fashion.

In the present day game, the top players defend their image rights almost as fiercely as any other part of their vast pay packets, aware how lucrative sponsorships and endorsements can be, but in

1960 the footballing world was a very different place. Had the decision to place a footballer 'in charge' of storylines been made a few years later, then perhaps Denis Law, who always had more of a Roy Race-style haircut, might have got the nod, but in 1960, playing for Manchester United held just as much prestige as it does today; Charlton, who was younger than his talented team-mate Dennis Viollet, the season's top scorer, was the natural selection.

Rightly known as one of the gentlemen of the game, Bobby seems to have managed to persuade people not to dwell on the fact that, in his first three months as a scriptwriter, he kidnapped an entire football squad, route-marched them through the jungle, made them play three games in four days, and then flew them home to play five in sixteen. In light of the storylines he was supposedly writing, a worrying side to his character was being revealed – people wished us to believe that beneath that famous comb-over was a man willing to inflict all manner of hardships on other players.

Even putting the humorous side of Charlton's appointment to one side, it was a brave decision by the powers that be, accepting as it did that the whole thing was no more than a story, and required the services of a writer. As obvious as it sounds, such an admission had never been made in the life of the comic before, and a discreet veil had been drawn over the logistical side of affairs. Admitting that someone wrote all the adventures, even though that person plainly didn't, was tantamount to letting light in on magic.

By the time the following season arrived, in September 1960, the issue of writers was a very live one. The work of journalist Don Pike and newspaper editor Andrew Stenning, combined with entrepreneur Lance Vigors, saw Roy come as close as he'd ever been to parting from his Rovers.

Having failed to win in their first six games, and with their only signs of form coming in the FA Cup, Melchester were having a tough time of it, even before chairman John Mason's businesses all took a turn for the worse. Vigors bought Mason's shares, despite already owning Shermall United, in whom he had invested a fortune to bring them up to First Division standard. Part of Vigor's plan would be to relocate Melchester to Shermall Stadium, which was considered more luxurious and modern than the historic Mel Park. Shermall would move in the opposite direction. Had the idea been to generate friction and rivalry between the fans and players of the two sides, it could not have worked more smoothly, but by the time another one of those endless mystery fires put Shermall Stadium out of action, only two months after the Rovers moved there, the atmosphere was poisonous. Mystery fires, along with kidnaps, were a popular plot device, enabling months of storyline to be ditched at the drop of a hat – or match. The bane of the Melchester Fire Brigade's life was the saviour of the Roy of the Rovers scriptwriter's.

It was also one of those issues about which the comic was curiously ahead of its time. Although not strictly speaking a ground share, but a ground swap, the events which panned out in the comic hinted at several issues which would plague the game in future years; moving away from a club's traditional, and some would say spiritual, home, and the effect of owners entering the game who had made their money elsewhere, appearing not to possess any feeling for what football was actually about.

Inevitably, Shermall were then drawn to play Rovers in the FA Cup semi-final, and more inevitably still, two Shermall players were kidnapped in the run-up to the game. Football in 1960s Melchester had more 'accidental' fires and kidnaps than a Colombian turf war. At half-time – these things were *always* sorted out during half-time – Roy decided to solve the mystery of the kidnap; an FA Cup semi-final poised at 1-1 was not enough to fully engage him.

It swiftly became clear that Rovers' new centre back, Don Pike, was really a journalist working for the *Daily Gazette*, posing (deep) undercover at Melchester at the suggestion of Stenning. Roy marched up to the press box, grabbed Stenning, and dragged him down to the Shermall dressing room, so he could explain that *he*, not Roy, was behind the kidnaps. They had been staged to increase publicity, although why the Cup Final needed extra publicity we were never told. On reflection, however, that was far from the oddest part of the plot.

The Shermall players were apologetic to Roy, realising he was in the clear, and true to form, a late Melchester goal saw them into the final. In one of Ben Galloway's more interesting team selections, Pike somehow kept his place in the centre of defence (despite being outed as an undercover reporter) only to injure himself, ending his Cup Final prematurely with Rovers 1-0 down.

Never one to be outdone, he found himself some crutches, and hopped up to the press box to cover the rest of the game, for both the *Daily Gazette* and the Roy of the Rovers readers. Two questions were raised by this. First, what was the original *Daily Gazette* reporter doing while this was going on, and second, having read his report, how did Pike ever get to be a football writer in the first place?

'My leg throbs with pain,' he writes. 'But it does not pulse so violently as this vast crowd with excitement as it watches the stirring battle below. Corstone are swarming around the Melchester goal. If only I were there to help them . . .'

It carries on in much the same manner for the rest of the final. When he was carried off the pitch, the reader's sympathies were squarely with Don Pike, yet by the time he finishes his report, they have been transferred to the poor copytaker, who will, in due course, have to transcribe Pike's flowery nonsense.

Suffice to say, by the end of the game, Roy has scored twice and Melchester win 2-1. It's another FA Cup triumph, in a year that can, genuinely, be described as turbulent.

In order to demonstrate the attraction Roy of the Rovers held for us as children it is worth getting back in contact with the real world. Put bluntly, the 'real' 1961 Cup Final, between Tottenham and Leicester, was less than a classic. Spurs won 2-0, the goals coming within seven minutes of each other towards the end of the game. Not so late that they could be considered late, thrilling winners, nor so early that they could have set the game up for a festival of exciting football.

There was, however, a sub-plot. Having already wrapped up the league title, Spurs' victory saw them become the first British team in modern times to do 'the double'. The season had been dominated by Bill Nicholson's side and victory at Wembley against Leicester had ensured them footballing immortality; it made them – whisper it who dares – a greater side than Melchester Rovers.

That could never be allowed to stand, and yet directly competing with real life was not an option, and until the comic began to lose its way, many years later, never would be.

The cunning answer was to engineer a relegation fight, which Roy won on the last day of the season, sealing survival with a late goal. It was tense, exciting and, most importantly, ensured that Melchester's season remained unmissable right the way to the end, just as Tottenham's had been.

When viewed against the context of the following season, 1961–62, we might have been left wondering whether the action couldn't have been rationed out a bit more carefully? Rovers finished in mid-table, which was, after the previous seasons, horribly dull, and disappeared out of the FA Cup in the fifth round. Their first European Cup Winners' Cup match saw them trailing the well-known fictitious Hungarians of Schonved 2-1, until Blackie fired a shot into the bottom corner.

Or at least, it would have reached the bottom corner, had the ball not burst on the way, eventually slumping pathetically to the ground a yard short of the line, with the keeper, presumably, first beaten then amused. The only piece of good news Melchester fans got from Europe, or indeed anywhere else, all season, was when Roy turned down an offer to go and play for Italian side Batori. Once more the links with real life were clear to spot – John Charles had been a huge success at Juventus, while Denis Law was at Torino. The £85,000 price tag might have been a vast sum for the Rovers to turn down (although Law had already twice been sold for more), but they knew that they could never find anyone who could get kidnapped as easily as Roy, while his habit of scoring winning goals and crucial hat-tricks was also endearing.

If attempting to overshadow Tottenham's achievements had been difficult the previous year, as the 1961–62 season developed a real life story was once again threatening to overshadow anything Roy and his side could manage. Whether deliberately or not, the writers wisely declined to compete with the exploits of Ipswich Town; newly promoted and tipped only for relegation by most experts, Ipswich were steered all the way to the title by their manager, a slightly taciturn man called Alf Ramsey. Had you made your way to the bookmakers and asked for odds on Ramsey taking England to victory at the next World Cup, and doubled it up with the prospects of him one day managing Melchester, the odds quoted in your direction wouldn't have been nearly as long as the stares.

The 1962–63 season was notable for featuring Roy's England debut against the footballing might of Caragua, albeit that he nearly got dragged off before half-time, when he momentarily forgot the game while trying to overhear the latest Melchester score shouted from the crowd. Once satisfied that all was well back home, he was like a man possessed, scoring two and creating the third. Among his many other firsts, then, Roy Race was the first player to worry more about his club commitments than his international career. An allegation that, in the current era, gets levelled against players as a criticism, was in Roy's day more like a badge of honour. Thrilled by this promising introduction to the international stage, he duly celebrated by returning to Melchester and collecting another league title.

There must have been a school of thought that entering any more competitions that involved foreign travel really wasn't a good idea for Roy and his colleagues, given the frequency with which they got themselves into trouble the moment they left the country. As readers, though, we lapped it up. Rovers were England's dominant footballing force by far, and the opportunity to go and do the same on a European stage was long overdue. There were sneaky Italian strikers and thuggish Spanish defenders to conquer, and besides, we quite enjoyed the kidnaps.

We watched on excitedly then as, hard on the heels of their league title, Melchester found themselves entered in the European Cup, progressing through, on a tide of Roy Race goals, to the last four. The semi-final saw them overturn a deficit from the away leg, as Roy scored twice to beat the West German side, Stalzburg, which left Rovers in a slightly unusual position, familiar to

Liverpool fans, of doing nothing in the league or cup, yet then finding themselves in Europe's biggest final. This involved travelling to Paris, which again, after the adventures in South America, one might have expected to be trouble free, but nothing at Melchester was ever that simple.

Blackie Gray had always come across as the quiet one of the duo – getting kidnapped because Roy was getting kidnapped, shot down because Roy was on the plane, and so on. Even when they were still at school, he was late for the kick off because the car got sent the wrong way as a result of Roy being in it. Although his playing career would go on to last every bit as long as Roy's, it was undoubtedly already time for a mid-life crisis, lest Blackie become the Michael Owen of his day, being in equal parts both successful and overwhelmingly boring.

The crisis arrived shortly before the European Cup Final, which was to see Melchester pitted against the Italians of Nettruno, and it took Roy of the Rovers into an area it had never previously dared to tread. While injuries, punch-ups, kidnaps and all manner of internal politics had, from time to time, made life with the Rovers more difficult that it ought to have been, in the early 1960s, the idea that a woman might be allowed to interfere with footballing matters was practically unthinkable. Women just didn't appear at football grounds unless they were serving meals in the canteen or drinks in the bar. When, years later, Ben Galloway got himself a female secretary, Roy was so shocked at this feminine invasion of a previously male bastion, he married her, but much more of that later.

Blackie, however, went one better and managed to get himself romantically involved with a French actress by the name of Suzanne Cerise. Strictly speaking, he became involved in the same way teenage boys become involved with female movie stars, with most of the action taking place in his imagination, but it was enough of a distraction to send Blackie into a temporary tail-spin. She was a perfectly caricatured cross between Brigitte Bardot and Sophia Loren, taking her nationality and coquettish nature from the former and her looks from the latter. This was, most certainly, new ground for the comic, and none of us, as young readers, was entirely sure where it was heading.

It was not completely new ground for football, however, which had experienced a narrowing of the gap between itself and showbusiness four years earlier, when England captain Billy Wright married Joy Beverley, of the Beverley Sisters. To a younger audience, the wedding of David Beckham and Victoria may be the major collaboration between the two industries, but Billy and Joy beat them to it by almost half a century. Having captained England, earned more than one hundred international caps and completed in excess of 650 appearances, all for Wolves, without receiving a single booking, Wright was a very Roy Race-type figure, albeit without the goalscoring prowess.

Blackie, meanwhile, was batting well above his average with Madame Cerise, and this may have altered his thinking somewhat. Given the frequency with which he supplied Roy with scoring chances, it was something of a miracle that he didn't pass her gently and delicately into the path of his lifelong chum, out of sheer force of habit.

Having looked briefly at the background against which Roy's adventures first appeared, and the world of entertainment into which they fitted, the fact this storyline introduced a degree of glamour into Roy's existence seems entirely fitting. Nineteen sixty-two was the year the Rolling Stones played their first gig, the Beatles signed their first record deal, James Bond arrived in British cinemas and Marilyn Monroe died and promptly became an icon. The cult of celebrity was becoming ever-more important, or so it seemed, and Roy was determined to stick to the role of a principled, steadying figure.

Back in Paris, Blackie was reading from a slightly different script. The problems he faced were exacerbated by the fact that the object of his affections was not exactly free to receive them, given that she was already in a relationship with a stuntman called Ed Garrard. It is, in many ways, a typically Roy of the Rovers reaction. Having never run a storyline involving a woman before, when they did, instead of making it straightforward, they wrapped it around the additional plot points of a European final, a movie star, a besotted midfielder (who wanted to wrap himself around the movie star) and a stuntman. It was included to show us the Rovers acting in light-hearted, 'locker room' style behaviour, rather than out of a desperate need to associate football with glamour and celebrity. Were the same story run now, forty years later, the motives would inevitably be different.

There were, aside from all the goals and glory, times when the scriptwriters seemed to have just dragged a selection of random ideas out of a top hat, and, almost for a dare, decided to run them, all at once. It's certainly the only way to explain the proliferation of kidnaps, and seems to offer a reason for this particular storyline, apart from showing the team acting laddishly, every bit as plausible as any other suggestion. The end result of all this nonsense was Ben Galloway standing in the centre of the dressing room of the 'Paris Stadium' surrounded by Melchester players, getting changed in preparation for a huge game. Surrounded by ten players, to be precise, rather than eleven, thanks to the absence of an actress-chasing, stuntman-avoiding midfielder.

With seconds to go before they headed for the pitch, in staggered a slightly bedraggled looking Blackie. It is, in hindsight, a miracle that he ended up with such a dull reputation, given his habit of charging into dressing rooms, chased by police, stuntmen and a dozen other pursuers besides. The secret life of Blackie Gray made the secret life of John Major look decidedly mundane.

'Gray,' thundered Galloway. 'If we lose against Nettruno, I'll see you never play in first-class football again.'

'I can only say that I'm sorry, Ben' he stuttered, looking sheepish, before Roy broke in with a simple demand – 'Get changed'. So simple, in fact, that it teetered on the edge of being insultingly obvious. Then again, as he hadn't been the one turning up late for a European Cup Final because of a dalliance with an actress, he can probably be forgiven for being straightforward.

By half-time, Rovers were two down, and Roy, who always enjoyed a crowd in the dressing room to while away the break, hatched a plan as he walked back down the tunnel. Just as Ben was about to launch teacups around, the door opened – unscheduled dressing room entrances were almost mandatory at times of high tension – and in walked Suzanne Cerise.

'Wow – Suzanne Cerise!' exclaimed one player, leaping up in the air. Given the situation, the celebrating footballer was perhaps fortunate that Galloway didn't have him transfer-listed before he came back to earth, but he was determined to explain his delight. 'Just what we need to bring us some luck!' he cried. Suzanne went on to deliver a speech that put female emancipation back a decade.

'Mes heros! You win for me, yes? I have a surprise for you eef you do.'

If it was supposed to cause a magical transformation of the Melchester squad into snarling, angry lions, it first seemed to turn them into simpering lapdogs.

'Yes, mam'selle!' whimpered one, while Blackie, who had by now reverted completely into a 15-year-old with a crush on his teacher, merely gasped: 'You can depend on us, Suzanne!'

It was a pathetic spectacle, but it seemed to spur the Rovers into action. Whether it was the first appearance of a woman in the comic, or just because they were in the mood for a dramatic comeback, the writing was on the wall for Nettruno. There they had sat, Italian, tanned, well-dressed and handsome, hearing that a famous actress was coming down at half-time to pay a visit, and before they knew it, she was strolling past their dressing room and going to meet a bunch of pasty Englishmen who drooled and whooped as she walked through the door. It was easy to see why they felt so shattered.

Roy got an early goal, the equaliser arrived soon afterwards, and despite a tense interlude midway through the second half, Blackie, predictably, struck the winner, deep into injury time, to give Rovers the win. It was their first European Cup, arriving two years before (in real life) Celtic became the first British side to win it, and three before Manchester United did the same as an English club. United, of course, won it in a game in which Bobby Charlton merely played, not one he wrote, which makes Melchester's victory so much more special . . .

If the players had any colourful ideas about the manner of Suzanne's surprise, though, the following day delivered something of an anticlimax. Ed Garrard, the stuntman, was the only man for her, and she was going to marry him, but would love Blackie to act as Best Man. It seems like a classic slap in the face, but Blackie somehow managed to look delighted. The Rovers players formed a guard of honour for Suzanne and Ed as they left the church the following day, after what must have been a very swiftly arranged wedding, holding an arch of football boots aloft, for them to walk under. Even by the standards of Roy of the Rovers, it was surreal.

Among the glamour of a film star and Hollywood stuntman, there was an almost deliberate lack of it from the footballers. Having them in their kit was their way of reminding us that football came first, ahead of anything else, and nothing as trivial as a wedding would make them change their view. If we once more spin the clock forwards forty years, the player who most seems to fit this description, the one who you suspect would most happily want to carry on playing in the street long after the fans had disappeared, is surely Wayne Rooney. Often the best player on the pitch, always charging around like the keenest kid in the playground, when Rooney got married, the pictures were sold exclusively to a glossy magazine for millions of pounds. Even today's most single-minded heroes might balk at the thought of attending the wedding in their kit, though.

What was arguably stranger still, however, was the degree of seriousness that some people insisted on attaching to the episode. Many years after the story appeared, an essay about the role of Roy of the Rovers appeared in an academic work called 'A necessary fantasy?' The subject of Suzanne Cerise and the Paris episode are considered at length by the authors Alan Tomlinson (no relation to Barrie) and Christopher Young, and their conclusion leaves the reader in no doubt that they are unimpressed:

> In the course of the story, Suzanne Cerise is viewed both positively and negatively: she causes Rovers' first-half deficit, but inspires them to win in the end. However, the message is clear: A woman's word is ambivalent. Cerise's promise of a surprise turns out to be a grave disappointment, in view of which there can be only one solution. This comes from the mouth of Roy at the end of the episode: 'Phew, now Blackie won't have Suzanne on his mind any more. He can concentrate on football.' After an exploration of women in their role as inspiration and disappointment, they are firmly relocated at the margins of the male environment.

While we may have a degree of sympathy for the view – as has already been said, women took a long time to play any more than a fleeting role in Roy's world – the authors perhaps miss the point a little, in order to make theirs. Roy of the Rovers didn't set out to make a statement about feminism, or anything else, it just reflected the world in which people lived. Besides, their first-half 'deficit' was clearly caused by poor defending and a strong wind, not the poor treatment of a strong woman.

Trying to attach hugely profound meanings to football-related subjects is rarely a successful venture. It was only football, and it was only a comic, and even as children, we understood that. In fact, we probably appreciated that quite a bit more as children than we do now as adults. The eyes we use now, sadly, know a bit too much about the world to languish in such naïve wonderment, and we expend time and energy that we once used recreating Melchester's adventures, trying to look for a deeper meaning in them.

Mercifully, in order to lead us away from the dreary world of analysis to the bright lights of fantasy, it was time for another kidnap. To prepare for the next season, Melchester went on a tour to South America. Even as they taxied down the runway, a million young readers cried out: 'No! Don't! You'll all get kidnapped! Again!' But to no avail. This time it was a trip to Malagos, to play against Bagota, and those sneaky rebels were at it again, seizing the side, and dragging them off into the jungle to play a friendly.

Melchester played more pre-season games at gunpoint deep in the jungle than they ever did in more mundane settings, and the route marches and weapons which ensured these contests happened in the first place rather strained the word 'friendly', but somehow, the matches always went off without interruption. It is hard to imagine that nobody complained about either the depiction or the inclusion in the story of a bunch of mercenaries, who were once again black and living deep in the jungle, caricatured with huge, toothy grins and pneumatic, fleshy lips. It was, however, a different age and some storylines, and this one in particular, reflect that more starkly than others.

The Black and White Minstrel Show, which nobody would contemplate putting on screen now, still had another ten years to run on BBC Television. Indeed, such was the blindness towards the possibilities of offence being caused, or perhaps the lack of interest about the risks of gratuitous insults to an entire race, the show had won the Golden Rose of Montreux in 1961 for Best Light Entertainment Programme. If, far from failing to upset people, such a show actually won awards, then concerns about stereotyping in a children's comic were never likely to receive much of a hearing.

This time the Rovers beat the rebel side 17-2, in a game which must have left Roy frustrated, simply because there was neither need nor opportunity for a dramatic late goal in order to win it. As thanks for playing the game, not that they had much choice, Roy and his side were taken to their intended destination of Bagota by their former kidnappers, in order to play the original game as scheduled. After a couple of days in the jungle, however, the ordeal, combined with their lack of rest, left Rovers a shadow of their normal selves. Weary and error-prone, they were losing at half-time until Beppo and Bruno, the leaders of the gang who had held them, arrived in the dressing room.

By this time the Melchester dressing room had been fitted with a turnstile, to cope with the flocks of people who turned up whenever they cut up an orange and pondered a substitution. While their previous half-time visitor, Suzanne Cerise, had used her charms (and their hormones) to get the best out of them in the second half, Beppo and Bruno had a more direct approach – drugs. The team were plied with carioca juice, which had, they were assured, extraordinary rejuvenating powers. The complaints about the characterisation of the locals could now be extended to include shades of either witch doctors or drug pushers, depending on your view. It worked, though – instantly restored, Rovers tore into Bagota, emerging 2-1 winners. Roy scored with an overhead kick in the last minute – his standard reaction in the aftermath of a kidnap.

Within ten years of first featuring as a comic book hero, Roy had achieved many things, including England appearances, European Cups, FA Cups and league titles. His involvement in at least five kidnaps of varying degrees of seriousness, however, is the one aspect of his life over which the authorities might retrospectively want to cast an eye.

Looking to alleviate the constant fear of crime, the writers evidently decided that a more humorous touch was required. Bobby Charlton was no longer pretending to put together the scripts, no doubt scared about what had been revealed about him by the turbulent events he had supposedly scripted over the last few seasons. In stark contrast to what had gone before, some levity was introduced.

The arrival of Jumbo Trudgeon, or to give him his full name, Lord D'arcy Plantaganet Trudgeon-Marclay, at the start of the 1964–65 season as an inside left was designed to amuse, rather than elicit dramatic gasps. Jumbo was supposed to play it for laughs, rather than goals, and the role was written to perfection. A multi-millionaire, he interspersed occasional moments of genius on the pitch with a Bertie Wooster-ish ability to cause well-meaning chaos off it. Known to all as Lordy, he spoke in the way Dick Van Dyke adopted in *Mary Poppins*, and was every bit as believable. We loved him, because he was as different from anything which had come before as it was possible to imagine, both in the immediately obvious, such as the way he dressed and spoke, to the deeper levels, evidenced by the way he reacted to situations. He was one of the first real surprise characters in the comic, and from the earliest days the writers knew that they were on to a winner.

If a situation looked impossible, Lordy could always be relied upon to find the crucial pass – 'Nil desperandum! Belt it, Roy, m'boy!' When launching a shot towards goal, he was always optimistic – 'On me word . . . Keep the change out of that!'

Lordy was never stuck for words. Until, that was, the day in 1965 when Mel Park was hit by an earthquake midway through the second half, leaving four-foot-wide cracks streaked across the surface. ''Pon my word, the pitch is breaking up!' reflected Lordy, side-stepping sharply to avoid sinking into the depths of the earth. The earthquake, caused by subsidence, proved to be the end of football at Mel Park for the season, and Rovers' bid for the league title faded away as a result. As straightforward as it is to trace most of the occurrences in Roy of the Rovers back to an event in real life, the earthquake episode proves impossible, having seemingly arrived from a scriptwriter's imagination untainted by the outside world. Obviously, it could never happen again – could it?

As poor as their league form had been, in the FA Cup Melchester were once more unbeatable. By the time they got to the final, against Eastoke, who were going for the double, Roy had injured his knee, and could hardly walk. Exactly how the Rovers' reserve striker still failed to make it into the starting line-up is a mystery, but as ever, Roy started the game. Effectively playing with ten men, Rovers were soon a goal down, until Roy fashioned the inevitable recovery. Unable to kick the ball, he set up the first with a dummy, and then headed the winner, true to form, in the last minute.

In the writer's defence, there must have been a sneaking suspicion that the summer was going to provide a hard act either to live up to or to follow. Rovers might have been dramatic in the way they claimed the FA Cup in May 1966, but in July of that year, England were busy winning the World Cup, in a game complete with last-minute equalisers, dubious goals, late winners and hat-tricks, and you didn't even need to suspend your belief to enjoy it. But what of the striker who had scored twice on his international debut the previous year? The man who had scored more goals, more dramatically than anyone else in English football? How was he not in the team?

The answer was simple. If you wanted to believe that Roy's adventures were real, then just to be on the safe side, they got him injured shortly before the tournament, while winning the FA Cup. That nasty knee injury might not have stopped him from dummying and heading his way to glory in May, but it wouldn't stand up to the battering of a whole tournament, so for Roy, the World Cup was a non-starter. That though, was just an insurance policy, because to be on the safe side, the comic strips never once referred to the whole tournament.

Print deadlines made it impossible to comment on events of the day within any sort of sensible time frame, so the safest thing to do was to ignore the whole thing. Ironically, then, while England's footballers were winning the world's most famous trophy, England's most famous footballer was turning a blind eye to it. The comic would repeat this tactic in years to come, as Ian Vosper (who alongside Tomlinson was the comic's most famous editor) explains later, and one which, once the reader grew used to it, seemed to make perfect sense. In fact, that's as good a description of the whole Roy of the Rovers concept as you'll ever need – once you get used to it, it all makes perfect sense.

Melchester's response to England's triumph in the World Cup at Wembley was to win the European Cup Winners' Cup the following year, 1967, at Hampden Park. With a certain inevitability, Roy scored both goals in the final. For once, however, the second arrived with some way still to play – and the last-gasp drama was provided by a Tubby Morton save, rather than a goal. It was a radical departure, although not as dramatic as the end to their league season. Every now and then, as we have already seen, it was decided that it would be a good thing if Rovers flirted with their own mortality a little, and got involved in a relegation struggle. This tended to occur during seasons in which they had already won a trophy, as to do otherwise would mean a year of complete failure, and that just wasn't acceptable.

Rovers would often have to endure extraordinarily mixed fortunes during the course of a single season. The 1966–67 season was possibly the greatest example of this, when they returned home from their European glories to fight a relegation battle. They should have escaped by beating Toncaster, but Jumbo had taken several other players to the away fixture in his chauffeur-driven Bentley; when it broke down, Rovers were forced to play without them and, as a result, lost.

It left them facing Melboro, their local rivals, and needing to win 4-0 to survive the drop. Were they to be relegated, the summer tour to America would have to be cancelled, although given their record on foreign tours, this mightn't have been a bad thing. After a string of kidnaps, for many of the players a season of Second Division football could have been preferable to a third, successive abduction, doubtless at the hands of a crazed cowboy.

It wasn't a thought anyone dared utter near Roy, however, and in the event, having led 4-0 at half-time, they extended their lead to finally beat Melboro 7-0, escaping the drop with characteristic style. Miraculously, the tour passed off without major incident – North America was evidently a safer bet than South America – and for once, rather than leaving them glad to be alive, pre-season saw Melchester emerge full of life, and ready to put the domestic shortcomings of the previous year firmly behind them.

The swings of fate afflicting the Rovers may seem unlikely, but it is worth looking at the league tables of the time to remind ourselves of just how unpredictable football once was. In the modern era, there have been (for thirteen years) only three clubs who can win the title, and this situation will carry on until the money is pulled from one of them, or equally vast amounts are poured into another, fourth contender. The game that Roy used to remind us was the greatest in the world is drunk on money; predictable and surprise-free.

Looking back to the era of earthquakes at Mel Park and English World Cups, that decade brought eight different winners of the First Division title, and eight separate FA Cup winners. The last ten years have brought us three different Premier League winners and five separate FA Cup holders. It may well be that Roy's adventures look absurdist and escapist because that is exactly what they were intended to be – we shouldn't ignore the possibility also, though, that they seem so bizarre and random because the real world now serves us up such predictable fare.

By Christmas 1967, someone had been studying the record books, and came up with a statistic which generated improbable excitement: Roy Race was only two goals short of becoming the highest goalscorer in Melchester history. The furore it caused was immense. He had, according to the statisticians, scored 298 goals for his side in a little over ten years, one short of the record. If this caused any disbelieving murmurs among the readers, it was more likely to be because the figure seemed too low, rather than too high. Just counting the last-minute winners, surely it should already have been around the 400 mark?

It was an episode that seemed tailor-made for Roy to claim the glory, as the nation waited for him to score the goals which broke the record. Instead of just scoring the goals and accepting the praise, however, Roy took the opportunity to deliver a lesson in the evils of greed. The side desperately tried to feed him the crucial pass, and time and again it was intercepted or he was marked too tightly.

Eventually, at half-time, Roy explained that, as he was being followed by defenders wherever he went, he should be used as a decoy. It worked to perfection – at least, until the writers could resist it no more, and let him score twice anyway, just to get the whole record business out of the way before the last game of the season.

Once more, Rovers were second, playing the team who were top, and the odds were stacked against them. Roy was injured, but hobbled about the place, eventually poking out a toe as he lay helpless on the ground, to set up young substitute Alec Blackburn to score the winner and claim the title. There is, to this day, no record of anyone betting against them to do so.

As the 1960s drew to its end, Melchester had time to add just a few more select pieces of silverware to their cabinet, and a few more tales to their legend. In August 1968, Ben Galloway signed a new centre half, Douglas Ballard, for £150,000, a club-record fee and, quite purposefully, no doubt, precisely equal to the then record English transfer fee paid by Leicester to Fulham for Allan Clarke. If it couldn't mirror events as far as World Cups were concerned, the writers ensured the comic stayed firmly in line with reality with regard to other matters. As if to highlight the dangers of publishing so far in advance, however, no sooner had Rovers matched the record fee than Clarke was off, to Leeds, for £165,000, breaking the record once more. Trying to keep up to date was evidently more difficult than the creators of Roy's world made it look.

Ballard was marked out from early on as a classic comic wrong'un, and nobody who knew the history of Roy was expecting him to remain in such a state for long. Reform or rejection were his two options, and after a dramatic two months, Galloway had endured enough, and sacked him. Quite why he didn't try to sell him and recoup some money was never made clear, but it didn't really need to be. At Melchester, if you were the wrong type, they needed you out of the door before your nefarious ways could infect the rest of the dressing room.

In his place, Galloway signed Lofty Peak, who would hang

around for years to come and never utter a word out of place; just to make the difference between him and Ballard quite clear, he was known as the 'Gentle Giant'. Melchester's other centre half, 'Bomber' Reeves, was out of action after falling out of the plane while celebrating on the journey home after their European Cup victory over Shevnik Sparta (it was on the runway at the time, thankfully), so they were a little too thin when it came to the back four to complain.

They reached the final of the European Cup in May 1969, and again it was played in Paris. Memories of the last time they played there, and Blackie's disastrous run-in with Suzanne Cerise, flooded back, but obviously, such a thing couldn't happen twice. It didn't, as Blackie instead conspired to get himself concussed after being kicked in the head by a horse, days before the game. On reflection, the last time he had been swooning and swept off his feet in Paris was preferable to this. Come the final, though, against the mighty Portuguese side Santova Rapid, Blackie was fine, and took his place in the starting line-up.

Unfortunately, another knock on the head saw him return to his befuddled state, rob the ball from his own centre half, and charge the wrong way down the pitch, before thumping a shot beyond Tubby Morton, for the greatest own goal in European football history. We sat at home and flicked from page to page in disbelief, dreading both a second for Santova, and the end of that week's adventure arriving, leaving the inevitable cliffhanger. Substituted, as much in disgrace as distress, Blackie watched as Santova packed their area and defended for their lives. This would become a common feature of Roy of the Rovers whenever the side faced European opposition, albeit that this appears to be its first example.

Roy wanted you to know that Continental sides were sneaky. If they went ahead, they didn't try to extend their lead, like proper footballers, but defended, like blaggards and cowards. It was, Roy always believed, something of a character defect, probably caused by the pencil-thin moustaches they wore, in order to distinguish themselves as foreign. Just to illustrate the point, at most stages of the game Santova had all eleven men in their own area.

Even in years to come, Roy never quite grew out of his suspicions surrounding sides from abroad – not even when he started signing their players, as the editor of the time, Ian Vosper, cheerfully concedes.

'Yeah, I'd admit to that. And their crowd would always shout out "Caramba!" which indicated that things had gone well. Or badly, actually, come to think of it. In fact, it indicated that something had happened. I'm not sure we ever narrowed it down to whether it was something good or something bad!'

Eventually, as Blackie sat on the bench, little cartoon birds flying around his little cartoon head, tweeting, Roy worked out a plan. From a short corner, the ball made its way across to Roy, who, being outside the area, was unmarked. He let loose a pile-driver from 25 yards, which the keeper found impossible to see through the crowd of bodies. We know this because, in the best traditions of the comic, he had time (in between it being struck and it flying past him for the equaliser) to cry out: 'Out of the way. I have lost sight of the ball!'

From there on, Santova were forced to play more expansively, and as we all knew they would, fell to an inevitable defeat. A second European Cup of the decade left Melchester Rovers (captained by the greatest striker in their history, and English football's most popular figure) as the envy of every team in the continent. For Roy Race, the Sixties couldn't possibly have finished on any higher a note. Or could they?

December 1969 saw them scheduled to play in the World Club Cup Final, against Sao Madro Macional. Who would have thought it possible ten years ago, when Ben Galloway's rebuilding plans were still little more than scribbles on a piece of paper?

Unfortunately, by this stage, there are no points left for guessing how they got on. When a young, nervous substitute called Chalkie White was called on after just ten minutes, only to immediately concede a penalty, we still knew it would all be fine – we knew, and yet we were still nervous, because the writers achieved that fine balance week after thrilling week. And, even though we guessed that Chalkie would settle wonderfully into the role, encouraged by Roy – before scoring the winner, running on to Roy's pass, minutes from time – the excitement was no less intoxicating.

In December 1969, England were already the champions of the world, and now Melchester Rovers had joined them, as the greatest club side on the planet. We had never needed con-firmation of this fact, but now we had it anyway. The greatest player in the world played for the greatest side in the world, and they had the trophies and the goals to prove it. As they celebrated on the back of a bus, touring Melchester with the trophy, Roy tried to coax a smile from his manager:

'Try to smile, Ben. Force yourself. This is the greatest day in Melchester's history!'

The response was a Galloway classic: 'Things aren't as good as they look. A lot of things about that match worried me. There'll have to be big changes.'

Ben might have been a genius when it came to deciding how things would pan out on the football pitch, but even he understood who the real bosses were. The glamour might have belonged to the characters, but the power lay, as it always would, with the writers . . .

CHAPTER FOUR

THE ARCHITECTS

'I always thought what made Roy great was that he kept the ball on the floor and played proper football. Couldn't have someone like him playing for someone like Wimbledon or Sheffield United, with the way they used to play, could you? A big wallop upfield, then "Chase that, Roy".'

Paul Smith

As much as we enjoyed imagining that Roy and his Rovers were a real team, playing games and enjoying triumphs somewhere nobody but the readers ever looked, the reality was, of course, different. Melchester's last-minute winners weren't created by the precision of a through ball or the power of a shot, but by the imagination of writers and the skills of artists. When the young Roy first kicked a ball, it was because Reg Eves thought it would be an intriguing basis for a story, and when he shaped to go left and then right, we believed it because Joe Colquhoun's drawings added an image to our imagination.

While Frank S. Pepper originally sat down and dreamed up a young boy playing football for his youth club, the chain of command which brought about the new storyline would be incomplete without a man called Derek Birnage, who rested slightly above Pepper, but below Eves in the company hierarchy. All of them deserve credit for first bringing Roy Race to the world. Birnage was the editor of *Tiger* in 1954, and was instructed to put in place the creation of a football story which was closer to real life than anything which had been tried before.

Roy marked a departure from the fantastic – believe it or not – style of story which had been Birnage's stock in trade up to that point. He had previously written strips such as 'Two-Wheeled Whirlwind', 'Big-Hit Briscoe' and the gloriously named 'Mystery Ice-Ace of the Arrows'. He was born in 1913, to a family that had publishing in the blood. By the time he died, ninety years later, he had become a sufficiently important figure in the world of comics, and by definition popular culture, to warrant obituaries in *The Times*, the *Daily Telegraph*, the *Independent* and a number of other papers besides.

The desire to produce a publication of some kind was plainly in Birnage's genes, as his father edited a religious, highly conservative and incredibly successful paper called the *Sunday Companion*, which in the years following Derek's birth sold upwards of half a million copies each week. After being educated at boarding school, the young Derek worked at a junior level in comics before spending six years at war. Initially, on returning, he had little interest in going back to his former job, and tried his hand running a toy shop with his wife, only for the business to close and comics to come calling once more. Had Derek Birnage been better at selling toys, the world might never have discovered just how good Roy Race was at scoring goals.

Having set Roy on his way in 1954, Birnage eventually took over the writing duties himself in 1959, and scripted the stories for four years. One of his first jobs was to hire Bobby Charlton to pose with a typewriter, and pretend to write them himself. For this, Charlton was reportedly paid 15 guineas a week, while Birnage, who actually did the writing, in addition to just about everything else, received only 11. If it caused his enthusiasm for either the business of comics or the game of football to dim, he never allowed it to show.

It was, despite a long and respectable career in the publishing business, the most successful project with which he ever became involved, and to this day ensures a small part of Derek Birnage, about whom nobody seems to have a bad word, lives on for ever. His role was eventually taken over by David Gregory in the mid-1960s, when Birnage moved to become the editor of *Shoot*, but while Gregory by all accounts steered the *Tiger* ship safely and un-contentiously along, it was the sub-editor he hired in 1967 who will forever have a special place in the hearts of Roy of the Rovers readers.

Little did he know it when he strolled through the door at the interview, but Gregory's decision to employ Barrie Tomlinson was an inspired one. For Tomlinson it was an early step forward on a journey that was to carry him to the very top of his profession, yet as with Derek Birnage and his inability to sell toys, but for a moment of chance, he too might never have found his way into the world of comics:

It all started when I saw a newspaper advertisement for a job in Fleet Street, which just said 'beginners wanted' and no experience was required, so I thought I'd give it a go. That was with Amalgamated Press, and next thing I was a sub-editor on *Lion*, and then moved on to being a sub-editor on *Tiger*, and eventually editor. From then on, things just kept going, and I can't imagine ever doing anything else.

I look back, and I'm so glad I answered that advert, because I've not really regretted a minute of what's gone on in the 45 or so years since I did. Comics are about judging the readers, working out what you think they want, serving it up as well as you possibly can, and then listening to them while you fine-tune the idea to the way they like it. I've done that for years, and it's worked out all right, I think.

Tomlinson is as genial as you might expect of a man who has spent most of his life doing his dream job. His emails have a habit of arriving with the cheerful header 'Greetings!', and while softly spoken, it takes only the briefest glimpse at his track record to realise why the world of comic publishing holds him in such regard. He is, after all, the man who first plucked Roy Race from the *Tiger* chorus line, and, following an instinct, made him into a star. He, as much as anyone else, was responsible for adding an entire phrase to the British sportswriter's lexicon.

'It does make me smile still, and it's a great compliment that the phrase "Roy of the Rovers" whether it be a Roy of the Rovers moment, or real Roy of the Rovers stuff, has entered the language. When you launch a magazine, obviously that's the last thing that you're thinking about, but it's really nice when it happens. I can't think of it happening too many times before.'

Having picked up the baton from Gregory, Tomlinson set about making his new title as well known as he possibly could. Before doing anything, he sat back, took a long, hard look at the comic landscape, and worked out how best to set about making sure that *Tiger*, and Roy in particular, became household names. Years later, with his methods justified many times over, he recalls it all with a quiet modesty.

'It had a lot to do with timing, and very fortunate timing at that.

When we were coming to the fore, many of the people in the media who held key positions had been brought up on a diet of comic book heroes. That meant we were always going to be looked on favourably and with a bit of affection, which was something we used hugely to our advantage.'

The secret to Tomlinson's success, as much as anything, was his consistency of approach. When a problem arose, or a dead-end seemed inescapable, he remained calm, studied the options, and refused to believe that anything was impossible. He had inherited a character who he could see had potential, and he weighed up carefully how best to extract that and to develop it. He knew, perhaps above all, the importance of using the comic's allies and its better known and more influential fans. Sometimes, it seems, with extraordinary consequences. He says:

> Even before Roy had his own comic, back in the days when he was in *Tiger*, when I was the editor, he had a bit of a select following – people were intrigued by the ups and downs and the way things changed so dramatically the whole time. Not all of them were the sort of people you'd expect, either. I remember being at a function and being introduced to the Duke of Edinburgh, and he said to me: 'It's all a bit soap opera with Roy, isn't it?'
>
> I had to laugh, because he had a point, I just hadn't expected him to be the one to make it. When we launched the comic in its own right, though, he proved that he really did know what he was talking about, and that it hadn't just been polite chat, by sending us a letter, which we included in the first issue.

When that first issue arrived, Tomlinson ensured the profile of his leading man became larger still. It was, as he freely admits, a policy born out of necessity, rather than choice, but nonetheless, the originality of the basic idea behind his strategy still raises a smile, in admiration of its sheer simplicity.

> I asked the big bosses what our advertising budget was, as I thought we needed a bit of publicity to help with the

launch, and it was made clear to me right from the start that our advertising budget was pretty well non-existent. There wasn't any way we could make the best out of the new title without some sort of publicity, so we started tinkering with things, and running the sort of stories we knew would attract the attention of Fleet Street. Then, when they came to us hoping for a quote 'from Roy', I'd appear as 'his friend' and the novelty of it all would increase the interest tenfold.

I'd explain that he was too busy to speak to them directly, but he'd asked me to pass on whatever the message was they wanted to hear. By being careful about this, we built up a very good relationship with the media, and I became known as Roy's friend.

From that promising basic premise, many editors would have been happy to sit back and admire the fruits of their labours. It was such a simple idea, cost so little to implement and worked so well, that there was scarcely any need for a phase two, but Tomlinson wasn't the sort to rest on his laurels. No sooner had the initial plan showed itself to have potential, he was working on ways of fine tuning and developing one of the comic book world's earliest public relations campaigns.

Another trick we used to use, which worked brilliantly – far better than we'd ever imagined it could – would be to get Roy to write letters to newspapers, complaining or making observations about all manner of topics which had come up in the world of sport. They would invariably get back in touch with us, and ask if they could have a longer conver-sation, in order to put together an article about it. What made me smile was that, while they always pretended to appreciate what was going on, they still managed to sound a little upset whenever Roy wasn't available, although they did eventually accept that I would, as Roy's friend, be able to speak on his behalf.

That started with the *Evening Standard*, who ran a piece, and to be honest, to this day I can't remember exactly what it was about, but 'Roy' wrote in to complain about it. They got back to me, as I've described, we went through a routine that became completely standard to us, and by the time the exchange was finished, we'd had lots of publicity, without harming anyone or spending anything. It was good for all parties – we got the exposure we needed, the papers got the publicity they wanted, and nobody got hurt.

As shrewd as Tomlinson's campaign was, it remained, crucially perhaps, very much in the spirit of the comic. Its beauty lay in the fact that nobody ever really felt cheated – as he says, the paper got the 'quote', the comic got the publicity, and everyone smiled at the thought of a cartoon footballer with opinions. Having said that, what may seem obvious today wasn't always quite as clear to people when the plan was first hatched. Tomlinson continues:

> I was surprised at how long they seemed to take to catch on to what we were doing. They might have been laughing up their sleeve, and treating us as the village idiots, but firstly, we still got what we were after, and secondly, I was the one speaking to them, and I never got that impression. Whether it was because they wanted to believe in Roy or not, I'm not entirely sure, but they acted as if they did. I think they just began to think of him as a real person who had me as his spokesman, and thereafter they never really questioned it. Roy was probably quoted more often than any other cartoon hero, and sometimes about quite serious things!
>
> It was interesting, because though it was clearly a joke, people just didn't seem to want to acknowledge it as such – as if they were somehow letting the side down, or ruining the act by admitting that he was a cartoon character. It reinforces, I suppose, the idea that they were comic fans as children, and didn't want to change when they grew up. Roy was something they could believe in, and that was what they were going to continue doing!

Roy offered opinions on everything from football violence to a new England manager, but perhaps the finest tribute to

Tomlinson's plan came when Roy's impending marriage to Penny was announced, and Denis Law offered an opinion on how married life might affect him as a player. By the time one of the planet's finest strikers starts offering opinions about your cartoon character's career, it's safe to assume that your publicity plan is doing something right.

The results were often stunning, assisted considerably by the innocent times in which Tomlinson worked. With a smile and a degree of charm, Barrie was gently pulling strings and making things work to his advantage at every turn.

> Much of what we did could only have happened in that particular age, it has to be said. The world is far more commercial now, particularly the world of football. These days football teams and footballers themselves seem to be tied into deals with certain companies or brands, and they won't do anything, not even just for a minute, unless there's some money in it for them, or it's part of an ongoing contract.
>
> We just relied on the old-fashioned tactic of asking people politely if they'd mind helping us out, and in the first place, because it was a more innocent age, they did so, and gladly. As time moved on, Roy became better known and so we were able to ask bigger and more important people to do things which perhaps took them further out of their way, and represented bigger sacrifices in time, but we were very lucky, and people were very good, because we almost always got what we wanted in the end.

Not only did they get what they wanted, but they got it for a fraction of the cost it would otherwise have amounted to. It would be easy, and tempting, for Tomlinson to sound boastful about his achievements in this aspect of the comic alone, but his voice is puzzled, rather than triumphant. To this day, it seems, he cannot quite understand why nobody else tried to promote their publications in a similar way.

'Nowadays a PR company would charge a fortune to come up with the sort of system we had in place for promoting the magazine,' he says, 'and all of it would be money you really didn't need to spend. A lot of the things we did to promote Roy have never been copied, and that shows a lack of imagination.'

As Tomlinson made his initial plans to launch Roy's adventures in a comic of its own, so the character began to develop visually, into the blond, muscular figure we recognise today. This was in large part due to the work of David Sque, who drew Roy from the early months of 1975, crafting his adventures for more than a decade. He took over from Yvonne Hutton, who drew the strip for eight years, until the end of 1974. Hutton and Sque had been at art college together in Poole, and discovered a mutual love of illustration and design.

Indeed, it seems to have been an early misplaced compliment, when someone described one of Sque's paintings as an illustration, which offered the first hint of what he was to go on and do for a living. At the time Sque was, by all accounts, rather offended at his work being described in a way he took to be rather disparaging, but a lifetime's work, earned through his talents as an illustrator, may just, by now, have cushioned the blow.

In the early days of both Sque's and Hutton's careers, achieving any sort of reputation as an artist was made incredibly difficult as a result of the rivalry between IPC Magazines, who published *Roy of the Rovers*, and DC Thomson, based in Dundee, who published many of its comic competitors. Most of the artists were freelance, but their styles obviously stamped themselves very prominently onto their characters, and finding someone who could take over the strip (should they leave) without the change being immediately evident was difficult.

Given the headaches caused by having to replace them, the comic editor's worst nightmare was for one of his artists to get poached, and as a result, precautions were taken. None of the artwork was signed or credited, in order to make it more difficult for rival publishers to identify potential poaching targets. It was a sign of how insular and, to an extent, paranoid the comic world was at the time, and also how secretive the publishers liked to be. People earned a living from it, but in the majority of cases, they did the job because they loved it, and not because it offered any imminent promise of riches.

Sque had worked with Tomlinson on *Tiger*, drawing a story called 'Martin's Marvellous Mini', and when Yvonne Hutton gave up doing Roy, Sque landed the job after persuading Tomlinson that he could draw more than just motor racing stories. It was quite a feat of persuasion, because in those days there were so many artists, the editors could afford to pigeonhole them. Having overcome this hurdle, though, he spent three months drawing Roy in addition to 'Martin's Marvellous Mini', at the end of which, he was exhausted. He approached Tomlinson to apologise, and explain that there was no way he could continue to do both, so he would have to drop Roy.

With the strip increasing in popularity all the time, however, this wasn't an option Tomlinson was prepared to take. In order to keep Sque onside, Roy increased in size, and 'Martin's Marvellous Mini' became slightly less marvellous, as the story reverted from colour to black and white, before dwindling away altogether. Thus, to the list of 'if only's' Roy has collected over the years, we can add that *if only* David Sque had been more determined to continue with a comic strip about a rallying mini, our hero might have grown into something quite different from the muscular, blond figure we all came to know so well.

Sque was as uninterested in the game as his predecessor, Colquhoun, proving that very little in the world of comics, even an artist's lack of interest in his subject, is ever original.

When I got the job, people said, 'But this is football! You're not interested in football!' and I said to them, 'No, I can draw anything.' People are people and figures are figures – just put a football shirt on them or whatever! Now, of course, I was sworn to secrecy and couldn't tell the Sunday papers that I didn't like football when I was doing the national footballing hero in comics! Obviously I've played it, but I'm a doer, not a watcher.

It wasn't, as Tomlinson explains, purely to do with secrecy that the two competing publishers knew so little about each other.

Funnily enough, our world wasn't quite like it might have been for other sports journalists, because we never got to meet up with any of the 'opposition'. I never met anyone from DC Thomson, and they were based up in Dundee, so I suppose that's not surprising. It's not like newspapers, though, where journalists go to the same events and bump into each other all the time. We did our own things, at opposite ends of the country, and as such, we never had any reason to bump into each other. There were no functions where we would have had reason to meet.

While there were downsides to being a freelancer, however, there were also considerable positives. Sque, who one suspects would never much have enjoyed working for someone else, is the first to admit it, and his stories of the internal politics at IPC underline why. The idea of Roy marrying Penny, he recalls, came from Tomlinson, but was immediately rejected by his immediate boss. A month later, in a large meeting with the senior figures at the magazine, the same boss went ahead and presented it as his own idea, taking the credit from Tomlinson. With all the politics it entailed, it wasn't a world to which Sque felt well suited, and sitting at home in his studio was probably a far safer option.

Having received the script, Sque would set about dividing up the page, calculating how many frames each would hold, before sketching, inking, colouring and inserting the speech balloons which brought the words into life. On occasions, particularly keen-eyed readers might spot an advertising hoarding around the edge of the pitch, promoting the services of 'Jennifer's Salon' or 'Jennifer's Hairdressers'. There are no prizes for guessing the profession of Sque's ex-partner, Jennifer, but he always had very neat hair, apparently. Tomlinson explains:

There was a very different feeling to comics produced back then, I suppose, because of the techniques we used. There wasn't any of the digital imagery and technology that exists now, and we used to rely on a process that was more labour intensive, but looked different on the page as a result. It also came with its own stresses and strains, of course. We didn't get copy emailed automatically in, and relied on the hard copy arriving via trains, or the post, or however else it was supposed to be getting in.

With Sque drawing the strip in *Roy of the Rovers*, and Yvonne Hutton, by this time, drawing the one which appeared in *Tiger*, it was an occasionally frantic working environment, as Tomlinson recalls.

> For my part, I stayed as editor for a couple of years after Roy launched as its own identity, but you must remember I was editor of *Tiger* as well, so I was already doing two jobs. It was always the intention that I would stay as long as it took to see Roy safely launched, I suppose you could say to get it safely out of harbour, and then to take a more general role, which would allow me to oversee a number of different titles. As time progressed it became clearer to me that what I wanted to be was the mastermind of the two titles, but with people in place who possessed the day to day skills to keep it running smoothly and make sure it developed along the lines we would discuss when we had meetings.

His 'general role' was admirably wide-ranging. In the early 1980s he appeared on BBC One's *Nationwide*, talking to Sue Lawley about Roy's recent marital problems, and acting in the role of Roy's agent, while wearing a natty three-piece suit and dark framed glasses. It brought Roy to a wider audience than ever before, and showed once more the wisdom of the decision to send his leading man down the aisle.

> What we created was something that people wanted to remember. When that morning came round when the paperboy pushed your copy of *Roy of the Rovers* through the letterbox, it was an exciting thing. That comic was anticipated by people who treated it in much the same way that they treat television cliffhangers these days.
> We even had our own little running jokes, I suppose you'd call them, and they were especially good in the summer. Roy

and the team went off, year after year, on a summer tour to
somewhere in the Far East, and they would always get caught
up in something dodgy, or kidnapped or whatever. And yet,
in true comic style, they'd firstly, always escape, and secondly,
always go back next year for more of the same. It was like a
tradition!

And yet, as with all traditions, it took someone to come up with
the idea in the first place. Tomlinson simply seemed to think up
more than his fair share of them.

From its earliest days, *Roy of the Rovers* had a small table buried
away in its pages, inviting the reader to fill in their marks for each
and every story. The publishers acted upon the collated ratings,
promoting stories that appeared to be successful, and on occasion,
axing the ones which failed to live up to expectations. Its ingenuity
was matched only by its simplicity, and once again, the idea could
only have come from one man.

> The idea of recording feedback, and asking the readers what
> they thought of the various strips, was considered a bit
> revolutionary, funnily enough, but it was something I'd
> thought about for a long time, and it never seemed anything
> other than a sensible, and particularly simple, thing to do.
> Roy was supposed to have a dialogue of sorts going on with
> the readers, and in order for that to seem believable, we had
> to get to a stage where he was seen to be acting on what they
> said.

Barrie Tomlinson created the best possible foundations for *Roy of
the Rovers*, before, as he says, taking on a more supervisory role and
leaving other, capable hands to deal with the day to day problems
of describing the adventures of the nation's favourite footballer.
There might have been those who saw it as the end of a golden era,
and that the only way from here was downwards. There had been
many times in the past when people had predicted the end for Roy
and his team-mates, feeling that, in a short-lived medium, they had
outlasted their welcome. Not to Tomlinson, though.

'I always thought there was a place for Roy,' he maintains. 'And for a variety of reasons, somehow, we managed to find it, year after year. Perhaps we were lucky? It's hard to look back and know, if I'm being honest. I'm proud of what we did, though. Yes. I'm very proud actually.'

Once again, Tomlinson is being a little modest about both his achievements and his standing within IPC. As his talents were recognised and his ability to come up with endless ideas became better acknowledged, he was a man in demand. Eventually, despite already running *Roy of the Rovers* and *Tiger*, his workload caused him to take the backward step he had always desired. It could, given how well things had already gone at *Roy of the Rovers*, have been an awkward time, but as far as Sque was concerned, the new man fitted in just perfectly.

'Barrie went on to supervise six publications at one point: *Lion, Tiger, Roy of the Rovers* and three more that he'd taken over. So he was group editor. And my editor, who came in to do Roy, was Ian Vosper. Lovely, lovely guy.'

A lovely guy indeed and, as the next decade was to show, a perfect heir to the kingdom Barrie Tomlinson had created. Roy Race would be latching on to late crosses, finding an inch of space, turning and firing home late winners for a while longer yet.

CHAPTER FIVE

THE SEVENTIES

'There was always a late winner. Always. I think some of them might have arrived after the game actually ended – they were that late. They loved a late goal. And a kidnap. Obviously.'

Charlie Hyam

Roy was practically an old hand by the time the 1970s arrived, having already been active in the game for sixteen years, earning no fewer than four league titles, four FA Cup Final triumphs, two European Cups, two World Club Cup Championships and a Cup Winners' Cup medal. I entered the new decade with rather less of a track record, having been born just a week or so into the 1970–71 season. I make no apologies for arriving on the scene after Roy had already put thirteen major medals into his trophy cabinet.

Thus, the events so far have required a journey back into the archives to ensure that Roy's adventures are chronicled as accurately as possible. Of course the characters, barring a few, and certainly the teams and style were immediately familiar, but I cannot pretend to have read each adventure as it happened. From the mid-seventies onwards, however, fine detail from re-reading old comics mingles with the memories dredged up with each passing page.

In the Seventies, we had the newspapers delivered to our house. Previously a mundane event, it was raised to a weekly peak of excitement by the presence of a copy of both *Roy of the Rovers* and *Tiger*, sandwiched between the newspapers. They were removed from their hiding place before the papers had even reached the doormat, and myself and my brother would hurtle off to our bedrooms to devour the week's adventures – he with *Tiger*, me with *Roy of the Rovers*.

After an hour or so, a stand-off would take place, with the swapping of comics handled so seriously and carefully it made a hostage exchange look like a vague arrangement. It is that hour that everyone who ever read the comic remembers most – the moment you first got your hands on it and snuck away from the world in order to follow the fortunes of your heroes, who had been stuck in suspended, inked animation since the previous week. The world of literature may well have offered us greater and more sophisticated thrills since that day, but I defy anyone who once experienced it to remember the thrill of opening a fresh, new week's worth of *Roy of the Rovers* and not find a wistful smile appearing on their face.

My timing, for once, had been rather good, as the Sixties had left Roy with quite an act to follow. The dull, grey, real world was looking an awful lot brighter since England won the World Cup, while the fantasy world Roy inhabited had surely been mined to exhaustion. The previous decade had seen Melchester Rovers inundated with tenders for work from cabinet makers, as they collected three league titles, two FA Cups, two European Cups, a Cup Winners' Cup triumph, and, to top the lot, not one, but two World Club Cup wins, the most recent happening days before the start of the new decade.

Even with their fates crafted by a team of writers and artists, topping the last ten years would be the sort of challenge only a fool would take on; a fool, or Roy Race. With the warnings of his respected and formidable manager, Ben Galloway, echoing in his ears, Roy knew there was much work left to do if the current squad were to achieve their full potential. It had been a glittering decade for the Rovers, but the challenge now was to see it as a foundation, rather than the finished article. All that silverware, warned Ben, even while the celebrations for the World Club Cup were still going on, represented the start, rather than the finish, of his plans for the club.

At the time, the players probably failed to take their manager's words sufficiently seriously, and who could blame them? Every time they stepped onto the pitch they seemed to leave it victorious and feted, and even when things seemed as if they were going awry, Roy could be relied upon to pop up with a last-minute winner. For the writers, however, even though we, the readers, seemed to demand a constant diet of victory and triumph, there had to be some degree of balance and the occasional upset had to be entertained.

Despite this, ultimately the demographic of the readership meant Melchester could never go too long without enjoying some success. It was what made the story so attractive to people. We understood the importance of the issues Roy and his manager raised – of taking nothing for granted and never becoming complacent – but they were no substitute for a late winner and a dramatic victory against all the odds, and they never would be. Children know what they want, and the writers of *Roy of the Rovers* knew exactly how to give it to them.

It was at about this time that the cyclical nature of Roy's plotlines became truly apparent. There are, ultimately, only so many things you can script a football team to do and, in terms of dramatic impact, and without leaving the pitch, there are only really two – winning and losing, as comics don't *do* draws. Given the nature of the story, it was obvious that there were going to have to be more victories than defeats, and that in order to make those stand out, they would have to be achieved in the most extraordinary way possible.

Already, the limitations on the writers become clear. Roy's habit of scoring last-minute goals had largely developed because there was no other way to keep Melchester successful without becoming dull. It may sometimes have bordered on being far-fetched, but given that it was running in a comic, and not attempting to be taken seriously as a piece of fiction, that was preferable to becoming boring.

Stock scenarios were born, which could be relied upon to turn the wheels of the story for season after season; and with the average reader probably staying with the comic for only three or four years, most options, if recycled wisely, were read only once. Looking back and assessing the stories en masse is a slightly unfair way in which to consider how the comic worked, unless you keep in mind that the experience of most readers was of a select few of the adventures, enjoyed in an intense period of several successive years. To complain otherwise is akin to leaving the theatre having enjoyed a show, and then getting upset when you pop back the following night and discover that the same actors are saying the same words.

Admittedly, this doesn't forgive or explain the plethora of kidnaps, but in Roy's defence, the concept of having to recycle stories isn't one with which many comic strips ever had to contend. The vast majority went through the range of possible adventures once, and then, looking or feeling tired, they folded. Roy of the Rovers seemed to still be steaming along happily once this circle had been completed, however, so it simply set about going round again. Besides, if having gone through that process we still need someone to blame, we could always just point the finger at Bobby Charlton.

Perhaps I'm worrying unduly. John Gardner, who 'read it proudly for longer than I really want to admit', found the rolling, regurgitating style of the storylines almost comforting.

I'd have been a bit let down if, having won the league once, Melchester went into a slump for a decade before developing another side to challenge once more. I remember the thrill of them winning what, in one particular season, seemed like game after game, and the fact that they went on to do it again the next year didn't bother me in the slightest.

I even loved the kidnaps, because they weren't like proper kidnaps, because the kidnappers were generally rubbish – nobody ever had too much difficulty escaping. I knew what I wanted from *Roy of the Rovers*, and it delivered it. And loads of other comics tried to be dark and moody and unpredictable and they never lasted half as long. How does that phrase go? It did what it said on the tin!

This was certainly true, and it was no surprise that, in the wake of their World Club triumph, Galloway's doubts about the quality of his side were proved correct. Melchester's league form was unimpressive, and to finish outside the top three was less than they might have expected. Then again, it wasn't one of their intermittent relegation fights, which so often seemed to follow great triumphs, so perhaps a degree of reality was starting to creep into matters.

They still had the FA Cup to contest, having reached the final with Roy scoring only a measly seven times along the way. They were pushed close in the fourth round, being taken to a replay by non-league Woodburn Spartan, but recovered to put matters right with a 7–0 win at Mel Park in the replay.

Roy, Tubby Morton and Geoff Giles all got picked for the 1970 World Cup squad, although injury was to rule the great man out of a competition in which he could surely have made such a difference to England's chances. Given the goalkeeping difficulties England endured, it's hard to see how Tubby might not have influenced matters as well, but it wasn't to be. The writers, a cruel, hard bunch, decided it would be Tubby's *On the Waterfront* moment – his big chance stolen away from him because someone else decided it wasn't going to be his night. The only difference really being that, in order to wreck his dreams, Tubby didn't get to take a dive.

They were playing against Seaford Athletic on a hot Wembley day in the first final of the 1970s, and when normal time ended the sides were level at one apiece. Extra time was required, with the Rovers' players wondering how they would last the pace. Galloway's response was very similar to that which Sir Alf Ramsey opted for four years earlier when the World Cup Final had required an extra half an hour to separate England and West Germany. Sir Alf marched out onto the turf, cast an eye over his players and, mindful of the effect conceding a last-minute equaliser might have had on them, weighed up carefully whether to opt for the carrot or stick approach.

'You've won it once. Now go out there and win it again!'

The stick seems to have won. Galloway went down a similar route.

'All of you, listen to me. The FA Cup isn't won by softies. Seaford have had an exhausting time, too. I pride myself on producing the fittest players in the game.'

Ben didn't say anything else, nor did he have to. Rovers scored three times in the last fifteen minutes, and the trophy was theirs. The Cup win saw them qualify for the European Cup Winners' Cup, and further glory beckoned. Victory over Rythoven Olympic of Greece in the first round was impressive, not least for overcoming the issues surrounding their name. It must have been a tricky business, naming Rovers' opponents through the years, and especially in the European games; it's fair to say that the process was not always an unmitigated success. 'Rythoven' sounds too Germanic to come from Greece, while the addition of 'Olympic' appended on the end, to hammer the point about their country of origin, seems slightly unnecessary had they only thought to get the place name sounding right in the first place.

The second round saw Roy scoring a second-leg hat-trick to overturn a two-goal deficit and end the European dreams of the utterly fictitious, but splendidly named Racing Lombardo, of Italy. The West Germans of Hagenburg fell next, well-named but, unbelievably for Germans, not very good at penalties. With extra time failing to separate the sides, Tubby Morton saved three spot kicks, while Roy, Blackie and Tubby himself, who had always harboured dreams of returning back to life as an outfield player, scored to put Melchester through.

The semi-final was a desperately tight affair, against the believably, if not brilliantly named Portuguese side Argarvo Rapido. It was the second time Rovers had played a Portuguese side, and the first were called Rapido as well, so it was obviously a suffix that pleased the writers. It seems superfluous to record that Roy claimed the winner late in the second leg, but of course he did, setting up a final against Standard Wasserdram of Belgium in West Germany's famously imagined Menkdorf Stadium. Wasserdram were strong and physical, but poorly named, simply borrowing the 'Standard' from Standard Liege, and for the second time in one cup run, sounding more Teutonic than perhaps befitted a bunch of Belgians.

One of the great traditions of Roy of the Rovers was the way it summarised the story so far in a text box attached to the first pane of action. It wasn't unique, as many comics adopt a similar device to get newcomers up to speed, but the way in which it went right back to basics always raised a smile. Each box opened with the words 'Roy Race was skipper of Melchester Rovers . . .' and thereafter managed to compact everything that had happened between that point and wherever the previous week left off into a couple of sentences.

It was a masterpiece of brevity, and this particular offering warned us not only that Albert Hurer, the Standard Wasserdram striker, was the main opposition threat, but that his side had seen two goals disallowed within the first ten minutes. Rovers, it told us, were at risk of getting beaten out of sight. We knew that wouldn't happen, especially not in a major final, but put the thought into a child's mind, and they stay on edge until the final frame of the story. It was a very simple formula, but one Roy of the Rovers, in particular, understood perfectly.

Many comics, and indeed adult performers, are unable to present something to children without first ruining the impact, hinting that the joke is a bit beneath them, as adults, but worth being told just for the benefit of the children. The writers of Roy of the Rovers felt no such compunction, nor did they want it to be thought of as something that worked on two levels, as so much of children's entertainment now does. Roy was meant to work on one level – the level of the reader, and they loved it, because it delivered, without apology, precisely what they wanted.

In later years, we might hear phrases such as 'with a mighty leap, he was free' and chuckle at the absurdity of the action they conjured up, but in childhood, we held our breath, waiting to see how our hero could possibly survive. Identifying such things as childish is seen as a sign of maturity in modern society, but it needn't be. Given who the stories were aimed at, it was simply appropriate. All of which is just part of the reason why, when we delve back into the stories, such affection surfaces – Roy of the Rovers was one of the things, through our collective youth, that never talked down to us, and never made anyone ashamed of being young.

So, we read on, worried about the threat of the obviously powerful Wasserdram side, our young minds concerned at how Andy Croydon, Rovers' inexperienced centre half, would deal with the dangerous figure of Albert Hurer, and keen to see how Roy would solve the problems. That he wouldn't solve them never crossed our minds, which is why we bought the comic in the first place.

It became clear to all in the first forty-five minutes that Hurer was cleverer than the hopelessly named Croydon; in fact, so much cleverer that poor young Andy didn't even know he was being fooled. Rovers went a goal down midway through the half, when Hurer dragged him off on a dummy run, leaving the way clear for his strike partner to score. In the circumstances, half-time might have been an appropriate moment for Andy to keep quiet and hope nobody noticed him, but an ill-timed phrase was required to set the scene for a lecture from Roy, and so that's what he delivered.

'Well, at least Roy, I've made sure that Hurer wasn't allowed to score!' declared a beaming Andy Croydon, announcing himself instantly as foolish, grovelling, smug and stupid. Fortunately, everyone in the dressing room knew that half-time in a European final was a good moment to let Roy explain exactly how football worked to Andy, otherwise he could easily, and understandably, have been beaten to a pulp by his team-mates.

'Andy, that's just it!' Roy protested. 'We've fallen into a trap. Hurer's been running as a decoy, to take the pressure off the other attackers!'

In an instant, the penny dropped with Andy. Ever the brilliant tactician, Roy had shown him the importance of looking around, trying to see what was happening on the pitch, and not ignoring everyone apart from one player. Unfortunately, it probably also taught him that inappropriate half-time remarks are rewarded by tactical enlightenment, rather than violence from one's colleagues, but that error would surely be corrected in time.

In the second half, Andy was so determined not to become distracted by Hurer alone, that he treated him with something approaching disdain. Spurred on by Roy's words, he set up the equaliser for Roy, before, in the last minute, Roy dragged half the Standard defence with him to the far post, allowing Terry West a free header at the near post to win Melchester the cup. A decoy! The irony!

Roy Race had not just spotted the problem, he had solved it, educated one of his young players, and then turned it around to use it against the opposition. That was why we loved him, that was why we bought the comic, and that was why the people who wrote the stories were so very clever. In the space of three pages of cartoon, a footballing parable had been passed on, and a trophy secured. If you can read it now, and not still smile, you've a heart of stone.

The following season, 1971–72, was, by any standards a major one, both in the life of Roy Race, and his side. For a start, a new character arrived in Melchester, and it was a puzzling debut. Penny was Ben Galloway's secretary, and occasionally appeared in the background, doing secretarial things. They never even gave her a surname – unless it was triple-barrelled 'Penny Ben-Galloway's-Secretary', but that seems unlikely. She was just plain Penny the secretary, or at least she should have been, but she appeared too often for anyone to believe that she was a character who wouldn't eventually play a further, more pivotal role. Characters didn't just appear in the strips for no reason; apart from anything else, the need to save space and compress the story as much as possible made it impractical.

It was clear Penny was destined to play a larger role, although quite what was something of a mystery. It obviously couldn't be romantic, because Roy was a comic hero, and they didn't do romance. Not in boys' comics, anyway, and certainly not when there were football matches to be won. Girls were creatures to be spurned at every opportunity – to scare with creepy crawlies, pull the heads off their dolls and tear down the posters from their walls. We were boys. That was what we were supposed to do.

We had to wait another four years for Penny's role to be given some degree of permanence, but in the meantime she continued to drift in and out of storylines, becoming friends with Roy, and then disappearing into the background once more. As adults, our naivety at failing to spot the marital train heading down the track towards us is both endearing, and worrying.

By the time 1972 creaked its way around to May, the Rovers had once more reached the FA Cup Final, where they would face Cranville United. Roy had scored five goals in the last four rounds, and had claimed the winner in every tie since the third round, so by his standards it had been a quiet competition, without so much as a hat-trick in sight. Indeed, for the last three rounds, only Roy and Blackie had made it onto the scoresheet at all, which must have had old (as he would have been by then) Alf Leeds popping his geriatric head into Ben Galloway's office and inquiring about a bonus. That schoolboy game he saw, all those years earlier, had proved to be a very worthwhile trip.

Before the side could concentrate on the FA Cup, however, there was another league title to win. Rovers hadn't emerged empty-handed from a battle to win the league for the best part of fifteen years, and yet we still wondered if they could pull off a remarkable triumph. Molton United (who, like so many of Rovers' opponents, seemed to have – quite literally – come from nowhere) were a point ahead, but had only one game left to play, while Rovers had two. If Rovers could beat Fordhampton, then their fate was in their own hands; while they did that, if Molton lost to Carford City, Roy would go on to the FA Cup Final with a league title already sewn up, and in search of the double.

Far be it from anyone to suggest that they could look back and second guess what the writers were thinking of, but the year before Arsenal had won the double in bright yellow shirts and grey, dull, real life. That had thrown down a gauntlet to Melchester. You couldn't countenance a real life side doing things with greater style than the Rovers, which meant only one outcome. At the time, it was a different story, and one with endless possibilities.

What was curious, before we even got round to worrying about the game, was the new role played by the previously unobtrusive Penny. Shortly after kick off, she appeared in the dugout, carrying a message, and wearing the miniest of miniskirts and a short coat. She stood out, as nobody else was dressed similarly.

'The news from Molton isn't so good for us,' she told Ben. 'They scored in the first ten minutes.'

This told the regular reader two things. Firstly, as ever, when it came down to the crunch games, the first piece of action would always go against Roy and his side. It gave them a mountain to climb, but that's what they always did, and without an extra challenge, the drama felt far less urgent. Secondly, despite having taken his side to numerous European and domestic glories, Ben Galloway had yet to invest in a radio, and relied on his secretary to bring him messages about other games.

In modern day football, managers are kept in contact with every last, tiny detail of everything that could possibly affect their side, and a dozen things that couldn't possibly, but make them feel important. Sam Allardyce stands on the touchline looking like a man in a call centre, having endless conversations with mysterious, Bluetooth-enabled contacts as the game goes on. Ben just had Penny, and when you contrast the results, Allandyce might have done well to take a leaf from his book.

As half-time arrived, Ben was busy telling his side the bad news about Molton's game, when Penny – obeying the time-honoured Melchester tradition that the dressing room must always have an unscheduled visitor during the break – arrived to let them know that Molton had been pegged back, and were now level. It seems strange that, when Suzanne Cerise turned up, everyone whooped and cheered, in between panting, swooning and promising to try harder in the second half. Penny, who was far better looking than Suzanne, but had chosen typing and filing over acting, turned up, miniskirt, long boots and all, and nobody batted an eyelid. There's a scene the academics chose to ignore when putting together their critical analysis of Roy's attitude to feminism. Nobody even patted her on the bum on the way out of the door.

It was time for a stirring speech, and also a reminder for all those readers for whom maths wasn't the highlight of the school day, of what was required. By anyone's estimation, these were two separate speeches, but Roy moulded them together in his usual, Churchillian style.

'If they draw – and we lose – that would mean we'd go into the Cup Final knowing we'd still got to win our last league match to do the double.'

So, with the story explained, and all the possibilities clear to even the dimmest player and reader, the Rovers stormed out for the second half, and claimed a 2-1 victory. As they sat in the dressing room, reflecting on their win, Ben wandered in, as if he'd just remembered something he had been meaning to tell them.

'I've just had the final score from Molton. They went down 2-1,' he offered, matter-of-factly.

Roy, always on the ball, did the calculations: 'That means we've overtaken them and they can't catch up! Rovers are the league champions! We're halfway to the double!'

This was new and uncharted ground for Roy of the Rovers'

fans. We had been used to a diet of glory and triumph, and even when it was interspersed with defeat and disappointment, it was always exciting. Seasons never petered out into meaningless games, because at the very least, there was always a final of some kind to be contested. This year, though, by any standards, the season was reaching quite a climax.

It would be unfair to suggest that the subsequent Cup Final followed a well-established pattern. Unfair, but true. Melchester were a goal down, had made a bad start, and in Eddie Eager, they had a young player, brought in at the last minute, who appeared to be suffering an attack of nerves which could impact on the whole side. An equally well-established pattern was about to raise its head, however, as Eddie decided to atone for his earlier errors. Plucking up his courage and making a forward run, Eddie looked to have carried the ball too far, losing possession on the edge of the opposition area. Then, with a desperate tackle/shot, he somehow planted the ball beyond the Cranville keeper for an unexpected equaliser.

In doing so, Eddie managed to wrench his knee, and had to be substituted, but his dramatic cameo had paved the way for a Melchester double. Substitute Chalkie White promptly set up the goal to send Rovers ahead. But then they allowed Cranville a way back in, just before the break, as they took their foot off the pedal, and found themselves pegged back to two-all. We have no record, sadly, of who chose to enter the dressing room during this particular half-time, although if the Queen was at the game, she surely couldn't have resisted the chance to offer a few words.

The second half saw Blackie send the Rovers into a 3-2 lead, and Tubby Morton leap to make a late save, denying Cranville an equaliser which would have been greeted with boos from young boys everywhere. Eventually, though, the final whistle arrived, confirming that Melchester had done what Spurs had achieved eleven years earlier, and Arsenal had done the previous season, by winning the double. If Ben Galloway really had concerns about the ability of his squad, then season by season, they were doing what they could to ease his worries.

While still not produced in colour, apart from occasional frames on special occasions, the style of the strips was, to many readers' eyes, as good as it had ever been, and possibly as good as it ever got. Yvonne Hutton, just as Joe Colquhoun had been when he first started drawing Roy's adventures, wasn't a huge football fan. She died tragically young, some years later in a car accident, but all fans of the comic have reason to thank her for bringing on the look of Roy so far, so smoothly, during her time drawing him, between 1967 and 1975. In the early days, he had been quite grey and dour looking, with lots of detailed crowd scenes behind the action that, while interesting in their own right, occasionally made a whole page feel slightly claustrophobic. Hutton lightened the feel considerably, by cutting down on many of the background scenes, and leaving the players, quite often, to be portrayed against a white, or at least considerably sparser and lighter background.

When conversations were important to the plot, she focused just on the heads and shoulders of the participants, adding to the impact, where once the frame would have featured background detail and extraneous features which would have lessened it. It was still a distance away from the colour and style which David Sque would bring to bear in years to come, but by creating a link between the early work of Paul Trevillion and that which Sque was to go on to produce, Hutton played a major part in the developing appearance of Roy Race and his team. Trevillion is a fascinating character, arguably worth a book in his own right. The creator of the famous comic strip quiz 'You are the Ref', his career has included record deals, world records and inventing golfing techniques. As a young man he was invited to draw Winston Churchill, and following on from Roy Race, he drew other sporting legends, such as Pelé, George Best and Tiger Woods. Of all the people who ever drew Roy, nobody ever went on to achieve quite the same heights as Trevillion.

The continuing overhaul was in evidence in the writing and in terms of the characters just as much as it was in terms of the artwork and the appearance. At the start of the following season, Ben Galloway decided it was time to take on some assistance, and appointed former Rovers player and army lieutenant Tony Storme as coach, while also chopping and changing his squad. Among the departures were recent double-winning heroes Eddie Eager and Chalkie White, while joining the club was the Cranville winger Mervyn Wallace, who would go on to great things with the Rovers.

The arrival of Storme, although not exactly a mirror image, could well have been influenced by the decision of Jack Charlton to go into management at Middlesbrough, having finished his playing career with Leeds.

While the season that followed wasn't a huge domestic success, in Europe, Rovers were the side everyone wanted to beat. Wanting to do something, however, and succeeding at it, are two different things. They reached the final of the European Cup against the Portuguese side Corados, which translates as 'Don't trust those sneaky foreigners, because they're all up to no good'. On the way to the final, Roy had claimed six goals, including his traditional semi-final winner, but Wallace was proving to be a star new signing, scoring three himself, which was one more than Blackie.

Corados were a composite of everything Roy had spent several years trying to warn his readers about when it came to European sides and players. They were very skilful – possibly more skilful than Melchester – and they were incredibly tactically astute, which Roy's writers evidently saw as being tantamount to gamesmanship. Rovers were 'foiled by tight marking', which is just one of the ways European sides show their wanton disregard for the entertaining side of the game, by refusing to allow the opposition to score spectacular and thrilling goals against them.

Then there was the physical side, where their defenders put in huge, burly challenges, trying to discourage the Melchester attackers from their trickery, almost as if it were a European final. Finally, there was their comical, pidgin English, which they used to conceal their true intent. Geoff Giles was only small, yet the Corados forwards refused to make allowances for the Melchester centre half, thus exposing their fiendish side. We never found out why Ben played a little centre half in a European final against a giant centre forward, but Tony Storme must have been to blame, making the selection while Ben was out buying a radio.

As the caption recalled, 'Geoff's burly opponent hoisted him back to his feet in a rather patronising way.'

'Keep your hands to yourself, mate!' growled Geoff, only to receive the cheery response: 'Sorry. No spikka Inglees!'

On the touchline, Ben scowled. 'I bet there's nothing they don't know about Geoff's record for losing his temper. They're trying to get him rattled!'

If it is hard to understand exactly what Ben was getting so upset about, it is harder still to see why Geoff Giles insisted on making himself such an easy target. What is clear is that the writers understood their audience perfectly. In the early 1970s, Europe was there to be caricatured, right down to the last bossy German, cowardly Frenchman or overly emotional Italian. Even when Geoff made a goal-line clearance, and was congratulated by his opponent with a pat on the head and a 'Bravo amigo!', he riled at the gesture, only to be greeted with another, smiling 'No spikka Inglees!'.

Somehow, the attacker would be getting his comeuppance – we knew that much. But how? At half-time, a plan was hatched. In the second half Geoff continued to pretend to get upset, receiving endless 'No spikka Inglees' responses, before finally launching his scheme.

'Roy – over to you – on his right!' Geoff called, as he prepared to pass. His marker moved right, proving that he was a sneaky, cheating foreigner who had been able to speak English all along. A million young readers made a mental note never to trust a footballer from abroad ever again. The huge attacker went the wrong way, the dummy was bought and Rovers had sown uncertainty among the Corados ranks. In an instant their cunning façade crumbled, to reveal their nasty side – something else Roy liked to warn us about.

As their discipline faded away, Roy scored one, set up the other for Mervyn Wallace, and the European Cup was Melchester's. It had been a spectacular season, and when Roy and Blackie, with their skills as international diplomats, each scored to give England a 2-0 win against Italy in Rome, nobody was surprised. It seemed to be an appropriate way to round it off.

Rovers started the following season looking as far from the formidable unit of the previous year as it was possible to get. If they weren't getting it right in terms of results, however, when it came to appearance they fared better, and in terms of football kit, managed to stumble across something quite iconic. The yellow stripe down the left hand side of their red shirts, paired with a matching stripe down the right hand side of their shorts, and a third band of yellow down the centre of their socks, was a look that the majority of readers will forever associate with Roy Race and Melchester Rovers. Emerging ever more certainly from the black and white era, with colour frames featuring with greater frequency than ever before, the modern era of Roy of the Rovers was starting to gain momentum.

As yet, nobody had even suggested it might make a comic in its own right, but there was no doubting its place at the fore of the country's sporting comic strip stories. To confirm its confidence as a story, the writers' ability to hint at what was to come, before shamelessly doing it anyway, was as clear as it ever had been. As they lined up for the first game of the new season, we started to hear about a new character – Charlie 'The Cat' Carter. Charlie was a goalkeeper, though (in the considerable shape of Tubby) Rovers already had a goalkeeper. Why did we need to be introduced to Charlie?

It took the writers about half an hour of the first game of the season to break Tubby's leg, and a couple more days to inflict a serious car accident on the hapless reserve keeper, Peter Baker. Once more, it was a lesson worth remembering. For all the moralising and preaching Roy could occasionally be scripted to deliver about the evils which threatened the game, and the need to keep its best interests close at hand, when they needed someone bumped off, there wasn't a contract killer who could compete with Roy's writers.

Still the team's form kept deteriorating, though, and as the players began to talk about a jinx they feared had beset the new kit, Roy was forced to finally produce an early picture of the side, showing that they won matches in such a strip years ago, and they should stop worrying, and do so again. There followed an upturn in form, and a first (and less serious than that which was to follow) meeting between Roy and firearms.

It was a convoluted storyline, featuring the affable Jumbo Trudgeon, a by-pass, a demonstration and an ex-army figure called Colonel Chadwick. A shotgun was accidentally let off, all jokes about Racey's Rocket were temporarily suspended out of respect, and we waited anxiously to see if he would recover from his terrible wounds. After seven days of living on our collective nerves, the next issue popped through the letterbox, and Roy was happily declaring it little more than a scratch, and preparing for the first game. Even as we tempered our relief with annoyance at being caught out by the 'with a mighty leap he was free' plot device once more, we steeled ourselves for the rest of the season. The league may be gone, but with Roy unharmed, was a cup run out of the question? Were we ever really in doubt?

There were some major changes behind the scenes, as Ben Galloway 'moved upstairs' as football writers have described it for years, to become general manager of the Rovers, and Tony Storme became team manager. I don't think we were ever convinced by Storme, at least not since he returned to the club in a coaching role. When the team posed at the start of the season he wore a tracksuit, which was fine by us, and an absurd, floppy hat, which I think it's safe to say was not. It was as if someone was trying to tell us that he was a bit odd and unusual happenings were on the way. We logged this away in the back of our minds – we knew the form.

The League Cup, which had never really featured all that highly on Melchester's list of priorities before, was claimed with a 1-0 win over Highwood, with Roy scoring the winner, having been strangely out of form, scoring only the nine goals in the run up to the final. By the time they reached the FA Cup Final as well, with Roy netting a mere five along the way, there were problems for him to deal with, though. The board had promised Rovers £5,000 each if they won the final, and the players talked about little else.

It was a footballing parable waiting to happen, and when Rovers went one down in the early stages, it gave Roy the chance to lecture his side about the evils of money, when set against the glory of the game. Slightly priggish, perhaps, and given the frequency with which Rovers went behind in all manner of finals, a speech he could certainly have pre-prepared, but delivered with outraged gusto nonetheless.

At half-time, however, there was the customary visit to the dressing room, this time by Ted Manning, a director of the club. Upset at the effect the £5,000 carrot had on his side, he upped it to £7,000. Roy was furious. He had already promised to give his prize money away to a youth club and, enraged by Manning's gesture (the last footballer in England to be upset by the promise of more money) set about winning the game. He equalised early on, delivered another lecture, and then claimed the winner. Had there been moneylender's tables on the pitch, he'd have turned them over, too.

It was a very strange interlude, and for a while, Roy and his side seemed to be overtaken by a string of them. Tubby Morton came back to training, and briefly got back into the side, as Charlie Carter pursued an unlikely – and frankly absurd – ambition to become a pop star. Having become entangled with an agent called Larry Sharp, Charlie was being actively lured away from Mel Park, and eventually, with his head swimming with the options, Charlie was dropped, with Tubby returning to the team. When Roy took Charlie on one side, it was clear why he had become so distracted.

'I could earn as much as £50,000 in the first two years, Roy!' Charlie announces. 'Pheeeew!' replied Roy. 'No wonder you're tempted. Earnings like that could set you up for life!'

And so the dilemma went, until Roy got a friend, Marty Miller, who understood the world of showbusiness, to have a look at Charlie's contract. Just as he was about to sign his career away, Charlie had the small print of the contract explained to him by Miller. He was, as we all suspected, being set up to be fleeced. Once put in the picture, Charlie reacted in the mature and dignified way we expected of our heroes, even those who had so recently had their heads turned by fame, and threw Sharp into the Melchester team bath.

Charlie's haircut, an extraordinary combination of spiked hair, a partly straightened mullet and a whiff of hairspray which made its way clean off the page, was based, surely, on Rod Stewart's, while the other, peripheral showbusiness figures were composite characters of the sort of colourful types who filled the world of entertainment in the early 1970s, all wide lapels and loud suits. It was different – certainly not dour or sensible, but there was a feeling that some of the footballing content had been lost.

Andrew Thompson is now a software development manager but remains, more than thirty years on, unhappy at the Melchester goalkeeper's flirtation with the world of pop music.

I was ten years old when that story started, and I'd been a reader for eighteen months or so. I remember being really irritated by it. My sister used to have her comic delivered with my copy of *Roy of the Rovers*, I can't remember what it was, but it was full of pop singers with long hair. Because I was a boy of a certain age, I hated it, absolutely everything to do with it; all I wanted was muddy knees and a football.

And then, all of a sudden, it was as if a part of her comic had come and invaded mine! I didn't want a pop star story. I wanted my football story back. I can remember it as if it were yesterday. I was so relieved when it finally got back to normal again.

And there rests the case for those who argue that there was no need to worry that readers might find some of the stories repetitive. This reader found the prospect of a little variation far more worrying than the threat of yet more of the same.

All we needed was for Charlie to find his way back into the side again, but with Tubby playing so well how could the writers possibly sort out such a problem? Need you ask? An injury, they reckoned, finished Tubby's career. The writers had done for him properly, this time. Thankfully, Roy had a job for him all lined up, managing the Melchester 'A' team. In a more cynical age, Roy could have been questioned for conspiracy to commit GBH on the unwitting Tubby, who seemed to get badly hurt with remarkable and highly convenient frequency.

It wasn't the spate of serious injuries, and the timing with which they seemed to occur, which troubled the Rovers fans throughout the forthcoming season, however, so much as the actions of their new manager. Whether Storme, a former soldier, was feeling a touch of much-delayed shell-shock, or whether he had just gone temporarily mad of his own volition, we never discovered, but some of the decisions which emerged from the office of the Rovers' manager over the course of the first few months of the 1974–75 season were, to say the least, bizarre.

The odd, not to say surreal decisions Storme proceeded to make, adds further fuel to the theory that the story was becoming too big to be housed as part of another comic, and perhaps, if it were to achieve its full potential, needed a home all of its own. Apart from the footballing action it conveyed, the story was also, once more, being used to carry various comedic and far-fetched plotlines, as if forced to introduce humour, whether or not it felt it appropriate.

Storme's actions in dealing with an injury to Jumbo Trudgeon were a perfect example. He had always appeared a little odd, although we took his insistence on wearing that obscure, safari-style hat in the team photographs as evidence of his military background. When Jumbo got hurt, though, and a replacement was needed to fill the void until Melchester's most well-to-do player returned to fitness, Storme looked not towards the dug-out, but the big top.

Sammy Spangler was a circus juggler, whose act involved all manner of balancing feats with a variety of objects, prime among them, footballs. Somehow Storme convinced himself, and more remarkably, the board, that these skills were transferable, and could be hugely effective on the pitch. It was a mad idea to start with, but when Roy got injured against Highwood with the game seemingly over and Rovers 4-0 up, we thought that Spangler, who was substitute, would at least get an easy introduction to professional football.

There are certain things a side require from a substitute. A degree of versatility is obviously helpful, and an ability to burst onto proceedings and make an impact as the opposition begins to tire is another. Prime among the things you need from your substitutes, though, before any of these other attributes, is that they turn up. It was at this formative yet crucial hurdle that Spangler stumbled. When Tony Storme turned round to tell him to get his tracksuit off and get ready to play, Spangler had wandered off, and failed to return.

Rovers were pegged back from 4-0 up, to eventually draw the game 4-4, and the end, for both men, was in sight. If it was already unlikely Storme would survive after the fiasco, it became inevitable a week later, as Rovers prepared to play non-league Sleeford Town in the FA Cup. Adopting the maxim about getting straight back onto the bike after a fall, Storme decided the best way to cure Spangler of the nerves that had seemingly precipitated his dis-appearance the previous week, was to put him in the starting line-up. So, against a side with nothing to lose, on a ground bursting at the seams with fans, and with the need to maintain their composure and professionalism absolutely paramount, Melchester Rovers kicked off the game with a circus juggler in midfield.

As plans go, football has seen better. They tumbled out of the cup, 2-1, and taking his cue from the past actions of his juggling midfielder, Storme fled the scene. Given that the option was to explain the rationale behind his selection policy to Ben Galloway, it was a good decision. People might, however, have expected poor Tony to reappear when he thought Galloway had calmed down slightly. They were mistaken. Days went by, and with the manager still absent, the board made a decision. Things couldn't carry on like this – Storme had made a mockery of the club, and they were going to react, if only to restore some dignity to proceedings.

Roy became player-manager, but the lack of information about what had happened to Storme unsettled him, and he was unsure about stepping into a role that had not, formally at least, been vacated by its previous incumbent. Then again, he was a cartoon character, and if the writers decided it would be a good storyline to appoint him as manager, Tony's chances of ever coming back were decreasing by the minute.

There was a brief reappearance by Storme shortly afterwards, when, while heavily disguised, he passed a note to Roy at half-time, offering advice as to how the Rovers played the second half, but it was clear that the writers were unconvinced by the character, and needed to see him safely off the premises. Mercifully, they opted against killing him off, which given what happened to Tubby, whose knees were capped every time Charlie Carter needed a run out, must have been a distinct possibility.

Instead, he emerged from hiding on the eve of Rovers' appearance in the Cup Winners' Cup Final of 1975, to announce that he was leaving football to go into business with his brother. We never discovered whether the business venture, which involved leisure centres, was a success, or indeed, whether he employed Sammy Spangler, but given the problems he had caused Melchester Rovers, Tony Storme was grateful simply to escape with all his limbs intact.

The final, in one of the occasional brushes with reality Roy enjoyed, was played at the very real Hampden Park, against the very fictitious Greek side Niarkos, and marked Roy's first major test as a manager. It didn't look all that promising in the run up to the game; he rued only bothering to learn about Niarkos's semi-final opponents (the Spanish side Atletico Tandora) leaving him to plan tactics for a side about which he knew practically nothing.

Having spent the majority of the game trying to work out who was playing where, and who the opposition danger men were, Roy eventually opted for the tried and tested tactic against European sides of pushing a defender upfield, and watching the opposition swarm forwards, before chuckling at their naïve ambitions, and scoring on the counter attack. It was a dilemma for Roy. Sometimes, as with Corados, the cunning Portuguese side he had beaten a couple of years earlier, foreigners were shrewd and tactical. This, we gathered, was negative, dull and decidedly sneaky – something an English side would never countenance.

Then, along came Niarkos, and Roy seemed to be luring them forwards in a way some might consider shrewd and tactical – something which, when done by Melchester, was a way of taking football to a new level. You might consider that Roy was occasionally guilty of double standards when it came to continental sides, but you were probably too busy cheering on the Rovers, as they scored the two late goals which claimed them yet another European trophy.

It should have been the start of a well-deserved holiday for Roy, but he found himself back in international action again just months later, playing in a European Nations Cup game against France. He had a friend, Jules Bernard, who played for the French side; he was probably the only foreigner Roy trusted. Jules was worth millions, for reasons that we never understood. His wealth had certainly attracted attention, though, enough for a good, old plotline to raise its head once more; shortly before the start of the game, Jules's nephew got kidnapped.

Roy and Jules plotted together – an unlikely alliance that, for some reason, they felt would solve the crime more swiftly than involving the police. While it seemed promising, by the time kick off arrived, neither Jules nor Roy was aware whether the nephew was safe or not. Strangely, they decided to play on in any event, Jules arriving as a second-half substitute to inform Roy that their plan had been a success, and the boy was free. Jules celebrated by thinking of the happy, family reunion that could now take place, while Roy ran rings around him to score two goals and win the game.

It was an obscure pre-season storyline, and reminded us that, while we were all too ready to mock the continual cricket matches and doom-laden foreign tours which otherwise occupied Melchester's summer months, at least they were tried and tested episodes. Happy as we were that Jules hadn't had to endure receiving bits of his nephew posted back to him at regular intervals, the whole thing was over and done just a bit too swiftly. We liked our drama stretched out a little bit more, and given that we knew, ultimately, Roy would escape with a mighty leap, both literal and metaphorical sometimes, who could blame us?

Besides, Roy should have taken a break, and lounged around on a beach for a while, because having played football seemingly all summer, in between frustrating organised gangs of kidnappers, his management skills were suffering. Rovers lost the first five games of the following season, and their league challenge was over before it began. They made an important signing, however, with the writers opting to introduce a touch of grit into the side, sending a tough Scot called Duncan McKay to Rovers, where he would stay for many seasons to come. Duncan called people 'Laddie', and had a beard and headband. Had he been allowed to play with haggis in hand, just to further reinforce the image, he would surely have done so.

Duncan provided crucial stability to the Rovers, while Roy,

after his disastrous start to the season, seemed finally to have got the hang of management. He led Rovers in a dramatic and desperate charge up the table, which eventually left them in second place, short of the title by just one measly point. Defeat to Westhampton, who were virtually doomed to relegation, killed off their chances, but it wasn't, even then, the biggest news of that particular campaign. Earlier in the season, we had seen the end of Jumbo. He was allowed to retire with a degree of dignity, rather than be killed off in a freak Deep Heat accident, but it was still a sad day. Jumbo had been absurd when he arrived, then he'd been funny, and suddenly, before we knew it, he'd become part of the wallpaper. It was quite a loss, if you were young and easily impressed.

It should have been a crucial time for the readers, as Roy moved into the next stage of his career, managing the team while still proving that he was the best player in the game. We were distracted, though, by the fact that Penny, the secretary with an eye for the main role, was still popping up in the story at regular intervals. She seemed to get along with Roy very well – very well indeed, actually – until one day, to our horror, they announced that she was going to marry him! On Cup Final day!

'I quite fancied Penny, if I'm being honest,' says Stephen Davidson, who, as a teacher, may now regret, when he next meets his pupils, being quite so frank. 'Maybe that was what told me I was a bit old to still be reading the comic – I must have been about 14 at the time, but I enjoyed the football side of it, I had done for years, and I couldn't give it up. I was hooked.

'Mind you, even then, I think I knew it was a bit odd to be young enough to read a comic, and old enough to fancy the main character's wife-to-be.'

It was, clearly, an odder sensation than many of us were going through, but the confusion, if not the reason for it, was widespread. It was hard to know what to think. In 1976 the real life Cup Final offered an extraordinary David v Goliath clash, as Southampton took on Manchester United and, in Roy of the Rovers style, beat them. Not for the first time, when the real world offered genuine competition as far as drama was concerned, our favourite comic declined to take the challenge head on, but found an angle of its own, to counteract whatever reality threw at it.

Cup Final day, after all, was a sacred event, full of specially branded and utterly peripheral nonsense that children loved. It began at about mid-morning, and after numerous interludes chronicling how the sides reached the final, there would be a spot of Cup Final *A Question of Sport*. Having survived this brush with knitwear, there was usually a little bit of behind the scenes footage, showing footballers lounging around a hotel, before they disappeared for a while, emerging back in flared trousers and jackets which were all lapel and no body, for the journey to Wembley and, if we were really lucky, a camera on the coach.

By the time we'd seen them inspect the pitch (looks very flat and grassy, could be some cramp later on in the day) we'd had all we could take. The game was always rubbish, and the children were always chastised for pointing it out. The *A Question of Sport* picture board was the high point of the day most years, and from 11am it was all downhill.

But, it was the Cup Final, and as such it was special. And now Roy Race, of all people, was mucking it up, by using it as the launch pad for a wedding. We didn't know enough about this woman – admittedly she always seemed to know the football scores, but was that enough? She could know the goal difference for all we cared, just as long as she didn't upset the delicate balance of our comic world. Many of us felt a touch betrayed.

Roy's hat-trick in the semi-final had made it such a special prospect, but the wedding hung over it like a cloud. It was almost as if the prospect of what was to come weighed down the players, who could see a man they had always considered strangely androgynous and wedded to his football, getting wed to the secretary. Had we been able to express it in such terms, well, actually, we wouldn't have done. We were just upset a girl was gate-crashing our comic.

There would be a lot of adjusting to do, and nobody could blame us. This had never been done before, marrying off a comic hero. Not once, in the vast history of sporting comic action in this country had a hero gone off and got married. They were busy winning things, or shooting Germans (or aliens) and making stirring speeches, and suddenly, Roy thought he could combine heroism with marriage. We knew the comic precedent. We knew how distracted Clark Kent got by Lois Lane. And *he* was a superhero.

The final started badly, with Melchester going behind, and their bid to get back into the game never quite came to life. There was a dispute about a bouncing ball and whether it had crossed the line. Ten Rovers players claimed it had, while Roy lectured them for not playing to the whistle, and explained that the referee's decision was final. You could, if you were being particularly biased, claim that Penny was clearly already turning him soft, but in fairness, he'd been making similar observations long before she arrived on the scene.

Come the final whistle, the Rovers players looked utterly dejected, until Roy reminded them of the ceremony they had to attend later in the afternoon. Grinning, he strolled towards a group including big, tough Duncan:

'So . . . Heads up, Rovers! I don't want to see any Cup Final blues on my final day of freedom!'

'Freedom?' queried Duncan, who, like the big, tough defender he was, plainly took little interest in such things, before remembering: 'Gosh, I almost forgot! Roy's getting married!'

Being told that the Cup Final defeat didn't matter, because there was a nice wedding to attend may not have been the most cheering thing Duncan ever heard. For what it's worth, the audience wasn't hugely chuffed, either. The Rovers took their duties seriously, though, and still in their kit (they must have smelt glorious), they formed a guard of honour outside the church. It was the most surreal, single illustration of the Rovers side ever drawn, and as the years went by, there was serious competition for that role, as well.

It was crunch time for Roy. In many young minds, the season had been a horrible failure, and a marriage was in serious danger of allowing far too much light in on far too much magic. What he said next could determine how seriously we took him. We were desperate for Roy not to sell out, to say something that reminded us where his priorities really lay.

'Well,' he said, turning to his bride, as they walked back down the red carpet. 'I can't say the season has been a complete loss, Penny!'

At the time we probably cheered the sentiment, but adulthood (allegedly) brings with it greater depths of subtlety and discretion.

How, we wonder, did she manage to throw her bouquet to the crowd, when the temptation to shove it in her new husband's football-obsessed face must have been overwhelming?

She'd have had to be quick, though, as Roy responded to her bouquet by kicking a ball into the crowd.

'Let's hope a youngster gets it!' remarked Noel Baxter, thus confirming that, while he'd only ever been a member of the supporting cast, as far as the Melchester squad were concerned, he'd also always been a bit of a manager's pet. 'It might be some kind of omen for him!'

And then they disappeared off, to hold the wedding reception in the Melchester Supporters' Club, which always seemed a bit cheap, given that he surely got a discount. Would things ever be the same again, or had our hero lost his edge for ever? We waited nervously to find out.

CHAPTER SIX

STANDING ON HIS OWN TWO FEET

'As a nine-year-old, the best thing in the whole world was to get together your complete collection, which was probably a hundred comics or more, and then sneak a day off sick from school. Your mum would insist you stayed in bed, and so you did, happily, going through a whole season at a time, story by story. That was as good a day as you could have.'

Tony Hedling

Even though Roy had seemed intent on getting value for money from his wedding with the less than salubrious reception venue, there were others who had more glamorous plans for his future, both on and off the page. As the new season arrived, in the August of 1976, a chain of supermarkets decided to spice up the league by offering £30,000 to the first player to score fifty goals in a season. Placing the reward into perspective is easy – just a year or so earlier the writers had presented us with the torn figure of Charlie Carter, who considered giving up the game because his potential earnings from music could have reached £50,000 'in the first two years alone'. In the real world, Bob Latchford scored thirty goals in a season for Everton, two years later, and collected just £10,000 for his efforts.

Roy had, of course, interrupted his honeymoon in order to go and play for a European Select XI, but all talk was of the possibility of him collecting the prize, and the battle which would rage between Blackie and Mervyn Wallace, who many thought (and the writers ensured) would push him all the way. Of more major importance to the fans, however, was the way in which they would learn about this race for the goalscoring crown.

A month after the competition was announced, there was a further announcement, this time impacting on real, rather than fictitious life. Our suspicions that Roy had gone as far as he could go in *Tiger* were confirmed; our fears that the story was too big for the comic were shared by the management. We had worried that he overshadowed the other tales, that his deeds earned too much attention for him, despite his best intentions, to be a comic book team player. Having grown too big for the comic which had housed him for more than twenty-two years, where now? Was this the end for Roy of the Rovers?

Of course it wasn't. The solution the writers and editor came up with, however, was more daring and extensive than a generation of impressionable young readers dared to dream of. For the next few months, Roy of the Rovers continued to run in *Tiger*, as it had done for more than two decades, but it did not run there exclusively. On 26 September 1976, a new comic hit the shelves, with a familiar face on the front. *Roy of the Rovers*, the weekly comic, as opposed to merely the weekly comic strip, was born.

It was exciting in its own right, but coupled with the continued existence of *Tiger*, it meant the temporary opportunity to double up on your comic intake, claiming a double dose of Roy and his adventures, as Barrie Tomlinson explains:

> I was the editor of *Tiger* before Roy of the Rovers was dreamed of as a comic in its own right, and over the years I had persuaded the powers that be that the comic was better suited to being purely a sporting comic, and less of a mix of sport and action stories. We had some real success with *Tiger*, and as time moved on I came to the conclusion that it would be a good idea to refine it a bit more, and have a purely footballing comic, and no other sports in there.
>
> When the management asked me to have a proper look at this idea, I very quickly came to the conclusion that there was only one story to lead the new title. From that idea, and having looked at all the other popular football stories we had at the time, *Roy of the Rovers* was born, or at least, was born in its own right as a comic.
>
> We had to put in place a few insurance policies, if you like, to make sure it didn't do too much damage to *Tiger*, so (and maybe it was a bit novel) we had Roy of the Rovers running in both comics for a while, overlapping. We had the same author, which meant that the chances of the storylines conflicting with each other were minimalised, and thankfully the two artists had very similar styles, but it was a bit of a venture for us, running the same story in two different places

at the same time, all of it with different storylines. It did take
a bit of looking after.

Tomlinson's achievements in the comic world are many and
varied. Of all the moments of inspiration he came up with,
however, the decision to separate Roy from *Tiger*, and then to
manage to float the two successfully, both in their own right, was
a triumph, both of vision and execution.

Roy of the Rovers, standing on its own two feet, so to speak,
represented something that nobody in British comics had been
prepared to do before. The only comics that had survived while
concentrating on just one subject were war-based. *Tiger* had been
a sporting comic, but given the range of sports it featured, it could
hardly be said to be limited by that choice. Roy, however, was
taking matters a step further, and while there were doubts, for
Tomlinson it represented an ambition, rather than a problem:

> It was quite a challenge at first to produce a comic with, let's
> say, eight stories, all about football, because that hadn't been
> done before. I had always felt it could be done, though, and
> there was the space in the market to do it. As a single story,
> Roy's was popular enough to convince me that it could be
> done on the back of it. What really made it work, though,
> was the fact that we managed to stumble across a few very
> strong stories to go alongside it. Some of them became really
> long-running stories, like 'The Hard Man' and 'Tommy's
> Troubles', and that gave us a very strong base.

The spine of the comic, however, would always be Roy, and his
adventures with Melchester. A twenty-two year head start in *Tiger*
ensured a secure place in the public's affections, and even within
the first few issues, it was made perfectly clear that while Roy
might have a new home of his own, the sentiment and feel of the
story would not be changing a jot.

Roy Dalton was twelve years old when the new comic arrived
on the shelves, a day after four schoolboys in Dublin decided to
name their new group U2, while Czechoslovakia had just become
European champions, having beaten the Western half of a

Germany which was still very much divided. For Dalton, it was evidently one of childhood's great moments:

> I can remember it very clearly, and yet I obviously never took on board any of the reasoning behind it. I was twelve, and delighted. That was all there was to it.
>
> One week, I had a hero who lived in a comic with loads of other characters I liked, but never worshipped in quite the same way. Suddenly, as if from out of the blue, my hero had a comic of his own, a bundle of stories that felt as if they were written just for me, and I still had the old comic I'd always loved. It's the excitement I can remember, I suppose, rather than the detail. It was as if I'd got to the end of Christmas Day, and they'd announced that there would be another one, tomorrow. It was honestly that good.
>
> When *Tiger* came through the door, it was the best moment of the whole week. I'd be off, upstairs, and camp in my bedroom – I always read it in my bedroom, because I'd be undisturbed – until it was finished. Every last word and picture. Suddenly, the end was only the halfway point, because there was another one to start. Somewhere, someone had pinpointed the best part of my week, and decided to make it last twice as long. I'll never forget, as odd as it might sound, that moment. I'm smiling to myself now, just thinking about it.

Roy Race had no intention of letting young Roy Dalton down, as the new title launched with a fresh impetus. The money from the race to fifty goals competition, if he should win it, would go to charity, although exactly where, he was not saying. There were still plenty of local youth clubs rubbing their hands in anticipation because they always seemed a likely recipient for any moments of benevolence the great man might be about to provide. Having just started the title, it would have been a foolhardy gambler who backed anyone other than Melchester that season, but even the most optimistic (or cynical, depending on your stance) probably wouldn't have backed them to go the first twenty games of the season unbeaten.

They finally lost in February 1977, getting dumped out of the League Cup in the process, then exited the FA Cup the following month, but the new title had learned some important lessons from seasons gone by. Having at one stage seemed safely away and clear at the top of the table, Rovers had a dreadful run in the latter stages of the season. They had racked up twenty-nine successive unbeaten league games by the time they finally lost, but once the dam was breached, the defeats flooded in. By the end of the season, they needed to win their last two games to clinch the title, which, on reflection, seemed to be just about the same position they were in most years.

By the final game of the season, victory over Tynecaster stood between Rovers and the title, while Roy stood on forty-nine goals, and Mervyn Wallace on forty-seven, as the race to fifty went down to the wire. Come the day, a packed crowd roared on the Rovers, watching Mervyn score twice in the first half to effectively wrap up the title, and leaving both players on forty-nine goals.

The crowd waited until the very last minute of the game for a resolution of the season-long debate, as Mervyn lobbed the keeper, and Roy, racing to follow up the chance, headed it home. The players celebrated the title, while the fans went suitably mad, but the man himself was curiously reticent, as if there was something he wanted to say, but couldn't find the moment. In the end, as he addressed the crowd after the game, speaking via a microphone from the directors' box, he explained his awkwardness.

'First of all, I want to thank the greatest fans in the world for helping us to bring the Championship trophy back to Melchester! But as far as the "Goal Rush" is concerned, you're cheering the wrong man!'

The stadium went silent – or as quiet as a stadium goes ten minutes after a late goal has just claimed the league title.

'What's he talking about? There was no one else in the running for the money!'

The voice came from the crowd, from a man, judging by the picture, standing at least 20 yards away. Roy, not for the first time, must have had ears like a bat . . .

'Yes there was . . .' Roy replied, 'Mervyn Wallace! Everyone seems to have forgotten that he had forty-seven goals to his credit, before this game began!'

The voice in the crowd wouldn't be silenced. Like Statler and Waldorf, barracking the Muppets, it refused to back down.

'So what, Roy? Mervyn only grabbed two goals this afternoon. He needed a hat-trick to win the "Goal-Rush"!'

'And he got it . . . including the last-minute goal which every-one thinks I scored!'

'What? You mean, you're giving the goal to me, Roy?' Mervyn asked, looking bemused.

'I've got to Mervyn,' confirmed a blond haired, footballing legend, suddenly worth £30,000 less than we thought he was. 'The highlights of the game will be on television tonight, and I'm certain the cameras will show that the ball had crossed the line before I touched it! It was definitely Mervyn's goal!'

It was a moment of touching generosity – or was it a man admitting the defeat he knew the cameras would eventually and inevitably reveal, so getting the plaudits for being a sportsman while he still could? Perish the thought. None of us cared that, in the real world, Liverpool might have been retaining their title, because, not for the first time, in the minds of millions of young boys, Rovers were showing how to do things with true style.

Mervyn went off on a lap of honour, shouting repeatedly about how rich he was, while Ben Galloway came over to whisper in Roy's ear, and suddenly, the player-manager was rushing off. What, we wondered, could the problem be? Why were they heading towards the hospital?

We soon found out, although what they made on the labour ward, of Roy tearing through the door, still in his kit, is hard to tell. Indeed, what Penny made of Ben – who after all was only her boss, not her father – charging in behind him, is equally unclear. We do know, however, that the matron, who looked predictably stern, informed Roy that:

'It's all over, Mr Race! Mothers-to-be can't wait for football matches to end, you know!'

These days, of course, they can. Or at least, they arrange to have the baby to fit around their Premiership father's fixture list, but in 1977, things were different. Penny was sitting there, looking understandably pleased with herself, but with the air, we felt, of a woman with a surprise.

'Roy, come and say hello to your son!'

'A boy! I've got a boy!' he replied, showing an excellent appreciation of the facts.

'And don't forget to say hello to your daughter!'

Roy looked almost as baffled as he'd been when Melchester went a goal behind in the Cup Winners' Cup Final, and sat down to take in the news. And, presumably, to think about how to explain how he, as a new father of twins, would explain how he'd given away £30,000 on a whim, about forty-five minutes earlier. Ben backed quietly away, out of the door and kept on going, thinking much the same thought.

There were those who feared that fatherhood would blunt Roy's competitive edge, although the naming of the children put paid to that. How Penny allowed him to get away with calling his son 'Roy Chester Race' is yet another mystery, while 'Melinda', his daughter, shows all the signs of having been named by her mother. First marriage, now children – we loved our comic, but it did sometimes seem determined to make us grow up faster than we'd intended . . .

Making gestures through the naming of his first born couldn't conceal the loss of form the Rovers were suffering over the first half of the following season, however. Their league title was meekly surrendered, all chances of retention gone by the end of 1977, and their domestic cup form was, to say the least, poor, as they slumped out of both competitions without leaving a mark. Excitement could have been considered thin on the ground, but with a new comic to promote, and a potential new audience to attract, the writers knew far better than to let things fall too silent. What was left for Roy to do, though? How could they combine his new role as player-manager at Melchester, with the international scene, which was clearly the only place left for him to go?

The answer was provided with the same clinical efficiency which had seen Tubby and a host of others depart the scene when their usefulness had ended. Just before an important international friendly, against Holland, the England manager had a serious car accident, and Roy took his place. By this stage of the strip's life, we understood pretty well how things worked – if you stood in the way of smiling, sportsmanlike Roy, sooner or later, injury, death, maiming or some other form of misfortune would overwhelm you. Had Roy known what the writers were doing in his name, we'd have had another lecture on our hands, but it seems he never thought to question how much of his good fortune was down to other people's desperate luck.

The writers needed to come up with something particularly clever to make it stand out as a storyline, and as ever, they were equal to the task. Roy had a long look at the players at his disposal, and decided this was no time for sentiment – the side would be picked on merit. Despite this, of the thirteen-man squad for the game, Melchester players filled eight places, with Mike Bateson and Nipper Lawrence from Blackport also getting called up, and Johnny Dexter, who Roy had long admired, called home from Spain, where he had been playing for Real Granpala.

It left two places, one for an out and out striker, and another for someone who could maybe play off the front two, just behind Roy and his strike partner – but who, among all the sides Roy had watched, could provide players to fill such roles? The answer was both brilliant and simple, as most good ideas are.

In the front row of the England squad picture, crouching next to Roy, is Trevor Francis, then of Birmingham City, with black bouffant hair identical to Roy's blond version. On the other side was Malcolm Macdonald, Arsenal legend, and particularly well captured by David Sque. The Dutch must have known they were doomed. Even if their footballing talents somehow proved to be insufficient, the writers would drag things around in England's favour by the end of ninety minutes. And, of course, if they couldn't manage that, they'd make sure half of the Dutch side perished in a hideous clog-related accident, just to be certain. If Roy was entering the international arena, they had to be prepared to be even more ruthless than before.

It was an extraordinary storyline in many different ways. Firstly, these were major stars of the time – Macdonald was enjoying a successful career with Arsenal, having won the last of his fourteen real life England caps a year earlier, while with Newcastle. While on the way to recapturing the form which had earned him a call up, Macdonald injured his knee and never featured for England again, thus making his appearance alongside Roy his 'last' international. However, having scored all five England goals in a 5–0 defeat of Cyprus some years earlier, (a feat even Roy never managed) Supermac's legend was already assured.

Francis was a hero to the fans at Birmingham, having progressed through the youth system to become a first-team star, before making his England debut under Don Revie. It was an event a few years later, however, which secured his place in the record books, when he signed for Nottingham Forest for a million pounds, the first British player ever to command such a fee. Between the two players, their fee for appearing in a comic (or similar) in the present day Premiership world would have been astronomical, but for *Roy of the Rovers*, their affection for the title was such that it was done for a 'nominal' sum. So nominal, that none of the people involved in paying it can remember what it cost, other than that it was little more than a gesture.

Not least among the ways the storyline was unusual was in its bringing together of the fictional and the real. This had happened only once before, with Bobby Charlton supposedly writing storylines, and it had much the same effect – reminding the reader that they were just that: stories. Given the issues with print deadlines, it would always be impossible to include Roy in real life tournaments, so friendlies such as this were the closest he got to the otherwise logical conclusion to his career. The appearance of Macdonald and Francis reminds us of the innocence of the age, million pound signings or not.

On the pitch, it all started perfectly for England, with Roy heading down into Macdonald's path ('Yours, Supermac!'), allowing the Arsenal striker to volley home a dramatic opener, made possible by Francis's astute early pass. In the current era, their agents would have negotiated exactly how many appearances, passes and goals each would manage, but back in the innocent 1970s, the writers simply shared it out between the two men.

The Wembley crowd, for reasons which never seemed clear,

started to sing 'You'll Never Walk Alone', although they didn't get the rest of the words quite right, making it more puzzling still. It certainly distracted the England defence enough to allow the Dutch to equalise shortly afterwards. Momentarily deflated, it looked as if Roy's big day might drift into disappointment, until we realised how carefully he had picked his side. Francis got a hat-trick, Macdonald scored twice, and despite not scoring, for his role in guiding England to 'its greatest night in years', Roy was clearly a hero.

As the Dutch captain, and Roy lookalike, Johan Seegrun pointed out, shaking Roy's hand, afterwards: 'We bow out to the better team, Roy . . . But I do not think those people will let you get away so easily!'

'Aye!' said Roy, looking at the crowds, and momentarily adopting a Scottish accent (the writer, Tom Tully, hailed from Glasgow, and nobody ever thought to edit out his occasional pieces of regional dialect). 'That's what I was thinking, Johan . . .!'

Our minds were full of questions. Had Roy been too successful for our own good? Would England come calling, asking him to be the next manager? Would the current manager recover, only for the public to demand that Roy remain in his place? If so, would the writers have any hesitation in finding another way of killing him off?

The answer to all these fears was a resounding no, but there were other issues lurking in the back of our brains. Why was Roy so friendly with Johan Seegrun? Why did we even need to know his name? Why, and this was the most worrying, did he have a speaking role?

The moment he opened his mouth and said anything more meaningful than 'No spikka Inglees' we knew Johan was there for a reason. For a while, the most popular theory was that he would soon be heading to Melchester, to form a blond, mulleted strike partnership; but with Mervyn Wallace having just scored fifty goals in a season, replacing him might have seemed just a little harsh. And then, slowly, and to the writers' credit, the story unfolded, as Rovers, despite their dismal domestic form, crept ever closer to a European Cup Final.

Having beaten Dorino Dynamos of Italy (again, not one of the better named sides in the comic's history), Rovers earned a place in the final against the Dutch side, Alkhoven. You'll have guessed who was playing up front for Alkhoven and it was Johan who ensured that Melchester finished the season empty handed, scoring in a 3-2 defeat. From the moment we were introduced to him, at the start of the England game, we knew Johan would play some role at some stage in the future, but we had always imagined it would be to the benefit of the Rovers. Now it was clear that he was something of a red herring, and when he re-emerged it was to dash our hopes, not consolidate them. Perhaps we'd taken things just a little for granted – Roy was still able to wrong-foot us.

And not just us, but possibly, we learned in the latter part of 1978, the whole of Melchester, not to mention English football. In hindsight, had Roy never heard of Basran, we would all have been better off. The kidnap tally over the course of his career was already unfeasibly high, and as events would show, this latest arrival on the storyline scene was unlikely to make things much better.

Basran was a Middle-Eastern state, which, as a result of its oil, had a ruling elite with more money than they knew what to do with. The Sheik of Basran was football mad and wanted to buy something English. After the seasons Melchester had enjoyed over recent years, it was hardly a surprise when they caught his eye, but he was after something more precise than an entire club.

The Sheik had been studying English football closely for a long time, with a view to developing the game in Basran and one day, given that finance was no barrier, turning it into a world force. When it came to planning his footballing revolution, there was only one man to turn to. Roy was offered a million pounds to become the head of football in Basran, a job that seemed to encapsulate everything from national team manager to chief scout, with the freedom to do exactly what he wanted, as long as the side could be seen to be making tracks towards the summit of world football.

All of this was played out against the background of real life England manager Don Revie's decision to leave the national side and go to coach the United Arab Emirates. This was possibly the largest single blow (the 6–3 crushing by Hungary in 1953 aside) to its pride English football had, up to that point, suffered. Revie had previously coached a Leeds side which had won the league and earned scarcely a single fan from anywhere outside a short distance of that city. You could choose any one of a wide range of adjectives – ugly and brutal will do nicely – and know that someone else has already used them in connection with Leeds' playing style.

The fury at his departure was such that the FA banned him from football for ten years, although a court soon reversed what was plainly an embittered sentence. Revie eventually stayed in the region for eight years, before returning home to nurse his sick wife, and then falling ill himself, eventually dying in 1989 of motor neurone disease. It is hard to imagine quite how much controversy he courted, although perhaps it was only once he walked away from the England job that people had a precise focus on which to pin their anger. Previously the complaints had been about the style of football he preached, and as such were limited to fans of the game. Once the word 'traitor' was bandied about, everyone could join in with the witch-hunt.

The parallels with the storyline linking Roy with Basran are obvious, and yet another example of how the writers would 'tweak' events in the real world, in order to fit them into Roy's. It was an attention-grabbing tale, and we all knew, despite the odd twist and turn along the way, that it would work out for the best. It was a classic piece of Roy of the Rovers writing, dragging in almost every conceivable character at one point or another.

It was also, in its way, an extension of the parable of 'Goal Rush' from which we had only just recovered (and as a result of which, Mervyn Wallace was still celebrating). Someone was trying to purchase a chunk of Roy's love for the game, and we waited nervously to see how he'd react. In 1978, a million pounds was an almost inconceivably large amount of money. It would be another year before Trevor Francis, his fee evidently boosted by his impressive display for England alongside Roy and Malcolm Macdonald, moved from Birmingham to Nottingham Forest for a million pounds (although the actual figure was £999,999), and the game was still far from familiar with multi-million pound sums.

In true parable style, the money became a distraction. Roy turned the Sheik down flat, insisting that for him, Melchester Rovers and his career were inseparable, and the idea of moving his family abroad didn't appeal, no matter how much money was involved; but the fans refused to believe that he could possibly reject such an offer. The distraction of the Middle-Eastern money, coupled with the downturn in results, was too much for the Melchester board to take, and with the club seemingly headed for a barren season, the board sacked Roy as manager, and reinstated Ben Galloway.

When Roy recovered his form, Galloway assured the fans, he would be placed back in charge of the team. It seems a wonderful way to ensure that he lost his form all over again, as the pressures of management were plainly not good for him, but fate, and more importantly the scriptwriters, had other plans. A month later, in January 1979, the Rovers faced (the very well-named) Dynamo Zarcov in the UEFA Cup. Zarcov came from a place we, as children, understood simply to be 'behind the iron curtain'.

Victory duly claimed, the aftermath, Roy decided, was as good a time as any to make his position clear. He may have temporarily lost his job as manager, but the Melchester faithful had cheered their hero to the rafters whenever he appeared, despite being fearful that he might be about to depart on a tide of pound notes, and he wanted to reassure them. To that end, his programme notes for the game against Carford City that month were slightly more interesting than the usual 'Today we welcome Fred Bloggs and his side to Mel Park . . .'

To put the record straight – I will not be accepting the £1 million offer from Basran – I wouldn't leave Rovers for all the riches in the world. On the table was a palatial home, swimming pool, all the servants we wanted, luxury cars – the works. But I have rejected them all.

A representative from the Foreign Office visited me the other day. He urged me to take the job, said that the Sheik might inflate the price of oil if I didn't! So, to the Sheik, the British government and to you all, I give the same message. I'm staying put.

It was as close to politics as Roy ever really got. We fight over oil prices now – back then, we squabbled over our footballers. The knowledge that their captain cared sufficiently for his side to withstand the entreaties of the government and the lure of the Sheik of Basran's cash, seemed to galvanise both fans and players alike. Roy started finding the back of the net again, scoring five in the third round of the FA Cup, but when Rovers went out in the next round, it became clear that any silverware heading to Mel Park that year would come via European competitions, and not domestically.

It wouldn't be easy (although few of us ever doubted it would be achieved), as the draw, pairing Melchester against the Spanish giants of Zaragosa in the UEFA Cup third round, was far from kind. It did, however, introduce a player who would remain a hero for seasons to come, like so many before him, having first arrived as an opponent. Paco Diaz was Spanish, dark-haired and moustachioed, in typical, stereotypical style. He was also known as the greatest player in Spain, and, being continental, in Roy's view, 'fiery'.

He scored twice in the first leg, in Spain, but Roy claimed two of his own to hand Melchester an advantage they capitalised upon when they won 2-0 at Mel Park in the return tie. Roy was impressed by Paco, however, and saw the benefits he could bring to the Rovers. Having been steered in the wrong direction with the Johan Seegrun episode, we knew Paco couldn't come back to haunt the Rovers, so maybe Paco was going to be the overseas acquisition we had once thought Johan was destined to be?

By the time our hopes were confirmed, Melchester were in the final of the UEFA Cup, after a straightforward semi-final win over (the splendidly named) Sorbonne, of France. Paco could not play until the second leg of the final, which was a little puzzling, as it seemed highly unlikely that he would be able to play any further part in the competition that year, having already exited it with Zaragosa. As it transpired, his presence on the bench was not the calming and settling factor it might have been.

Roy had dropped Mervyn Wallace for the first leg of the final, which seemed by any standards a strange decision. With Paco having just joined, however, there was a need on behalf of the writers to crank up the tension as hard as possible, and having him sitting next to Mervyn on the bench, knowing they could soon be competing for a place, did the trick nicely. Mervyn may, of course, still have been muttering about having scored fifty goals and getting dropped, for which nobody could have blamed him.

Things were not improved when Melchester's opponents, the German side, Rassburg, took an early lead; the slightly ill-advised decision to opt for an eight-man wall saw a pass to one of several unmarked players, and a headed opener. As the crowd murmured, Paco stood up from the bench and shouted at them. A pointless gesture, perhaps, but excellent for upping the dramatic tension:

'The fools! Couldn't they see that it was a great goal? No one could have stopped it . . . Not even Mervyn!'

Mervyn sat there, with a face some way short of amused, as Roy demonstrated once more that, when needed, he had ears of which a bat would feel jealous.

'The Melchester goal is wide open for a cross . . .' worried one spectator, until Roy leapt to head clear the danger, all the while thinking to himself, 'Not as wide open as all that, chum!'

Seconds later, two fans standing at the back of the stand discussed the problems Rovers faced:

'I blame Racey! He shouldn't have disturbed a winning team by dropping Mervyn Wallace!' said one, while his friend agreed, adding, 'Too right! Old Merv eats players like Hans Fischer for breakfast!'

Standing about a hundred yards away, in the centre of the pitch, midway through a European final, Roy heard every, stinging word.

'Fischer happens to be playing the game of his life!' he mused. 'On this form, I doubt any player in the world could hold him!'

It was bleak for the Rovers, and when Paco wandered around the dressing room at half-time, it was more than just his light brown, Starsky and Hutch-style leather jacket that caused offence, as he freely dispensed tactical advice. 'Let's hope nobody's injured,' said Duncan Mackay, 'Merv's so angry, we'd be better off playing with ten men!'

It was, then, with an air of inevitability, we watched Gerry Holloway collapse to the turf minutes later, much to the delight of the Germans in the crowd. 'Teufel!', exclaimed one, oddly, as it seems to be more of an expression of annoyance than delight, 'What will Roy Race do now?'

What he did came as no surprise to us, even as we sat there, surprised. Mervyn came on, scored the equaliser, growled at Roy a bit, and then set him up for the winner. Roy then admitted to Blackie that he'd set the whole thing up, and encouraged Paco to irritate Mervyn, in a bid to snap him out of the sulk he'd fallen into since Paco's arrival. As he explained:

'I hoped it would make Mervyn so white-hot with rage, he'd forget his sulks and grab the chance to show that he's as good as any foreign player! And it worked . . .'

The second leg was little more than a lap of honour for Roy and his team, and after Paco had admitted to Mervyn what he had done, and Mervyn had somehow resisted the temptation to strangle him, Roy scored a goal ten minutes from time that guaranteed them further European glory.

As the team celebrated after the game, the shadow of Basran appeared once more. Despite the season's European triumph, the fans were still nervous at the prospect of losing their hero, and their concerns were not alleviated, in the days after the final, by the sight of Roy and Penny flying to Basran to speak with the Sheik.

In the end he agreed to do some coaching during the summer months; Penny and the twins lived in luxury, enjoying the sunshine, while Roy threw himself around a training pitch with the best footballing talent Basran had to offer. It wasn't quite the relaxing holiday he needed, although with a hefty pay packet and extraordinary surroundings, it had been a tempting offer. We worried that Roy might have had his head turned by all this, but then thought of the money – unimaginable sums for a footballer to earn – and our own, young heads began to swim.

Much has been made of the effects of jet-lag on major players of modern times, with endless experts dragged out in the press to assess the damage constant flying could be causing to David Beckham's fitness, but as ever, Roy was there first. Years before anyone had heard of Beckham, when he was just a three-year-old, toddling around an East London back garden after his ball, the greatest footballer of the day was jetting halfway around the world to conduct a business deal.

If doing so much travelling, even before Air Miles had been invented, was an annoyance for Roy, he refused to let it show. By the end of the summer, not only had he set up Basran's first football league, but he had taken coaching sessions with the national team and negotiated a groundbreaking deal on behalf of Melchester. The Sheik was desperate to acquire Roy on a full-time basis, even sending him a Rolls-Royce, which Roy, having refused to accept, with characteristic generosity, auctioned for charity. Somewhere in the suburbs of Melchester, the world's best equipped local youth club was getting richer still.

Eventually, as part of the deal, Lofty Peak went to become the coach of Basran, with the promise of further contact between the country and Melchester to come. As far as Lofty was concerned, it was a decent result. Other players nearing the end of their careers had been either ghosted away to pastures grubby, like high-security prisoners, shipped off before anyone could notice they had gone, or in several cases, injured so badly they could never play again. Lofty, in comparison, got handsomely paid and sent to the sunshine. Tubby Morton, who kept having his legs broken and ended up in charge of the reserves, must have been furious.

The only way for the Rovers to wind up the decade then, the most glory strewn in their history to date, was to set about collecting yet more trophies and breaking more records. Which they seemed all set to do, when suddenly, the wheels fell off. They signed Vic Guthrie from Westbury Town, which given that he had a disciplinary record to make Vinnie Jones blush, seemed like a strange acquisition, but we trusted Roy's judgement.

Then, inexplicably, half the side were struck down with food poisoning – a plot that reality wasn't to catch up with until well into the 21st century, when Spurs collapsed, en masse, before the final game of the season against West Ham, thus missing out on a Champions League spot. Melchester paid the price of having to play with six substitutes, by crashing out of Europe to a team of Icelandic part-timers, Heklavik. Roy missed a last-minute penalty, before remonstrating with Blackie for requesting the kick be re-taken, and giving him a quick on-pitch refresher lesson on the laws surrounding spot-kicks.

It was, by common consent, the lowest moment in Melchester's history, and according to Roy, their worst ever defeat. It hadn't been such a bad run of form since getting his own title, however, and with his popularity still as great as ever, for Roy Race, the 1980s awaited. Twenty-five years in the game had been enough to whet his appetite. Now, the action could begin properly.

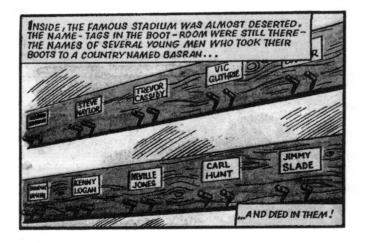

CHAPTER SEVEN

THE EIGHTIES

'I remember when the magazine did a tie-in with Gola. Even at a young age I was a marketing man's dream and was lured by free stuff on the front of magazines. I would say this was early '80s but you'd probably have a better idea of the timescale. I'm sure I still have the badge somewhere, "Roy of the Rovers wears Gola kit" – I should see how much it's worth on eBay.'

Mike Lawrence

Having to look back two and a half years since winning the last domestic trophy might not, to the average football fan, seem like much of a wait, but Melchester fans were never average, and such a description was never applied to their club. Slumps, though, are relative things, and after the Seventies had ended in desperate style, with Melchester crashing out of the UEFA Cup to the minnows of Heklavik, the Eighties hardly began any more promisingly.

The very early stages of January showed an upturn in fortunes, admittedly, and they slowly crept their way back up the league, but the FA Cup soon provided them with a banana skin. Chalkford Town were about as lowly as the confines of the game allowed them to be before becoming non-league. Unheralded, they lurked hesitantly in the lower reaches of the Fourth Division, in the glorious pre-Premiership days when there still was such a thing.

We were first made aware of potential problems when a Frank Bough-alike television presenter was handed a newsflash during the Saturday afternoon sports programme. Notwithstanding what we already know about the ability of one frame of a strip to convey huge amounts of information, this opening piece of artwork was a classic. The presenter is wearing a green blazer and tie, creating a look that seems perfectly suited to his role, being equal parts park-keeper, Alan Partridge and golf club secretary.

In front of our early 1980s presenter is a red telephone, because, as we know, until the mid-Eighties it was illegal to present live television programmes without such a device in front of you, lest there was a sudden emergency. Why, during the course of said emergency, the presenter couldn't be spoken to via his earpiece, the same as happened the rest of the time, was never clear. Perhaps as a tribute to the great days of the Batphone, a red telephone had to be on the desk at all times, reminding us of the extraordinary dangers of live broadcasting.

He was handed the newsflash, which was a piece of paper, freshly typed by one of the three (female – that's a goal pulled back for the feminist academics) typists sitting behind him, by a floor manager, who was, of course, male. He had to be male, as he had headphones to wear, along with an expression suggesting he was extremely important, and, given the news he had to convey, shocked. Why the producer didn't just read the scoreline into the presenter's ear, again, we're not sure, but in this instance, presumably he had to see it to believe it.

'I've just received confirmation of that incredible scoreline . . .' he gasped. 'Chalkford Town ONE . . . Melchester Rovers . . . NIL!'

Around Melchester, rather than remaining in their front rooms, people stood, inexplicably, outside electrical shops, and watched the sets in the window relay the news. A man in a car mentioned, hopefully, to a fellow motorist that it must be a mistake, only to be told: 'Not according to the radio, chum! Chalkford scored from a penalty in the first half!'

As the tension crept around the streets of Melchester, the Rovers pushed desperately for a late equaliser. Finally, with moments left, the Chalkford goalkeeper fumbled a shot, and left Paco Diaz a tap-in from five yards to salvage the draw. Paco, of course, was still struggling to come to terms with the English language, and so by the rules of comic writing, had to remind us of this at every opportunity.

'Is mine!' he cried out, as the moments ran out.

A few years earlier, Clive Thomas, officiating in the real life World Cup, had denied Brazil an equaliser, by blowing for full time while the ball was on its way into the area from a corner kick. Thomas pointed out that he was fully entitled to do so, and the rest of the world, in turn, pointed out that indeed he was, but it was still a very silly time to be blowing the final whistle. For the Roy of the Rovers scriptwriters, it had provided a dramatic idea, to be stored away for the right time, and as Paco lunged forwards, that time had come.

The whistle blew as he hit the ball, the equaliser never arrived, and Rovers had crashed out of the FA Cup in ignominious style. As they trudged off the pitch, Roy's extraordinary ears once more found themselves called into action.

'I feel almost sorry for Roy Race!' said one, about thirty yards back from the tunnel entrance, amidst a packed crowd. 'I don't!' replied his mate, standing next to him and, of course, holding a scarf above his head. 'He's had his fair share of glory.'

Roy, looked up, having located the conversation above all the din, and thought to himself 'Aye! And I don't begrudge you your day, Chalkford! Good luck . . .'

We still never knew, apart from the Tom Tully theory, why Roy occasionally became Scottish in moments of crisis, but his muttered 'Aye' was heard on several separate occasions, usually when Melchester had just done something particularly stupid. Having already gone out of Europe to the tiniest club in the competition, exiting the FA Cup to the smallest remaining side was, by any definition, careless. His mood wasn't helped by the chairman, Sam Barlow – who unfortunately looked uncannily like future serial-killer Fred West – arriving at the door to the dressing room to berate his captain.

Roy was furious and promised to win the league instead. On the great scale of footballing explosions, it left a little to be desired, although when the Rovers went into the final game of the season needing only a point to claim the title, few were surprised that Roy and Blackie both scored, to ensure the trophy returned to Mel Park. On the face of it, things were good – and the Eighties were welcomed with the league title. We had seen, however, the first signs of frailty from Roy, and with the advent of a chairman who put him under pressure, and the external troubles he had to deal with during the season, our hero was beginning to look vulnerable.

In the outside world, we were in the middle of a period of almost total Merseyside domination of the game, with the title heading there twelve times in the fifteen years between 1975 and 1990, ten of them to Liverpool, and twice to Everton. Liverpool's goalscoring hero of the time was Ian Rush, but with his black hair and moustache there was no confusing him for Roy Race. As Kenny Dalglish came more to the fore, comparisons in terms of both appearance and performance became more frequent, particularly when Dalglish became Liverpool's player-manager. As we will shortly discover, however, the true model for Roy's looks during this time was someone altogether more unlikely.

Promised a surprise if they won the league, other players might have awaited something pleasant from Sam Barlow once the trophy was safely hoisted, but Roy was too shrewd to let his hopes rise so high. True enough, the surprise was the first transfer between Melchester and Melboro, as Geoff Giles was sold, which was not perhaps quite the bonus Melchester fans were hoping for. To replace him, Roy signed Nat Gosden, who had the nickname of Grandad, due to having reached the extraordinary age of 35. Admittedly, he reached 35 with a balding head that seemed to be on loan from a 70-year-old, but it still seemed a little harsh, even by nickname standards.

And from such humble beginnings, the season slumped ever lower. Knocked out of the European Cup by Zalmo of Sweden (which, like all good team names, sounds almost authentic, but not quite) they then played with a strangely defensive mindset in the FA Cup against Kelburn, failed to get their usual late goal, and went out, 2-1. And those, in all honesty, were the highlights, because in the league they were awful. So awful that after all those years of last-gasp goals securing trophies, April 1981 was going to see a late drama decide if Rovers could avoid relegation.

Through a process of goal difference and applied mathematics too complicated to revisit, Roy and his side needed to beat Stambridge City by five goals in their last game of the season to avoid the drop. Despite the unlikely nature of this, there were still not many people prepared to bet on their imminent demise. Two early goals from the Rovers, and a display from the Stambridge goalkeeper, Len Coburn, which might have had match-fixing investigators twitching, seemed to set them on the road to unlikely survival, but slowly the tide turned.

As Roy unleashed another rocket towards goal, it hit Coburn on the shoulder, spun onto the bar, and landed back in his arms.

'The stroke of luck he was praying for!' moaned Roy. 'I've a hunch he won't be so nervous from now on!'

Roy was rarely wrong, and this was no exception; overtaken by some form of goalkeeping schizophrenia, Coburn proceeded to save just about everything that Melchester sent his way. Roy finally snatched another just before half-time, though, and with Rovers three up, we sensed their safety was guaranteed. When Paco Diaz converted a penalty with ten minutes to go, we knew where to look, and we knew exactly the sort of relief-tinged glory in which we were about to indulge. It was all set for Roy to score the fifth and save the day.

In the final minute the chance arrived, as Roy was pulled down in the area, and the referee pointed to the spot. But, unwilling to change Melchester's usual routine, Roy handed the ball to Mervyn Wallace, and told him to get the whole 'not getting relegated' business sorted out. Admittedly, there are those who could have seen this as an example of Roy backing away from his responsibilities, but he had his jaw set at that determined angle, and we dared not question him.

We did question him a bit though, when Coburn dived the right way, and there might have been a few more quizzical glances in his direction straight after the keeper pushed the ball onto the post. Vic Guthrie charged in to safely put away the rebound, but he made poor contact and slid the ball wide of the post. There were anguished stares all round, as the referee's whistle announced the imminent departure of Melchester Rovers from the top flight of English football. It took them just three frames of illustration to end more than two decades in the First Division, although given what was to come, that amounted almost to labouring the point.

After almost thirty years, it was the first real experience of failure Melchester had ever tasted. Previously they suffered the temporary disappointment of not winning a Cup Final, or coming close to claiming a league title yet falling just short, but this was different. This was complete failure with no mitigating factors, because in football, genuine tragedies aside, relegation is as bad as it gets. Five years earlier the same fate had befallen Manchester United, sent to the Second Division courtesy of Denis Law's back-heel, while a couple of seasons before Chelsea had gone down, but they were far from the artificially rich side they are now.

By the time Derby had surrendered to the drop the year before, County had become a pale imitation of the side they once were, making the job of identifying where in real life the idea might have come from a difficult one. The truth seems to be that, for once, finding a direct example is impossible. The beginnings of the idea might have rested with United's relegation, but it was brought to life through a desire to do something a little different. After season upon season of triumph, it was time for the readers to support their side through some disappointment, although it remained hard to take. In that season, 1980–81, real life saw Leicester, Norwich and Crystal Palace relegated. How, with all due disrespect, could we compare the might of Melchester to them?

It was a major decision to make, because the ramifications were, by definition, set to linger for an entire season at the very least. Had our hero been a boxer, the writers could have depicted him as being knocked down, only to rise in the next frame and claim a dramatic victory. Almost any other sportsman you care to think of could have achieved similar recoveries, but for a footballer, relegation meant having a comic spend a year with its hero in the Second Division. To their credit, the writers refused to allow Melchester that last-minute reprieve, and sent them crashing down. Interesting times loomed.

Strangely, against this background, Rovers managed to negotiate their first shirt sponsorship, as the sportswear firm Gola paid to have their eternally not-quite trendy name on the Rovers' chests throughout the course of the season. The trend for allowing a sponsor to slather a logo over the front of your shirt arrived in football in the early 1980s, as Manchester United suddenly tacitly recommended Sharp electrical products to everyone, Spurs swore by the restorative effects of Holsten Pils, and Everton allowed Hafnia to show the world that not all shirt sponsorships lead to an increased awareness of what the product actually is.

There wasn't even, by all accounts, that much of a financial interest as far as the comic was concerned in having the sponsor's name on Melchester's shirts. The money paid by Gola was negligible, but having a sponsor there allowed the comic to look up to date and modern – a feature which would have suffered had the kits remained pristine and different to every side in the real world. Had Gola known at the start how infrequently Roy would get to model the kit, they would have taken extra photographers to the first few games, just to get value for money. The period after Christmas was not going to be one of the more active of his career.

The start to the new season had been tough, coping with life in the Second Division, and dealing with a huge number of problems, both personal and professional, which all seemed to arrive at once. Added to this, had Roy been the sort to keep a Christmas card list, names would have been crossed off all over the place. Actually, one suspects Penny might have kept control of such matters in the Race household, as her secretarial skills merged in with her wifely duties, but she remained one of the few people who seemed not to have a vendetta against Melchester's golden boy. Five people, in particular, seemed to have an axe to grind with Roy, or, given the chance, to use on him.

Vic Guthrie, whose last-minute miss had helped seal the Rovers' departure from Division One, had managed to fall out with Roy over just about every issue which had raised its head in the intervening period. He was transfer-listed, out of favour, and generally doing all he could to live up to his billing of a 'nasty piece of work'. Equally supposed to be dangerous and unpleasant was Trevor Brinsden, who was a Seventies-style hooligan who appeared, by some form of *Life on Mars* process, to have been washed up in the Eighties. Trevor had a few unfortunate traits for a hooligan, the principal of which being that he wasn't in the slightest bit frightening. Bovver-booted and woolly-hatted, he had introduced hooliganism to Mel Park, and in return, Roy had intro-duced him to a lifetime ban, thus ensuring relations between the two were a little strained.

Arthur Logan was more to be pitied than scorned, having lost the plot somewhat after his son, Kenny, had signed for Melchester against his wishes. Arthur wanted his son to join the family estate agency business, rather than waste his time on anything as unprofitable as being a footballer – a further reminder of the innocent times in which Roy operated. He cursed and muttered about his son's manager, but nobody truly believed he was capable of anything serious.

The other two characters who were introduced to the story caused our, by now fairly accurate, antennae to spring to attention. Arnie Meckiff was a cousin of Roy's who lived in Australia, but had arrived in Melchester under a cloud and under suspicion, after a dodgy real-estate deal back home. There was no reason for Arnie to be in Melchester, other than as a prop for something else to go wrong – we'd seen it too many times before. Lastly, and oddest of all in many ways, was Elton Blake. Elton was an actor and had been due to appear in a television series based on events at Melchester Rovers, playing the role of Roy. For reasons, again, which weren't fully explained, Elton somehow lost the job of playing Melchester's hero, for which he seemed determined to make Roy pay. How any of us understood this as ten-year-olds is not clear, but we appear to have done so. Just.

This represented yet another change in the way Roy's life was being portrayed. Just a few months on from relegation, which could never have been considered seriously as a storyline before, we were seeing problems between him and Penny, and now hordes of people – or so it seemed – with major vendettas against him. There had always been the occasional 'wrong'un' for Roy to deal with, but now they were arriving thick and fast. The innocent world we thought we understood was beginning to get an awful lot more interesting.

So, with a host of people seemingly furious with Roy, we waited to see what would happen, because we were far too experienced in the ways of Melchester Rovers to believe that so many new characters could appear at once for it not to be for a very good reason. And, just before Christmas 1981, the most shocking front cover Roy of the Rovers ever produced came sliding through the letterbox.

'ROY RACE SHOT!' ran the headline, with the word 'shot' dripping with blood, as a revolver appeared in the bottom right hand corner of the page, and Roy, in his office, wearing jacket and tie, but falling backwards with his hands flung up, seems to get shot in the side of his head.

He was discovered by Vic Guthrie, who instantly became a suspect as far as the people of Melchester were concerned. The readers knew better, and understood that the sudden influx of characters made it highly unlikely that the suspect would be caught anywhere near the scene of the crime. In a hospital bed, unconscious beneath his bandages, Roy lay there as the readers, and indeed the whole country, waited to see what happened next. It was a year earlier that the fictional character of J.R. Ewing was shot in *Dallas*, and people were quick to see the joke the comic's writers were playing.

Even now, though, be prepared for a battle if you suggest that the idea was in any way 'stolen', as Barrie Tomlinson explains:

'We had to keep an eye on what was going on in the "real world" with Roy, but we weren't overly influenced by what was going on. We occasionally reflected things, obviously, most blatantly when *Dallas* shot J.R. and Roy got shot, but not slavishly so. We did it our own way, I like to think.'

Dallas was a huge television hit at the time, a worldwide phenomenon, with Larry Hagman and a cast of Identikit, perma-tanned thousands, all squabbling over oil prices. It is not to be confused with *Dynasty*, which featured Joan Collins and a cast of Identikit, perma-tanned thousands, all squabbling over oil prices. For reasons unknown, Roy of the Rovers decided to ape it, but, as Tomlinson so rightly says, 'in our own way'.

For a comic that had finished off the careers of so many characters without a moment's hesitation, if anything we were relieved that they hadn't done it quite their own way. If they had, Roy would certainly never have recovered, let alone played again. And yet, it is impossible to dismiss the episode as just a publicity stunt, or yet another example of how to create maximum publicity for minimum cost. The storyline gained the attention of the public in larger numbers than anyone could possibly have predicted and reminded everyone just how popular the comic was; and yet the whole plot was, in many ways, a bit of an experiment on behalf of the writers and editors.

'It was interesting,' said Ian Vosper, 'because it mirrored

everyday life, things that were on the television at the time and
suchlike. *Dallas* was big at the time, so we had an idea to do
something based on that, although in terms of plot, it took a lot of
planning and a lot of setting-up. The response it got was amazing.
Absolutely amazing.'

Paul Jones earns a living these days 'working in IT', although as
he is endearingly ready to admit 'it's actually far too boring to
explain what it is exactly I do'. He remembers the dramatic events
of December 1981 all too clearly, though.

I don't know what I made of the connection with *Dallas* at
the time. In fact, even if someone had mentioned it, I
wouldn't have thought twice about it. I still think the
shooting of Roy Race was a bigger deal than when someone
blasted Larry Hagman.

I can remember buying the comic with my older sister,
and just standing there in the shop looking at the words with
blood looking like it was dripping down them. I think she
was getting annoyed with me because she wanted to get on
with it and read *Jackie*, or whatever it was, but I was rooted
to the spot. I don't think a newspaper, or anything in the real
world, has ever had such an effect on me.

With Roy stuck in a hospital bed and, more pertinently, stuck in a
coma, suffering the longest injury lay-off of his career, a decision
was made to install a replacement manager, albeit on a temporary
basis. They could have gone for Ben Galloway, just as they could
have invented all manner of people, but while interest was still
high, the decision was made to aim for the top. Ian Vosper saw no
reason not to start his search with arguably the most famous
manager in the game. After all, he reasoned, what was the worst
that Sir Alf Ramsey could do?

Thankfully, we never had to find out, as he agreed without a
moment's hesitation. Sir Alf stepped into the gap left by the bullet-
riddled striker, and promptly recalled Vic Guthrie to the side, even
going so far as to have him wear Roy's famous number nine jersey.
The police might be investigating the 'Super-Brat' but Sir Alf saw
him playing an essential role. It made his World Cup defence of

Nobby Stiles look like small beer, but none of the readers thought for a minute that he was guilty. It would have been far too convenient, and other people fitted the likely profile far more neatly.

Things came to a head in Sir Alf's second game in charge, as Melchester, who were still unbeaten in the league, faced Keysborough. From the start, as the hospital turned the radio commentary up and placed speakers next to Roy's bed, Melchester attacked with everything they had. Defenders, midfielders and attackers alike joined forces to launch an onslaught on the Keysborough goal. Vernon Eliot got one, Paco Diaz got one, and, as even the policemen around the perimeter of the pitch threw their helmets in the air in celebration, the crowd began to sing Roy's name.

At the hospital the doctors and Penny watched on as they turned the volume up. Then slowly, almost indiscernibly at first, Roy opened his eyes. Within seconds the public address system at Mel Park crackled into life.

'Ladies and gentlemen, boys and girls . . .' (They had a very proper public address system at Melchester.) '. . . Our apologies to Keysborough for interrupting the game at this point . . . But we have just received a message from Melchester General Hospital. And it's the news we've all been waiting for! The greatest news in the world! Roy has recovered . . . He's out of the coma!'

The scenes were extraordinary. Players hugged each other, Sir Alf shook hands in the crowd, and even the opposition stopped to shake Blackie's hand. 'We're as pleased as you are, Blackie. Aye, Roy is something special to all of us.'

Blackie grinned, and tried, as did we all, to ignore that strange 'Aye' which appeared from time to time. The Rovers felt the need to celebrate, and they knew only one way to do it. Curiously, by modern standards, this didn't involve thousands of pounds' worth of drinks, a West End nightclub, a host of young women brought in for the occasion, and a flutter of hush-money pay-offs. They just scored goals. Again, and again, and again.

Blackie notched the fourth, Mervyn Wallace's goal made it seven and Blackie's second was Melchester's eighth.

'It sounds like the Rovers might be getting on top, Roy!' chuckled a slightly star-struck doctor.

'What's . . . what's the record for the . . . most goals scored by one team in a . . . football league game, Penny?' Roy queried.

He received a smiling rebuke for his question, although given that he'd been asleep for weeks, and he'd still to ask about his children or wife, he was perhaps lucky that she didn't dispatch him straight back to unconsciousness. Before she could reconsider, the star-struck surgeon rushed back in, with news that the record was 13-0. Rovers needed six more!

You can guess the rest. Blackie got a hat-trick, Vic Guthrie got a header, Vernon Eliot snatched his second and Duncan McKay claimed number twelve from the penalty spot. Had Mervyn Wallace done that a few months earlier, the Rovers wouldn't have been relegated and all of this might have been avoided, but nobody actually said as much, which was probably for the best.

Kenny Logan scored a header to make it 13-0, all while his father dreamt of estate agency fees, and when Roy demanded a deep throw into the box, deep into injury time, Duncan obliged, and young Kenny pounced to head the goal that broke the record.

As Mel Park went mad, the crowd spilled onto the pitch, unchallenged by the police, who, having been throwing their own hats in the air earlier on, were in no position to start moralising about inappropriate behaviour.

'Let them go, lads! This is one pitch invasion I wouldn't mind joining in myself!'

'Aye!' said a colleague, taking the 'Aye' count to hitherto undreamt of heights. 'We'll forgive them! Just this once!'

Sir Alf gave a radio interview, bemoaning the fact the side missed a few chances, and explained he'd be thrilled when Roy was fit and ready to come and put him back out of a job. The rest of the season was predictably celebratory. In a nutshell, Sir Alf took the Rovers thirty-four games unbeaten, Roy came back and they lost their first match, but as we recovered from the irony, he then returned to playing and scored two on his comeback.

They eventually won the league with Roy claiming a hat-trick in the vital, final fixture, and as the evidence fell into place, Elton Blake, the would-be murderous thespian, had his collar felt for attempted murder. It can't really have been a great time in Elton's life, as even this episode reeked of anti-climax – it hadn't even been

a particularly hard mystery to solve. As he'd never really featured
in the comic much before the shooting, his capture and subsequent
departure wasn't going to impact on anyone else, which put him
in a category all on his own. If Vic or any of the others had done
it, there would have been repercussions to deal with, but Elton
offered no such problems. All of which made it the first shooting
in the world, Scooby Doo stories excepted, solved instantly and
effortlessly by a bunch of eight-year-olds.

But with one exception, as Paul Jones is once more proud to
point out:

> I thought it might have been Roy's cousin – sorry to ruin your
> theory – because he was a cartoon baddie. It was good that it
> was the actor Elton, though, because once he was gone,
> nobody had to mention him again and we could just carry on
> as before. I don't think they ever told us what happened to
> him, but I'd like to think he was mad, not bad, because
> nobody could really want to kill Roy Race, could they?

One of the things the writers never thought to tell us as Roy was
lying in his hospital bed, hovering between fame of the
posthumous and living variety, was that Penny was expecting
another baby. She arrived in the summer of 1982, a year after the
royal wedding between Charles and Diana, and, with a future gong
at the front of Roy's mind, was named, rather obsequiously, Diana.
On the pitch, however, things were not going quite so smoothly.

Before the season even started, the Rovers played a charity cricket
match, which they seemed to do most years since they had grown
bored of getting kidnapped. The opposition always seemed to
include a travelling Australian fast bowler, who had just settled into
the village for a few weeks on his wanders, when the Rovers came
calling. He'd charge in, off an immense run-up, and let loose a
flurry of short-pitched deliveries, which had Melchester's finest
leaping about all over the place. At least one would crack a finger,
and the ball would clatter into heads and rib cages far more often

than it clattered into the stumps. Given the ease with which Roy was usually able to donate, playing cricket was a very dangerous form of charity work.

This game, for reasons which eluded everyone, was so well attended it ended in a pitch invasion, which saw an enthusiastic crowd knock over Vernon Eliot as they stormed onto the pitch, mobbing him so completely, his leg was broken. Many people left the Rovers in all manner of extraordinary ways, but until the shocking news came through that Vernon's injury was so bad it had forced him to retire from football, nobody had yet been culled by their own fans. Once more, we were reminded of the long arm of the writers, and their imaginative ways of disposing of those whose expiry date had come around.

Vernon was a figure worth mentioning in his own right, for reasons other than just what he achieved on the pitch with the Rovers. When he first appeared in the story, there was something about him that stood out; and something which marked out, from an early stage, the willingness of the editors and writers to do something revolutionary. Vernon was black, and at the time that made him unusual as a footballer in the top flight, albeit a fictional one. As Ian Vosper recalls, it wasn't a particular statement, but neither was it a one-off.

Vernon Eliot was, I suppose, arguably the first black player to play in the top flight of English football, but I don't think that was a particularly contentious decision. We just sought to mirror what we saw in the world around us, and it seemed odd that there hadn't been many black players before, so we created Vernon. Likewise, Paco Diaz, who arrived as a direct result of Ossie Ardiles and Ricky Villa, springs immediately to mind. We were influenced again by the outside world. That was why people felt an attachment to Roy of the Rovers, I think.

He wasn't quite the first, but the character of Vernon was certainly addressing an issue which English football, at the time, seemed perfectly happy to ignore. Arthur Wharton played in goal for Preston in the 1880s, becoming the very first black man to play top-level football in England, but shamefully there was a delay of ninety-eight years before Viv Anderson made his debut for the national side, becoming the first black player to play for England. At the time Vosper refers to, English football, unlike the society from which it drew its players, was predominantly white.

As for the question of foreign players, with clubs like Ipswich bringing in Arnold Muhren and Frans Thyssen, Manchester City signing Kazimierz Deyna and, as Vosper mentions, Ardiles and Villa at Tottenham, the very beginnings of the foreign influx of players had begun. It was very early days as far as foreigners in English football were concerned, so while he may describe himself as being 'influenced' Vosper is being very modest – the trend was in its infancy, but already he knew, in the finest traditions of the comic, to reflect it, adapt it and use it.

Whether he broke new ground by his presence in the side or not, Vernon certainly (and unwillingly) managed it when he was forced into retirement due to his badly crushed leg, caused by the crowd approaching from deep square leg. He became youth team coach, patrolling muddy, cold pitches full of young players on wet, Melchester mornings. Had he got squashed a year or so earlier, he might have bagged the Basran job, complete with sunshine and a swimming pool. Vernon probably felt even more bitter than Tubby about the mundane nature of his future footballing years.

The board offered Roy funds to buy new players, but he remained determined to pursue his policy of offering opportunities to the youngsters instead, and, like so many managers before him, his principles looked set to bring him more and more trouble. Melchester were hopeless, made up of veterans coming to the end of their careers (excluding the timeless duo of Roy and Blackie, obviously) and wide-eyed youth team players; while Roy's abilities to ever become a stay-at-home dad were brought into question by a series of episodes showing him suffering horribly, having to check nappies and the like. Looking back on the way his 'plight' was portrayed now, it may be that the feminist academics have just pulled another goal back.

The board were also working on developing Mel Park into a truly modern, all-seater stadium, the meetings for which added to Roy's workload, and for the first time in his career, the fans had begun to turn against him. There were disputes over selection, and Trevor Brinsden was organising protests against him. With hindsight, Roy might have been better off framing Trevor for the shooting, and letting Elton escape the net. Shaken to his core by what he had done, the old thesp was never again going to be much of a threat, but Trevor was a fanatic, and always likely to stir up trouble.

Suspecting that all was not quite as rosy as the public image Rovers presented made out, the chairman of Walford Rovers, Harvey Rawson, made an opportunistic bid for Roy's services – £3,000 a week in wages, and £5 million to spend in the transfer market. He was met with a degree of mockery and mickey-taking, which might not have been the board's best tactic. After a game in April 1983, which Rovers won at the death (despite Roy taking off the injured Charlie Carter and putting himself in goal), things came to a head.

The directors stormed down to the dressing room, and demanded to know what he thought he was doing. On one view, it was a reasonable request – they did pay his wages, and he had just played himself in goal; when it turned out Charlie wasn't all that injured after all, and had left the ground in a foul temper, questions were bound to be asked. The way they were asked was too much for Roy, however, who gave them a piece of his mind and stormed into his office.

On the desk lay a red phone – perhaps he presented live television shows from there? Perhaps he was so important, only a red phone would do? We never found out. What he did next would have shaken the comic to its knees – if we weren't there already, following the whole shooting/Sir Alf/coma/14-0 escapades of the previous twelve months. Roy called Harvey Rawson. Even Penny had laughed and said he'd never leave Melchester. He'd show her! And us! And everyone who needed showing!

One phone call later, and he was still Roy of the Rovers, which was handy as far as the prospect of a vast rebranding exercise being averted was concerned, but it was Walford Rovers, not Melchester. Taken for granted for too long, Roy had finally snapped. None of us, if we're being honest, really knew what to think.

There had been players who had switched from one rival club to another before, most notably Denis Law, who crossed Manchester from the red side to the blue. Arsenal and Tottenham have appeared alongside each other on the CVs of several players, among them Sol Campbell, Pat Jennings and Willie Young, while George Graham and Terry Neill managed both clubs. Liverpool and Everton have shared a handful of players and even Rangers and Celtic, as feudal a rivalry as exists in British football, both send out invites to Kenny Miller and Mo Johnston when the old players have a reunion. We had never imagined Roy adding to that list.

The message to the readers was clear, and followed along identical lines to the one delivered when Roy had been shot – or when any of the other recent, radical plot developments had taken place. Having done things successfully for the last thirty years, times had changed, and so had the comic. The essential principles remained unaltered and the standards were still high, but as far as plot was concerned, don't rule anything out.

Ironically, what happened next was predictable, but in the unpredictable way that the writers had been perfecting for so long. Roy's opening games at Walford were stunning. Still furious, he scored goal after goal, seemingly mentioning Melchester after every one. This must have annoyed his team-mates, although not nearly as much as his habit of storming off the pitch at the end of the game and demanding to know how the other Rovers, his real love, had got on.

Blackie had become player-manager at Melchester, a role for which he'd auditioned almost as long as Prince Charles has practised being King, and as Roy stayed in Walford, life in Melchester seemed to go on without him. He lived in a flat close to the ground, while Penny and the children carried on without him in their old house, having refused to move (I think we were supposed to vilify her for this). By the time she took the children away on holiday to Crete (on Valentine's Day – spiteful as well as unreasonable seems to be the message), which at the time was also seen as evidence of an impossibly luxurious lifestyle, it was clear that if Roy was being dragged in two different directions on the pitch, it was nothing compared to what was happening off it.

When he turned up at Mel Park to play in a testimonial game,

opinion was split. He was booed by part of the crowd and handed
a petition by thousands of the local schoolchildren, announcing
that they still believed in him. Roy was so moved, he went to Sam
Barlow, the chairman, to see if the row could be sorted out; it was
plainly in everyone's interests to end this episode and get him back
to Melchester. Sam, though, didn't look like Fred West for
nothing, and offered his former manager cold-eyed short shrift.
And we knew that Sam would come a cropper sooner or later,
because in a good versus bad shootout, Roy of the Rovers
(whichever set of Rovers that might happen to be) would only
allow one result.

It wasn't only the audience who needed it resolved. One gets
the feeling that Vosper, who instigated the storyline, had
underestimated the toll it would bring on him.

> Roy left and went to Walford Rovers, so we had to fill a gap,
> and keep two stories going – both how Roy was getting on,
> and how the Rovers were doing without him – because
> people would want to know. Who to get to replace him at
> the Rovers, though? How to run the events shaping two
> clubs in one strip? Why keep Melchester in the story, unless
> Roy was going to return? It became clear he was, I suppose,
> we all knew that, but it was hard work keeping that moving
> smoothly along while he was playing somewhere else!

Before things could get better for Roy, though, comic law dictated
that they would have to get worse. Rob Richards (the initials
weren't accidental) was signed by Melchester, and became an
immediate favourite, thanks to his goalscoring talents, blond,
flowing hair and muscular build. You could feel Roy getting
irritated as soon as that deal was completed. Coupled with that,
Paco Diaz left, upset at life without Roy; and after a picture was
published of Roy going to a dinner with his secretary, Sandie
Lewis, Penny went mad, flew home from her holiday, and accused
Roy of all manner of infidelities – or as many as you could allude
to in a children's comic, anyway.

Roy, as we all knew, was innocent of any wrongdoing with
Sandie, although given his history with secretaries, Penny, of all

people, should have known the risks. Since she'd left the job, everyone who ever came into his office while he dictated his programme notes must have thought they were in with a chance. Finally, though, in November, things came to a head.

Walford visited Mel Park and, despite not scoring, Roy led them to a 2-1 victory, which saw Sam Barlow storming around in a furious temper. Barlow picked on Blackie, who discovered a passionate side not really witnessed since the Suzanne Cerise saga, and gave Sam back every bit as good as he got. The humiliation was too much for the chairman, who stormed out of Melchester, pledging never to return.

All it took was a noble gesture from Harvey Rawson – who, after all, had a contract keeping Roy at Walford – and the whole turbulent episode could be resolved. Sensing this, the writers decided Harvey was in a benevolent mood and, as a gesture, Roy was released from his contract and promptly left Walford to return to Melchester. Penny forgave him over the 'wrong secretary' affair, accepted his innocence, and the family were reunited once more. He'd been gone for about six months, but finally the world felt right once more.

The 1983–84 season was concluded by Melchester playing Walford in the FA Cup Final, which was very exciting even though absolutely everyone reading the comic knew it would happen. The same could be said of the result. Walford went ahead, Roy scored a dramatic long-range equaliser, and as a classic game entered its dying moments, Neville Jones, young, gifted and black, who had taken over the mantle of Vernon Eliot, cracked a winner off the underside of the crossbar. Melchester had won the FA Cup, although, as was evident by the front of their shirts, lost a sponsor: Gola, presumably baffled by the welter of shootings, affairs and transfers, had made their excuses and left.

There can come a point in any comic's life where things just start to get a little far-fetched. Getting shot was just, as far as most were concerned, the right side of the line, although whether Sir Alf arriving to take charge fell into the same category, we were never so sure. By the time Roy went to Walford we thought things were back on track – even if it was shocking, it was at least a football story shocking us – although we probably could have done without the Penny stuff. We were still of an age where girls produced groans of a bad, rather than good, sort and weren't much interested in Roy's love life. We suspected someone was fishing for headlines a little too hard, and Roy's wife leaving him seemed likely to generate them.

The start of the 1984–85 season did little to change those views, when, in the name of 'celebrity involvement', Geoff Boycott became chairman. You may want to read that sentence again – I say that because I remember re-reading the front cover several times when I first learned the news, trying to take it in. Why he wanted to take a break from scoring runs very slowly to become chairman of a fictional football club was not clear. He wasn't even a pundit back then, so we hadn't yet witnessed his prowess at sticking car keys in pitches or talking about the 'corridor of uncertainty' – not that either would have changed our minds.

Nor, for that matter, was the question of why, of all cricketers, we got Geoff? Just three years earlier, Ian Botham had plundered his way through a mighty Australian side to claim the Ashes, as part of an England team marshalled and directed by Mike Brearley, so if we had to have a cricketer, and we weren't sure why we had to, why couldn't it be one of them? The only thing we were certain about was that, with Boycott at the helm, Rovers were far from impressive.

It was, to an extent, the beginning of the age of the celebrity chairman. Elton John had become Watford chairman some years earlier, in 1976, although even back then football had cheerfully accepted him as a proper fan, rather than a celebrity looking for a publicity boost. Frankly, the idea that Elton John's profile was boosted through a connection with Watford FC, then a Fourth Division side, rather than vice versa, was never convincing. There aren't many short, tubby, flamboyantly dressed, overtly gay men who get the sort of warm reception Elton John receives when he arrives at a football match, and the affection has been hard earned.

The true inspiration for the Geoff Boycott storyline was the rather less attractive figure of Robert Maxwell, blustering news-paper owner and covert pension thief. Maxwell took over as chairman of Oxford United in 1982, and immediately proposed to merge the club with Reading to form a new side known as the Thames Valley Royals. The plan was, as we now know, shelved after huge protests from fans, and helped highlight exactly how little interest Maxwell really had in the game, or at least, how much feeling he had for it.

Back at Melchester, Geoff was taking his time getting started – much like many of his innings. Their league form faltered, they went out of the FA Cup early on, and while Roy played well for England, Melchester's hopes for silverware rested on the Cup Winners' Cup, which, by default, they seemed to reach the final of whenever their domestic season had been a washout. They were to play the Spanish side Real Santana and there was 'history' between the sides.

Duncan McKay's brother played for Glenmore (who, amazingly, were Scottish), and had broken his leg, or to be accurate, had it broken by a Santana player in the semi-final. Duncan was making it very clear that a spot of revenge was on the cards. The Santana coach, Carlos Villar, had also been in charge of the French national side when Roy played for England earlier in the season, as well as playing against him in the European Cup some years ago, and had tried to have Roy fouled out of the game both times.

Their current style of play was evidently no different, and thanks to a thuggish centre half called Basora, Roy was getting kicked all over the place. It was an interesting, if unpromising development. Previously, foreign sides had been sneaky, but nobody could accuse Santana of that. They didn't pretend they wanted to do anything other than maim our hero, and they made a very good attempt.

As he set up Neville Jones to score the equaliser which took the game into extra time, Roy was hacked down by Basora, and lay there receiving treatment while tactics for the final half an hour were discussed. Luckily, Roy had known what to expect from Santana, and every player, he revealed, rolling down the remnants of his shredded sock, had his ankles and shins strapped with yards of tape, to frustrate their malevolent opponents. It took Roy five more minutes to be ready and, as Rovers played on with ten men, Carlos Villar listened to the nervous cries of their fans, a smile emerging from under his pencil moustache that, as a pantomime villain, he was legally obliged to wear.

'You have seen the last of your hero, gentlemen . . .' he thought to himself. 'The so-called King of Melchester! Villar has seen to that, yet again!'

But, minutes later, Roy was back, and Villar's temper finally exploded, as Rovers were awarded a penalty. He attacked the referee, and received neither an undeserved nor unexpected red card. However, Duncan missed the spot kick, so the sides remained level going into the last half of extra time. As they changed ends, Basora approached Roy, and asked for a chat.

'Make it quick, Basora . . . And make it positive! Your manager has come up with enough dirty tricks to last you lot the whole of next season!'

Swallowing what must have been a sudden and fierce desire to tell Roy not to worry about it, he'd just carry on kicking him like he had all evening, Basora instead made an admission: 'I know . . . We not proud of it! We only ourselves to play for now . . . The honour of Real!'

Roy was mid-preach, and wouldn't be stopped now: 'Not forgetting those fans up there! English, Spanish, Scots! A lot of them behave according to the standards we set on the pitch . . . So let's give them something good to remember in the fifteen minutes we've got left!'

Again, somehow subduing his desire to kick Roy there and then, Basora instead shook our hero's hand, and the game moved into a turbulent, end-to-end fifteen minutes, before a penalty shoot out was needed to separate the two sides. As expected, when it mattered, Duncan scored, as did Roy, and by the time Blackie slotted the final Melchester penalty, the Cup Winners' Cup was secured. As the caption on the final frame informed us, it was a 'triumph of pure football over thuggery'.

But, if Geoff Boycott playing forward defensives in the boardroom wasn't enough to convince us that lunacy was overtaking the Rovers, the events of the next season certainly were. Needing goalkeeping cover, Roy signed Bob Wilson, who, while a lovely man and fine broadcaster, had retired from football in May 1974, eleven years earlier, making him an unlikely recruit. Many thought Wilson, at just 32, had retired too early, but waiting more than a decade before offering him a way back into the game seemed a dubious tactic. For many readers, 1985 was the year Roy of the Rovers went mad.

Roy's other defensive acquisition, the late Emlyn Hughes, had retired from football the previous season, and hadn't played in the top flight for six years. Once upon a time he'd captained Liverpool, and done so to endless silverware, but the only team he'd skippered in recent years had been on *A Question of Sport*, and even then, David Coleman seemed to have the measure of him. We wondered whether Geoff was cut out to be a chairman. Wasn't it his job to point out to the manager that his two transfer targets were already retired? On the cricket pitch, he slowed things down through his mere presence – surely he could adopt similar skills in the boardroom to stop things spiralling yet further out of hand?

It was hard to argue that Roy was looking to the future when he made these selections, but compared with what was to come, they were perfectly respectable purchases. We had been given hints, through the recent acquisitions, and the new, cricketing chairman, but little did we know that the whole comic was about to descend into what, sadly, can best be described as farce.

Martin Kemp and Steve Norman were both still highly active when Roy brought them to Melchester in September 1985, probably in all manner of ways the juvenile audience was not yet aware of. Unfortunately, football wasn't one of them, as being full-time members of Spandau Ballet, making records, playing concerts and appearing on *Top of the Pops* precluded them from a tough training regime. With all respect to Kemp and Norman, it marked a sad moment for Roy of the Rovers, as the need to court headlines overtook the need to court any sort of realism.

There were many key moments during the life of Roy of the Rovers and, given its lifespan, inevitably so. It would not have survived for as long as it did had it not thrown up more than its fair share of talking and turning points, but acquiring pop stars to play for the side just smacked of the bottom of the barrel. It had earned its reputation on good, solid stories, occasionally far-fetched, but always centred on football, first and foremost. This was a novelty, and we knew it.

Sadly, it reflected the state of football at the time. The Premier League was still six years away – not that it was a miracle cure as far as the health of the game was concerned. The Heysel disaster, where thirty-nine Juventus fans were killed as Liverpool supporters rioted before the European Cup Final, had taken place just months earlier, and it would be five more years before English clubs would return to European competition. The standard of English football grounds was desperately poor, with hooliganism an increasing problem.

A fortnight earlier, fifty-six people died tragically while watching the game between Bradford and Lincoln City, at Valley Parade, in Bradford, when fire engulfed the main stand. Bradford were supposed to be collecting the Division Three title that after-noon, before a discarded cigarette fell through a wooden stand onto rubbish below, and an inferno erupted. In a matter of minutes, molten tar fell from the roof onto fans, flames engulfed the rear wall, and toxic smoke filled the corridors under the stand.

In four years' time, we would have to endure the sight of ninety-six people, who had turned up to watch a football match, dying at Hillsborough as fences designed to cage supporters in, caused them to be crushed to death. For the time being, in the space of two, dreadful weeks, ninety-five people had been killed at two separate matches – burned, choked and crushed. The Popplewell inquiry, held in the wake of the Bradford disaster, did away with any new, wooden stands, and by default, made many existing stands illegal – among them, ironically, those at Bradford's opponents that day, Lincoln City. The Taylor report, which followed Hillsborough, effectively did away with terraces. Disaster, and its consequences, had changed football's landscape for ever.

Many people debated, understandably, whether it was worth carrying on; whether football was doing more harm than good. What was certain was that the innocence, what little of it there was left in the game, had gone, swept away by exposure to tragedy. It was a bad time for a comic that had relied on a high degree of innocence, to launch what was, in essence, a bit of a joke.

Martin Kemp soon replaced Blackie, who despite being injured, could have been forgiven for feeling a little put out. One of them had spent the last ten years playing an instrument, while the other had spent the last thirty years playing football. Suddenly the former was being allowed, seemingly without incident, to replace the latter. With his fellow band member, Norman, stepping into a defensive role when required, this squad of retirees and musos battled through to the League Cup Final, where victory over Tynecaster would reward them with both silverware and, if they could avoid conceding, a new record for keeping twelve consecutive clean sheets. It was little wonder some of us were starting to question whether the whole comic had lost its sense of direction.

Rovers did, of course, win the cup and, thanks to a late Tynecaster goal being ruled out (having hit the net a second after the final whistle) they also claimed the record. During the course of the campaign, Roy had faced complaints from a number of his senior players, about rumours concerning his plans to break up the side before the start of the following season. Quite why they were concerned about changes to come, rather than by the presence of a couple of singers and a *Question of Sport* captain in the dressing room, we didn't know, but Roy reassured them that he wouldn't be rebuilding the team. From that moment on, we knew something was going to happen, and we suspected it wasn't going to be good. We'd heard these sorts of assurances before, and to the trained ear they sounded uncannily like the chimes of doom.

Our fears weren't allayed any by hearing of the plans to go to Basran that summer, to play a friendly. Even in the days before carbon footprints concerned us, surely they knew the risks they were taking? Could nobody remember the number of kidnappings they'd suffered over the years? Straight away, there were signs that bad things might happen. Firstly, the four new signings – the 'real' people – didn't get their contracts renewed, which given the run of results leading up to the League Cup Final seemed harsh. But, hang on – that meant only fictional people were going to Basran. Secondly, Roy was picked by Bobby Robson to play in the World Cup Finals.

Hang on. Again. That couldn't happen, because Roy never played in real international competitions, because the timings didn't allow it. He could beat packed defences, but not print deadlines.

That meant something would have to happen to stop him playing, and that nobody was making the journey who couldn't be written out at a stroke of the editor's pen. Oh dear. So, off they trotted, straight into the middle of a military coup, and into a kidnapping, which meant, despite their rapid and uneventful release, Roy missed the World Cup. This felt like everyone getting off very lightly, though. Surely, the players wouldn't get away with just a bit of inconvenience, no matter how traumatic?

Of course they wouldn't. On their way back to the airport, their coach was involved in a collision, which was unfortunate. The collision was with the car of a rebel terrorist, which was even more unfortunate. Rovers' plight was worsened by the discovery that the terrorist had been on his way to commit a car bombing. The irony that the coach had not been the intended target did little to cushion the blow, in every sense, as Melchester Rovers suffered the sort of cull that the writers, even in their harshest hour, had never before contemplated.

Suddenly, in the space of one, huge explosion, Tubby's career-ending knock, Vernon Eliot's cricket pitch squashing, and all the other misfortunes to have struck the Rovers over the years were placed into context. Blackie was seriously injured and Roy had a dislocated shoulder, but others fared rather worse. Eight players were dead – Noel Baxter, Vic Guthrie, Steve Naylor, Carl Hunt, Neville Jones, Kenny Logan, Jimmy Slade and Trevor Cassidy. The Rovers had been decimated, and even Roy, we thought, could never recover from this.

But, recover he did, and, with a comic to fill, the story continued. Whether it was ever quite the same again is hard to say. Previous mishaps had been light-hearted, even slightly farcical, but suddenly the Rovers had been hit by something a little too close to reality to be particularly easy reading. Comic strips of the time treated death lightly – the proliferation of war comics being just one example of carnage being reduced down to 'us against them' as people ran around, firing guns and throwing grenades, but Roy of the Rovers had always been different. Also, what with the Munich air crash, albeit many years before, football had experience of a young side being virtually wiped out in one, tragic swipe, while it was only a decade earlier that the Munich Olympics had seen the slaughter of eleven Israeli athletes and coaches. Even as youngsters, we knew that this certainly bordered on bad taste, and probably overstepped the mark.

The ending of David Sque's association with the title, and the decision to hire Michael White, didn't help things. White is an established and respected comic artist, and has designed everything from book covers to stamps, but his interpretation of Roy seemed to owe more to the world of heavyweight boxing than football. Whatever they gave him to assist his recovery after the disaster in Basran, it had turned Roy into a cross between his former self and the Incredible Hulk. Had he been real, he would have lumbered onto the pitch somewhere north of 16 stones. All over the pitch, the expressions and movements of the characters were suddenly more serious and grave than the innocent image we had grown used to.

In reality, there was little real problem continuing, because the 'dead' characters were little more than supporting actors in the ongoing tale of Roy's life. It was like mowing down the chorus line, but sparing the star; brutal, but not the end. For many of the readers, however, the effect was just the same. The real impact wasn't from this story on its own, but the combination of a series of ever more ridiculous storylines arriving one after the other. With worrying speed, the comic was losing much of the credibility we'd ever felt it had – previously it had been stretched, but now it felt as if it had been broken.

Roy used to have plausible adventures – just – but with implausible frequency. People did get kidnapped, and some people were footballers, so it wasn't beyond the bounds of plausibility that a footballer would be kidnapped. When it happened a second and a third time and so on, it was implausible. That was the way the comic operated, and we understood and accepted that. Suddenly, the adventures themselves were implausible, and that presented a major problem. That was my issue with the latest developments –

although, being the age I was, I wouldn't have described it as such. To me, sadly, it had just lost the plot a bit. A childlike reaction perhaps, but when you're a child buying a comic, that's all you need, before you become a child buying a different comic instead.

It was part of a bid to modernise the storyline and to make it feel pertinent to young readers, but it just seemed ill-advised and not terribly well executed. The style White adopted looked better suited to war comics, or to the new breed of science fiction comics. Roy had always been slightly straight and innocent, and the illustrations had reflected that. White's style was a bit like watching an older relative dancing at a wedding – full of good intentions, and intending to deliver what was needed, but ultimately it made you wince.

On the upside, having lost their sponsorship deal with Gola a few years earlier, the Rovers had now, in the wake of their recent tragedy, gained one with Nike; this was far more cutting edge, even if seeing Roy in recognisably branded boots took a little getting used to after almost thirty-five years of generically bland footwear. Unfortunately, this clashed with the storylines. Roy still spoke in the same way he had in the 1960s, and hearing it coming from a man in modern, high-tech kit jarred a little.

Rovers won the 1987 League Cup, by then the sponsored and second rate-sounding Littlewoods Cup, with their patched up team, and introduced a new generation of players to Melchester in order to fill the gaps. Blackie's son, Mark, known to all as Cracker, joined the side; as did Olly Olsen, a Danish midfielder; Bruno Johnson, a huge, black central defender; and Pak Soon, a left winger who originally hailed from Vietnam, to give the side a more cosmopolitan feel. And then, to partner Bruno in defence arrived Johnny Dexter, given the role of bringing glory back to the Rovers. Not that it had ever really left.

Roy put the seal on the title, scoring with two minutes to go, which was a minute earlier than usual, to defeat Stambridge City 2-1; at one stage in this game he had played in goal as a result of injury to the usual keeper, Andy Styles. As he collected the league trophy, Roy braced himself. There was, we suspected, a speech coming, whether it be out loud or in his head. We weren't disappointed.

'Congratulations to you and your whole team, Roy!' said the dignitary handing over the engraved silver plate.

'Thanks!' replied Roy. 'I'm also accepting this trophy on behalf of all the Melchester players who never made it to the start of the season . . . Vic . . . Carl . . . Noel . . . Neville and the rest. This is for you, lads . . .'

We thought things would never be the same again, and when the following season began, we were proved right. The strip had always occupied at least two pages, and run from left to right, moving from top to bottom of the first page, before moving across to the top of the second. Nothing novel in that, and indeed, you might think trying to read a cartoon strip any other way was very distracting. You'd be right, as well, which made the decision to run the story from left to right, across both pages, in far bigger panels, (meaning a page held five or six, rather than the eight or so it once had) was even more difficult to fathom.

Even with his adventures depicted in such a cumbersome way, there was no stopping Roy though. In 1987 he marked his 30th season in the professional game by playing up front for England, at Bobby Robson's request, and scoring twice against Turkey, before being carried off with a knee injury. Confined to the bench for the early part of the following season, Roy instead launched a campaign against hooliganism, which presumably gave Trevor Brinsden yet more reason to dislike him. Mel Park got a family enclosure, and the rest of the world wondered why hooligans were in the 'stands' and families were held, semi-captive, in an 'enclosure'.

There was a reason behind the hooligan storylines Roy had begun to get involved with, and as with so many of the issues the strip tackled over the years, it was based in reality and the need to acknowledge the horror of Heysel. The recriminations were enormous, the issues relating to hooliganism very serious, and the game was forced to examine itself like never before.

During this period, the writers of Roy of the Rovers obviously couldn't put together storylines which featured Melchester playing in Europe, and so, later than you might have imagined for a man who regularly scored more than forty goals a season, Roy's England career sprang back into life. Among the many pub quiz questions he may feature in, Roy's record of having surely been the first man to manage England before going on to earn a regular place in the national side, could just be a favourite. Try as they might, the combined talents of writers and artists were unable to fit the entire Melchester side into the England team, nor to make an England international seem as exciting as a Melchester game. We'd watched the England team win a World Cup, but still came flooding back to see what Melchester would do in the Cup Winners' Cup the following season – they were different, and there was no point mixing the two and expecting us to be quite so captivated.

The background to the alteration – the reason European games couldn't be portrayed – left the whole thing feeling rather flat. English football was at a lower ebb than ever before, so low that *Roy of the Rovers*, which itself had been the antidote on plenty of previous occasions, had been affected. The direction in which the comic had to turn in order to keep things interesting was revealing: after a lifetime of occasional disappearances, usually at the hands of different military groups, a different generation of the Race family was about to go AWOL. Within weeks of the family enclosure being opened, the Race family was split wide open, as his son, Roy Jnr, went missing.

He stayed absent for a couple of weeks, before Roy thought to go and have a look back at the house where they used to live, and found him hiding in a tree house. Roy Jnr had been dropped from his school team, and was ashamed of telling his dad, it transpired. There were hugs, relief and words of encouragement all round, but it was hardly a red letter day for the Melchester police. Having taken two months to solve the most straightforward shooting in English history, they'd now taken two weeks to think to look in the most obvious place in town.

Despite its tricky start, the 1987–88 season went well for Melchester, who were once more bereft of a sponsor after Nike went the way of Gola. For a side who won quite so much, in such dramatic circumstances, their marketing department regularly failed to step up to the mark. Everyone had a shirt sponsor, except the team who won everything. They might not have been paid very much by Gola, but once they'd been paid something, they weren't going to let the shirt go for free, so with no bidders, they were left with no sponsor. With circulation now starting to leak steadily away, why would anyone sponsor them?

It was all very curious, and made odder still by the fact that, by the time they got to the last game of the season, they needed only to win for the title to be theirs. The winner was claimed in the last minute as, under pressure from Roy, a Stambridge defender headed past his own keeper. Not the most glorious route to a title perhaps, but it was Roy's eighth, and by that stage we forgave him being a little blasé.

By the end of the Eighties, it was hard to believe that there was anything Roy could do that he hadn't already done. Even by the writers' own, impressive standards of rehashing and recycling the stories, there surely couldn't be much new ground to tread? When the season started with Mel Park suffering an earthquake, our doubts were confirmed. It had happened in 1965, while the game was going on, and now, twenty-three years later, it had happened again. This time it was apparently because of tunnelling work under the stadium, the time before it had been subsidence, either way it was designed to put a damper on a season.

With the huge crevice running through the middle of Mel Park likely to impede their brand of passing, attractive football, Rovers were forced to play their home games at Wembley Stadium, but it did little to inspire them. It took six months, until March 1989, to repair the pitch at Mel Park, and even after they got back, only the bravest opted to play in central midfield, with the flanks somehow feeling much safer. Their league form was below par, although an 8–1 win over rivals Burndean in the fifth round of the FA Cup was a highlight – especially as Roy set up four and scored another while playing with his broken arm in a sling, having come on as substitute.

As was traditional, Rovers needed to win their last game of the season, this time to stay up, rather than win anything, and did so yet again, thanks to Roy's customary two 'last day of the season' goals. Sadly, though, with circulation going down, it wasn't just on the pitch that Roy and his side were having a hard time of it. The storylines were, perhaps, beginning to show signs of having done too many laps of the block, and it was with this thought that we arrived at the end of the 1980s, as Roy signed Andy Maclaren, a Scottish striker who had been attracting headlines on both sides of the border with his extraordinary strike rate.

There were a few things we knew about Andy, some instinctive and some because a lifetime's experience with Roy had prepared us for them. First, he'd show great early promise, and then fall by the wayside. Roy would offer him some advice, and if he took it he'd go on to be a top player, and if he didn't, he'd stay firmly becalmed by the wayside, and eventually be written out. Even if he became a top player, he'd never be better than Roy, obviously, because that wasn't possible, but the need to ask Roy for advice if he was to progress was a device used to indicate that we all accepted he could never be quite as good as our hero.

Second, and hinted at with none too much subtlety in the picture 'taken' when Maclaren signed, Roy wasn't best happy at the deal. It had been brokered by Charlie Sutton, a pushy director, and Roy felt he already had sufficient firepower to cope without a new acquisition. Scoring four goals in the game before Maclaren put pen to paper was a none too subtle way of pointing this out. Sign he did, though, and then he had a huge tantrum when Roy left him on the bench for his first game, before coming on to score the winner.

With the crowd questioning his judgement, the directors failing to give him proper backing and many people asking if he was approaching his sell-by date (despite the vast number of goals he was still scoring) Roy faced up to the last decade of the 20th century. He loved a challenge, always had, but this was different. Maybe, just maybe, the clock was starting to tick a little more loudly than it had before. The next few years would be very challenging indeed and, for the first time, maybe claiming a last-minute winner wouldn't be quite enough to save him. For the first time since that surging run and dynamic finish more than thirty-five years ago, the fate of English football's most durable player was no longer exclusively in the hands of the writers.

CHAPTER EIGHT

FAVOURITE STORIES

'I ran a newsagent's in the late Seventies, just about the time it went out on its own, separate from Tiger. I might sound daft, but yes, I did used to have a look through, when it came in. About half four in the morning, before sorting out the bags for the deliveries. "Racey's Rocket!" Bloody hell, that takes me back . . .!'

Peter Chapman

As Roy was always the first to point out, teamwork is everything. There was a time and a place for individual brilliance (albeit that it was usually Roy supplying the brilliance, at a time and a place of his choosing) but if it happened at the expense of the team ethic, he considered it almost improper. There was nothing wrong with a crashing drive, thundered home from 30 yards, the ball spitting and swerving off his left boot, leaving a pen and inked vapour trail in its midst, but he always celebrated that little bit harder if the ball arrived in the net via an intricate web of passes.

There was, after all, an engagingly Corinthian air about Roy Race. If winning required cheating, you were better off losing and, frankly, less of a man for feeling the need to break the rules in the first place. It was his belief in teamwork, coupled with his unwillingness to claim any more of the limelight than was otherwise impossible to avoid, which summed up Roy's character. He never got booed, it seemed, even by opposition fans during the most heated and frenzied of encounters, but was appreciated for his skill and standing in the game. There was the occasional pointed comment, drifting down from among the packed ranks (always, it seemed, landing within earshot of Roy) and sometimes Melchester as a whole were berated from the terraces, but as an individual, few fans could ever bring themselves to boo a legend of the game.

When Roy of the Rovers came to be a comic in its own right, in 1976, it was clear that Roy's concept of teamwork, previously limited to the fictional football pitch, would have to work on a broader and more realistic scale. As energetic as he was, and as dramatic as his life could be, there was no way that he could fill all the pages of a comic with his adventures alone. It was time for that belief in team spirit to come into its own; for others to show what they could do in aid of the common cause.

Searching out a favourite *Roy of the Rovers* story *other* than Roy of the Rovers itself, is a task which separates the fan from the casual follower. If you were unfortunate enough to have the sort of deprived childhood that left you reading alternative comics, bluffing (by relying on just naming the star of the comic in the hopes your childhood misjudgements will remain undetected) will only get you so far. The real test, as all true readers understand, is to list a favourite story not featuring Melchester Rovers.

All football fans are well aware of this phenomenon. As Nick Hornby and a generation of subsequent British writers have since observed, the male obsession with making lists eventually requires some complication to be added to the process, as subjects are gradually mined in ever greater depth. After a number of years, certain answers become obvious and, as such, in the interests of debate, are excluded before the debate properly kicks off. As a Charlton fan, for example, I once witnessed my side earn pro-motion to the Premiership after a Wembley play-off final which finished 4-4 after extra time, featured a hat-trick from our very own Roy of the Rovers, Clive Mendonca, and was finally settled after the trifling matter of a sudden death penalty shoot out, which we won, 7-6.

Compiling a list of our greatest games after that particular afternoon was a fruitless task, culminating as it did with the same contest, time after time. For the same reason, Muhammad Ali and Sir Donald Bradman have to be excluded from lists of greatest heavyweight champions and greatest batsmen. The need to keep the debate alive, therefore at least vaguely unpredictable, justifies the exclusion of the obvious.

And so it is with *Roy of the Rovers* – the title track must be discounted. Thankfully, this still leaves a wealth of weighty and wonderful tales. In its heyday, Roy had a supporting cast any one of whom other comics would have cheerfully and gratefully poached to be their star attraction. Roy usually claimed the front cover, but given that it was his name above the door, it would have been odd had he not. What was certain, however, was that the moment the reader had finished with their week's fix of Melchester Rovers, there was still far more to entertain them.

There will be those who disagree, of course, disputing the teamwork analogy, because comics are completely different from football teams, created as they are by outsiders, dabbling and manipulating storylines in order to create results that most entertain them. In these days of billionaire takeovers of football teams, where a Premiership club is as much a status symbol as a flash car or an expensive watch, it may be that we're perilously close to a comic book football world, albeit for all the wrong reasons.

The problems attached to having too much money weren't ones which troubled Billy Dane. Billy, like Roy himself to an extent, (and certainly in keeping with several other members of the 'supporting cast' of the comic) had his personal identity swallowed by the comic strip to which he lent half of his name. If you ask men of a certain age, out of the blue, about Billy Dane, the light of recognition may not immediately shine from their eyes. If you ask them about 'Billy's Boots', the reaction is immediate. The name of the star is less important than the name of the strip – a curious version of the 'nobody's bigger than the game' mentality of which Roy approved so strongly.

Billy was an odd hero for a football comic, being unburdened by any sort of footballing talent – or, at least, being unburdened by any sort of footballing talent *when wearing modern football boots*. Many things may have come the way of Billy Dane as a result of his adventures, but it's fair to say a contract with a large, modern sportswear manufacturer, and a series of advertisements promoting their particular football boots, was never really on the cards. Billy could truly show what he could do on the pitch only if he was wearing the boots of a great striker of 'yesteryear' (as anything having happened more than a decade earlier was referred to in the comic).

The striker in question was 'Dead Shot' Keen who, to honour a time-old footballing cliché, had hung up his boots many years earlier; he shuffled off to rest his arthritic knees, caused by years of

volleying an unvarnished leather football which, when wet,
weighed about the same as a ten-pin bowling ball. His boots,
however, had decided that there was still life to be lived, football
to be played and that being hung up didn't suit them at all. When
fate intervened to offer the ageing footwear a further crack at glory,
a comic strip was born.

Young Billy found old 'Dead Shot's' old boots when he was
cleaning up his grandmother's loft. Given his ability with a ball at
his feet when not wearing the boots, he was probably cleaning the
loft on a Saturday afternoon, as the chances of anyone requiring
him to turn out for their football team prior to his find were
extremely remote. Billy didn't even look much like a footballer,
with his slightly wild, wavy black hair and, even at fourteen years
of age, what looked like the beginnings of a paunch.

And that was the glorious difference between the 1970s and the
present day. Now, if children look a touch on the podgy side,
people write warning letters to their parents, put them on health
awareness schemes and reward them every time they pass an ice-
cream shop without emptying it of its stock. In 1970, they got a
pair of dead footballer's boots, and became a ball-playing genius.
Life was simpler.

Peter Gravel is now in his forties and works in local government,
a fact he admits cheerfully rather than grudgingly, but years on, the
memory of Billy Dane, in particular, still provokes an enthusiastic
reaction.

I think the thing about Billy's Boots was just that it was so
very plausible, while being totally ridiculous. The way he
played the game and the sort of goals he scored were rarely
too far-fetched, and you could almost believe it was just a
story about a kid who was good at football. Then he took the
boots off, or as seemed to happen all the time, had them
stolen, and he was rubbish again. It was odd; he had the
world's most special football boots, and was forever losing
them.

When I was eleven, and this is something I've never
admitted before, I went through our shed at the end of the
garden, dreaming that I might find my own pair of magic

boots. I think eleven's a bit too old to believe in that, don't you? When my wife finds this out, she'll never stop laughing at me. Funny thing is, I don't regret it. I loved that story.

He wasn't alone. Something about the simplicity of the idea, and in particular the execution of the story-telling, left Billy's Boots with friends stretching right the way to the top.

'I loved Billy's Boots,' admits Ian Vosper, cheerfully. 'It came from *Scorcher*, originally, and found its way, to my delight, into *Roy of the Rovers*. I never quite worked out, if I'm being honest, how Billy was allowed to play in those old-fashioned style boots. Nor, come to think of it, why they never stopped fitting him . . .'

One of the most endearing of Billy Dane's traits was his ability to curtail the natural development and growth of his feet, in order that they remain safely inside his magical boots, and one of Vosper's is the ability to muse about his characters as if they were real people. The natural, some would say logical, answer to how did Billy never grow out of his boots is the same as with every other story in the comic. It never happened because the writers decided it shouldn't. Cartoon characters share one, essential trait, and that is that they do what they are told. Quite literally.

Vosper, though exhibiting an engaging willingness to suspend reality, expands on his query in whimsical style: 'He never grew out of them in all the years he had them. Then again, Popeye never aged, either. That's the beauty of comics.'

Which is indisputably true. The reason comics are so easy to fall in love with is the sheer manageability of their heroes and heroines. It is also true that as far as *Roy of the Rovers* was concerned, there were rather more heroes than heroines. Penny Race occupied an occasional role in the limelight, but her habit of losing her temper and fleeing abroad the moment Roy was photographed alongside his new, blonde secretary, made it difficult for an audience of male, teenaged football fans to feel much sympathy for her. No matter how we eventually matured and developed a wider perspective, the battle between football and feminism could have only one winner. In hindsight, I'm not sure we really gave Penny a fair crack of the whip.

Then again, we were only taking our lead from our hero, who seemed to have a slightly strained relationship with the world of women's liberation. When 'asked' in a profile piece for his pet hates, he responded 'Smoking. Especially women.' Doubtless he could still have enjoyable conversations with Sepp Blatter, who while not busy guiding FIFA through the murky waters of world football, offered the opinion, some years ago, that the women's game would surely advance itself far more rapidly if only the players would agree to wear tighter, shorter shorts.

Another character who may well have shared views with Roy was Johnny Dexter, or, as he was billed and titled, 'The Hard Man'. Johnny, essentially, did what it said on the tin. Drawn by Doug Moxted and written by the then editor himself, Barrie Tomlinson, Dexter captained Danefield United through hell and high water. Indeed, had Johnny been given his way, the side would rarely have ventured anywhere else but places resembling hell and ravaged by high waters.

Looking like Desperate Dan in football kit, Dexter was a mountain of a cartoon character. Created in 1976 and enjoying his heyday through the early 1980s, Moxted took advantage of the fashion for troublingly-tight football shorts to give The Hard Man the sort of legs normally seen on an oil rig. Perhaps as a result of him being almost everything Roy was not – hot-tempered, overly-physical, defender not striker etc. – he became a favourite with the readership.

Paul Linden proudly lurks just the junior side of 40, and appears to remember details of Dexter's comic life that even Dexter himself, had he been more than just pen and ink, might have forgotten by now. Like all true fans of the comic, he hasn't let anything as trivial as adulthood force him into suddenly believing that it wasn't all actually real.

The Hard Man was as good a story as *Roy of the Rovers* ever had, particularly when Johnny and Viktor [Boskovic, his manager and occasional nemesis] were at each other's throats.

It always made me laugh, and there were times, probably most of the time to be honest, that I turned to The Hard Man before I turned to Roy of the Rovers itself.

The thing with Johnny Dexter was that he always tried to act like the big, tough bloke, and he was always losing his temper, but it never really lasted for very long and to be honest, he never really did anything that bad, did he? He could have gone out of control, but Viktor knew what buttons to press and how to get the best out of him. He had to be on the edge the whole time, because that was the way he played and that's why he was such a good player.

This was never better illustrated, literally and metaphorically, than when the 1981 *Roy of the Rovers Annual* came out. On the front cover, rather than featuring Roy, scoring from improbable distance, it showed Johnny Dexter sliding into a tackle from behind, leaving a green and yellow hoop-shirted attacker leaping away in terror. It was the only time in the history of the annual that Roy didn't feature as the major cover image, and an indication of the importance of The Hard Man story to the comic as a whole.

The Hard Man was an intriguing diversion for *Roy of the Rovers*, as it not only featured an occasionally flawed character as its hero, but it mixed in large amounts of humour, sometimes almost slapstick, as the storylines progressed. Perhaps this was a deliberate device, to dilute the impact of a man who frequently broke the rules and yet still came out victorious. More likely, it was just a pleasing antidote to the main story, where Roy could on occasion be just a little bit worthy.

As if proof were needed that The Hard Man was an attempt to play it for laughs, they even went so far as to give him a comedy partner. Johnny Dexter may not have looked too much like David Walliams, but Viktor Boskovic, Danefield United's manager, was a ringer for Matt Lucas. Tubby and bald, Hungarian-born Boskovic paraded around in a tracksuit which just about managed to get over his space hopper of a stomach; he exhibited the sort of tantrums which frequently left even Dexter silenced.

He announced regularly that he was a genius, possessed greatness, and would tolerate neither fools nor doubters. His perception of what constituted either of the two categories was inconsistent. Fat, clean-shaven and hairless he might have been, as opposed to slim, swarthy and carefully coiffured, but *Roy of the Rovers* foretold the arrival of Jose Mourinho by about twenty-five years.

Johnny and Viktor had a relationship quite unlike anything else in the comic, and certainly a world away from the (occasionally dour) professionalism of Roy and his side. They met when Johnny left Danefield to sign for 'Spanish giants' Real Granpala.

'The only time I fell out of love with it,' reflects Linden 'was the Real Granpala stuff. The Hard Man was a British story, and it only worked on these shores.'

Linden's view was evidently identical to the writers, as, after a brief stay in Spain, Johnny and Viktor were on the move – although for some reason they returned home via an eventful trip to Italy, which Johnny, perhaps uniquely, had seen as a natural home for his robust style of play. Viktor predicted it would end in disaster, and when the deal fell through at the last minute, it was somehow fitting to see the 'Hard Man' flee an Italian prison (and quite how he got there was never clear) dressed as the least convincing woman the footballing world has ever seen. Italian defenders, it appears, never allow a striker to get away with anything, but their prison warders are unable to spot a six-foot-four, heavily built, swarthy woman with a deep voice when they see one. At least Roy always took his brushes with foreign forces of law and order seriously.

When the team played well, Viktor was not averse to launching garlands of flowers around the dressing room, and leaping on his players to hug and kiss them as they strolled off the pitch. When things went badly, just about anything that came to hand was launched against the wall, as the players sat in silence and considered their shortcomings. Most entertainingly of all were the moments of tension which caused Viktor to raise the back of his hand to his forehead, raise his eyes to the heavens, and fall to the ground in a dramatic, spiralling faint.

Quite how Dexter put up with this for so long is probably best explained in the same way as the mystery of Billy Dane's ever-expanding boots. It was a successful, entertaining story, the readers loved it and for a while it even threatened to overtake the title story of the entire comic. Put simply, the two of them would stay at the same club, annoying, infuriating and irritating each other until the scriptwriters decided otherwise.

But, by 1985, after nine memorable years, an enormous period of time in terms of the life of a comic strip, The Hard Man had run its course, as all stories but Roy's own tended to. The comic was being given the once over, and like wallpaper which had faded and begun to peel, while some of us retained an affection for its shabby ways, the people who mattered had decided it needed updating. Johnny Dexter, after years of service, dedication and thinly concealed, yet comic, footballing thuggery, was going the way of every other comic book hero – whichever way the writers decided. It was probably for the best, as one more season would have seen him due a testimonial, and a fundraising golf day was never going to be his scene.

The ending was brief and to the point – a new, younger centre half had arrived that summer, and Johnny was suddenly surplus to requirements. He demanded a transfer, and Viktor, with the melodrama we had come to expect from the great man, granted it. With a flourish, probably. The queue at Danefield's door was non-existent. Only one side put in a bid for Johnny, Burnside Athletic, who sat at the foot of the league.

Having been insulted by Viktor's decision to release him, however, Johnny had no option but to swallow his pride and leave, and in August 1985 he did. The only man, apart from Roy, to have featured on the cover of an annual, was, just four years later, playing in the lowest tier of English league football. If it were real, it would have brought a tear to the eye. As it was, for many of us, it probably did anyway.

In true comic style, having adopted a new kit and a new club, Johnny also adopted a new title, as 'Dexter's Dozen' was born. The sometimes bleak story of survival in the lower reaches of English football was conveyed in serious tones, and the artwork of Mike White, who would later illustrate Roy, took over from the comic panels of Moxted, in order to convey the new feel of the strip. The hand to mouth existence of the players, the sparse crowds, the issues surrounding distribution of wealth down throughout football's hierarchy were carefully and seriously considered. It became almost a campaigning storyline, full of emotions, fears, doom and gloom.

All of which obviously failed to win our affections as readers because, after just a season, Viktor was brought back and slapstick was firmly back on the menu. Our relief was enormous – there was enough time to campaign about serious things when we were adults. For now, there were newspapers that could ignore the perils of the lower leagues in a serious and considered way, leaving *Roy of the Rovers* free to ignore them in favour of pure, unashamed farce. The ratings, we assume, went back through the roof.

The story lasted for just one season – presumably the combination of drama, nonsense, tragedy and comedy eventually being too much even for a comic. Predictably enough, Johnny and Viktor went out on a high, as Danefield won promotion to a league still miles away from the summit of English football. Johnny was too good to spend too long trudging through the lower division dross, so a cunning route back to the top had to be created.

They could have just transferred him straight back to the top flight, but that would have left the 'Dexter's Dozen' moniker looking somewhat misleading. Not for the first time, their solution was surprising – they transferred the character of one comic to another. Only one man could have had the eye for talent to scour the country's lowest league and spot a man who could add the steel and bite his defence needed. Roy Race was bringing Johnny Dexter to Melchester Rovers. The Hard Man was leaving his dozen, and the two strongest stories in the comic were united.

'People might have thought it was a very novel idea,' says Barrie Tomlinson, with the benefit of a career full of novel ideas to compare and contrast with. 'But to be honest, it's the sort of thing that's been going on in comics since pretty much day one. There was a bit of development when we did it in *Roy of the Rovers*, I suppose, because it was done with established and senior characters, but it wasn't a completely new idea, even then.

'There had been a long time to merge Johnny Dexter into Roy of the Rovers, and have him sign for Melchester, and we just had to wait until the moment was right to do it. It was always destined to happen, though.'

Whatever the problems of developing the characters over time, ultimately they were just one more minor niggle in a list confronting the staff on a daily basis, trying to get the stories finished on time for the printing presses to spring into life. Even straightforward issues such as the look of the characters were more complicated back in the 1970s than they would be today, and for Vosper, putting the comic together sounds less like the fun one might imagine, and more like a terrifying clash of deadlines and sod's law.

Issues of drawing style were all important – that was all people had to judge the character by initially, after all. There were certainly times, in the planning stages of a story, when an artist would come along with some sketches, and we'd have to explain that the style didn't quite fit the way we'd imagined the story being put across. It wouldn't be just me there, though. There would be a group editor, and also some of the art staff perhaps, so it tended to be a collective decision. Everyone would have to work on the strip, so everyone had to feel totally confident about it before we even got started.

That could be a little awkward at times, but logistically it became a hundred times harder when the artists were from abroad, [such] as Julio Schiaffino, who was based in South America and drew Hamish and Mouse, because you could wait two or three weeks even to get your pencil roughs back.

As for the 'surprise move' of The Hard Man to Melchester, it seems it was a surprise to everyone except the editors, which is just another way of reminding us of the reality behind the fantasy world we were happy to live in. Vosper continues:

Johnny Dexter was always, whichever way you looked at it, a bit tongue-in-cheek, but Viktor, the manager, was a sort of portly Yul Bryner figure who played absolutely everything for laughs, so he couldn't really be put into the same category. I could see how Johnny could make the move to Melchester, though, and it was a good idea, but Viktor wouldn't have worked in any strip other than the one he came from.

The move was made certain when, in the most tasteful sense, some vacancies appeared in the Melchester squad, as a result of the terrorist attack which had caused them a few problems during the course of their pre-season break. Eight sets of new watercolours and players sketches were never used, as the list of the dead grew slowly. With each passing minute of an editorial meeting some-where, another young talent was sent shuffling off to the great changing room in the sky.

Roy escaped with a dislocated shoulder, while big Duncan McKay, who probably claimed he had seen worse on the pitch, was only slightly injured; but there was no doubting that, in the aftermath of the disaster, Roy would have to get busy in the transfer market. He probably sat by the roadside, waving the smoke from his eyes and trying to jot down a team from the remaining members of the squad.

Johnny arrived on a free transfer, which, given he was still under contract, must cast doubts on the negotiating skills of his agent at the time. Melchester won their first game post disaster, beating Deans Park 5-0, with Johnny scoring, as well as Roy (inevitably) and Blackie Gray, which called into question the description of his condition as being 'seriously injured' just three weeks earlier. An emotional and tense season was guaranteed.

Dexter stayed at Rovers until 1993, when, inevitably, he started to fall out with just about everyone. Legends that they were, however, nobody who ever enjoyed Johnny Dexter's weekly pantomime adventures with Viktor Boskovic will ever dispute that the golden days were behind him, or that The Hard Man deserved its reputation as the only storyline which ever threatened the comic's title tale in terms of popularity.

Just to complete Dexter's story, he ended up in *Match of the Day* magazine, as manager of Castlemere, who by pure chance and the good judgement of a diligent scriptwriter played Melchester Rovers in the 1999 FA Cup Final. Melchester won. Obviously. Some traditions are destined to be observed, whatever happens, which is why so many of us loved it and bought into it every single week.

Merging stories together went on to become something of a speciality as far as *Roy of the Rovers* was concerned; while Johnny Dexter making the move to Melchester might have been the highest profile as far as the publication was concerned, as Tomlinson and Vosper have already intimated, it was not unique.

Having begun in splendid isolation as two stories, in two comics, 'Mighty Mouse', and 'Hot Shot Hamish', ended up hopelessly intertwined. Kevin Mouse was an unlikely footballing hero, who managed to make Billy Dane look lean and trim. Mouse was as wide as he was tall, with a mop of greasy, black hair and the sort of stomach darts players dream of. He wore glasses with the thickest lenses the NHS could provide, and routinely held them together with lengths of sticking plaster, bound round each decaying hinge, mummifying them into solidity.

'Kevin Mouse was my hero,' admits Steve Prettle, who now earns a living as a graphic designer, yet seems only too happy to delve back into some childhood memories.

> I was a bit tubby when I was younger. Well, I was actually a bit slimmer than I am now, but I was still a bit tubby by normal standards. Built for comfort, not speed, I am.
>
> Mouse was funny, which made him different from most of the other stories, and despite it being all totally unbelievable, it looked realistic. No matter how ridiculous all his antics were, the backgrounds were very grey and serious, which made the events even funnier. And I know I probably shouldn't admit this, but I'm going to get all my old comics out tonight, which I've still got bundled up, and I'm going to spend the evening reliving my past.

Mouse played in the First Division, for Tottenford Rovers, but his worst moments came not at the hands of his manager, but at the scene of his alternative existence, as a medical student. St Victor's Hospital was the sort of place the film world went on to capture in the *Doctor in the House* comedies of the 1960s and 70s. It was a dictatorial regime, with everything running to a precise timetable, and everyone expected to look neat, tidy and orderly at all times, requiring doctors to fit into a firm stereotype.

The comedy came from the tubby, scruffy figure of Mouse, who always seemed to be arriving at high speed, several minutes late, causing outrage among the formidable duo of Dr Mender, who also ran the hospital football team, and the matron, 'Mad Annie', who was a combination of Hattie Jacques and Margaret Thatcher.

Kevin Mouse's life was one long, protracted juggle, as he tried and failed to satisfy the competing demands of Tottenford, the St Victor's side, Dr Mender and Mad Annie. The chaotic timetable life imposed upon him would have tested even a highly organised, suave and dashing young medical student to the limits, and Kevin certainly didn't fit that description.

While Mouse was hurtling around St Victor's, spreading chaos and amusement, his eventual comic partner was far away, in a completely different strip. Hamish Balfour was a vast man, larger than Johnny Dexter, and drawn in a similar style to Mouse, also by Schiaffino. The only thing more frightening than the size of his thighs was the extent of his mullet, which cascaded away down his broad back, and trailed behind him like a golden comet when he picked up top speed. Says Prettle:

> From the outside, it must have looked as if Hamish was destined to bully Mouse. One of them was huge and muscular, and the other tubby and bespectacled, but what with it being a comic, there was never any hint of that. They were great friends, in the way comic characters are – without any thought that they represented such an incredibly odd couple.
>
> Had Hamish stormed in to straighten out the people who were making his friend's life a misery, the problems would have disappeared in five minutes, but Mouse would never have asked him to do it, and Hamish would never have agreed. They played everything for laughs, and even when Mouse occasionally lost his temper, it was funny, rather than troubling.

Hamish played in the Scottish Premier Division, for Prince's Park, although never really seemed to leave the Highlands, where he lived a blissful and remote life accompanied by his pet sheep,

McMutton. Just as Mouse had a senior figure in his life, keeping him on best behaviour, Hamish had his manager, Mr McWhacker, performing a similar role. Silly names abounded, but it was a storyline for which Tomlinson always retained genuine fondness.

'I was a big fan of Hamish and Mouse, which I thought were a really important part of the comic, because they offered that same sort of lightness as the summer stories used to, but managed it all year round.'

It is a sentiment echoed by Vosper, who also makes an intriguing observation about the distinctive facial characteristics of Kevin Mouse.

Artists do sometimes look a bit like the characters they produce – now that may be because there's a subconscious desire to make them like that, or perhaps it is just coincidence, although funnily enough, for a while, Roy was drawn by a chap who looked just like him, in David Sque, and Julio Schiaffino was a ringer for Kevin Mouse! A little, tubby bloke with dark hair – if he'd had the horn-rimmed specs, he'd have been perfect! It was like looking at a real-life version of the picture.

Whether he looked like Kevin Mouse or not, the point about Schiaffino's talents is not lost on Tomlinson, who remains happy and willing to shower praise on an artist who, for the vast majority of their working life together, operated from the other side of the world.

'It is extraordinary that he managed to capture those remote parts of the British Isles, and the bleaker bits of the inside of hospitals quite so well, when he lived on the other side of the world and had never seen them. It just shows you what sort of talented people there were around and how lucky we were to have them working for us.'

One thing Hamish and Mouse always had in common, thanks to Schiaffino's eye for comic art, was a distinctive shooting style. The ball would be struck with the point of the toe, the precise departure point obscured by a large star, drawn around the area of contact to emphasise the power involved. The follow-through would then take the boot high into the air, well above head level, as the ball disappeared off, leaving a vapour train in its wake.

Hamish was reputed to hit the ball harder than anyone else on the planet, and routinely destroyed nets, crossbars and just about anything else that got in the way of his pile-drivers. He began his days in *Scorcher* before graduating to *Roy of the Rovers* via *Tiger*, where he had rested happily for several years. It seems hard to believe now, but there were those who couldn't see how, when it was first mooted, combining the two strips into one was going to work. They were seen as a supporting act, a slapstick routine that would fill some space for a while, but never a star turn in their own right, as Ian Vosper freely admits:

> There were a few stories that really surprised me. Mouse amazed me, because of his size and shape. I thought it had a comic angle to it that was perhaps better suited to adults than children, but they absolutely lapped it up. Up until that time, I'd always imagined that what would work in *Roy of the Rovers* would be 'proper' football stories, with no room for humour, or at least, not at the expense of any football content – certainly not a 'cartoonified' strip, so that was a huge surprise to me. Also Hamish, because he was this cumbersome, giant figure, with a ridiculous shot and a mane of hair, and I found it hard to believe that anyone could take him entirely seriously at first, but he grew and grew on people.
>
> We did his hair as a bit of a graphic joke, but looking back at those early 80s days, with [Glenn] Hoddle and the like, that sort of giant mullet doesn't seem to be nearly as silly as it once did.

The stories were originally billed under the perfectly accurate, but less than catchy title of 'Hot Shot Hamish and Mighty Mouse' but soon found themselves with the new, crisper heading of 'Hamish and Mouse'. It started, as so often with *Roy of the Rovers* stories, by getting straight to the point, and ironing out any potentially awkward plot-based stumbling blocks later. Mouse wasn't wanted by Tottenford any more and, having met Hamish on a trip to

Scotland, discovered that he could transfer to a Scottish hospital. With no offers coming in from elsewhere, he signed for Prince's Park.

Several years ago, the *Observer Sport Monthly* magazine compiled a list of the top ten comic book footballers of all time. Designed as a device to stimulate debate and discussion, the top ten is a familiar feature of the magazine, and always manages to quite deliberately 'accidentally' stumble into controversy with at least one of its monthly selections – a fine journalistic tradition, and one which they have carried on with style.

Lee Honeyball, the assistant editor, explained that, based on a straw poll of friends, *Roy of the Rovers* was, rather unsurprisingly, the perfect place to find comic book footballers, but that the greatest of them all wasn't the obvious one. Hamish Balfour came out on top, thanks to the comedy he produced, with Kevin Mouse in third place. As if to rub salt into the wound, Billy Dane, and his fortuitously mystical boots, came in fourth, while Johnny Dexter snarled and crashed his way into fifth, leaving Roy way down in sixth place.

Roy doubtless would have greeted the decision with a show of delight for Hamish, warm handshakes for Mouse and Johnny, and a ruffle of chubby little Billy's already messy hair. Sportsmanship and a willingness to accept the decision would have abounded, although his congratulations to second-placed Billy the Fish from *Viz*, who arguably pokes a degree of fun at Roy, would have been something to see. Make no mistake, though, underneath that cheery exterior, Roy would have been planning out the next forty years, to see how he could improve. Finishing sixth, in any competition, was not something Roy Race could readily accept.

He probably only avoided slumping a position lower still because the story he nudged just in front of concentrated on stopping rather than scoring goals. Gordon Stewart was, as suggested by the name, Scottish and in a (probably perfectly deliberate) twist was not just unlike the endless collection of error-prone Scottish keepers of the time, but was very good. In fact,

Stewart was better than just 'very good', which was useful, as his story went under the heading of 'The Safest Hands in Soccer'.

He lived up to this billing, week in and week out, for Tynefield City, in a strip that was drawn in such minimalist, black and white, austere tones, it was a good job he did, because had he been rubbish, the overall effect would have been deeply depressing. Gordon Stewart was never one to get involved in great dramas (apart from one, arriving shortly) such as befell many of the other characters, but just relied on saving shots – regardless of how hard, or how well placed.

Had it not been for Stewart, it's fair to assume that Tynefield would have been playing in the local park by now, such was the ease with which other sides seemed to cut them apart each week. The simplest of passing movements would routinely see their defence shredded and, as a rocket of a shot was unleashed from close range, there would still be time for the traditional conversation among spectators as to how little chance the keeper had of stopping it.

The next frame would depict the back of Gordon Stewart's gloves, holding a football, plucked neatly from the air, midway to what had seemed an inevitable meeting with the back of the net. Disbelief would spread around the crowd, which was odd, as he did the same thing every week, and Tynefield would live to compete another day.

Stewart played a part not only in capturing the imagination of young readers, but in influencing their spending patterns (such as they were) and birthday present requests. For a period in the late Seventies, no primary schoolboy would even contemplate making the journey to the playground without his 'goalkeeping gloves'. I had a pair, and wore them religiously, despite never, as far as I can remember, playing in goal, and I was far from alone in that. Whether stuck between the posts or not, half the school playground ran around in goalkeeping gloves, whenever a football was produced.

Made of cloth, with elasticated wrists, the gloves appeared to have sections of table tennis bat rubber stitched to them, supposedly in order to help us catch the ball more easily. Had they been kept clean, and had they been made of a more durable material, then perhaps they would have done, but in the hands of schoolboys (or indeed, on the hands of schoolboys), they were of little use. The rubber would get worn thin within days, and then dry out and crack, providing a surface that was far more slippery than the hands they covered.

Trying to save a ball wearing a pair of £1 goalkeeping gloves was far harder than in bare hands, but we would not be dissuaded. Some people will try to tell you that it was famous international goalkeepers such as Sepp Maier and Dino Zoff who made gloves popular. To purists, perhaps, they may have done, but to most of us it was Gordon Stewart who saw our pocket money used to bedeck our hands with something which made goalkeeping quite so difficult.

Eventually, in 1982, after five years of gravity-defying saves, Stewart was finally beaten by an editorial decision, rather than a close-range header, and the story came to an end. Five years without a great drama? Could any *Roy of the Rovers* strip manage such a feat?

Of course it couldn't. They brought him back in 1983, in the first episode of a new strip called 'Goalkeeper', although oddly enough, it seemed to be set many years after he had supposedly retired. The solution to this seemingly tricky chronological challenge became brutally and immediately apparent, as he got onto a plane that promptly crashed, killing our hero. When the writers needed someone disposed of, they made the mafia look indecisive.

From the violent introduction to the new story, we met Gordon's son, Rick, who, wouldn't you know it, was also rather promising. Rick did the unthinkable, and signed for Tynefield City's huge local rivals, Tynefield United. He survived for seven years, until 1990, saved just as many shots as his dad, and did just as little of any interest off the pitch.

One affair, shooting, kidnap or arrest between the two of them, and they could have had that number six position in the *Observer Sport Monthly*'s, top ten, but it was not to be. Their good behaviour, and all round dour approach to life meant that, no matter how good they were in goal, the number seven slot was probably as high as they were ever destined, or indeed deserved, to reach.

For all its tales of glory and excitement, with games played out in front of heaving terraces and capacity crowds, the lower leagues played quite a major part in the life of *Roy of the Rovers*. While Johnny Dexter and Viktor Boskovic visited them largely to explore the comic potential of minor football, however, other strips were more firmly set in the lower reaches of football's hierarchy.

Durrell's Palace is not a name that features with any great frequency in the record books. Largely because they are and always have been totally fictitious, but also because, even with the scriptwriter's licence to grant them as much success as was desired, they spent their lives among football's paupers. They were managed through thin and thin by a youngish chap called Dan Wayne, who wore the permanently haunted expression of a man who could see plenty of clouds and precious few silver linings.

Palace played in the Western League, and even at this lowly level they regularly faced bigger, wealthier and more substantial opposition. The story first appeared in the hallowed pages of the comic in the early part of 1991, although due to the printing deadlines which saw them produced months in advance, the first time Dan and his poverty-struck squad appeared in the annual was two years later. The storyline that time, that they were so short of players the local milkman had to play in defence for them, was typical Durrell's Palace fare, as was the winning goal he inevitably scored.

Dan had a loyal, if eccentric ally in Joe Croke, who acted as Palace's groundsman. And secretary. And scout. And turnstile operator. And you get the picture. Joe did everything, always topped off with a battered old bowler hat, and seemed to enjoy, if that was the word, a role which involved constantly panicking about every fresh problem, regardless of the fact that Dan always came up with a solution sooner or later.

Dan's solutions tended to be so straightforward it was something of a mystery why nobody else ever thought of them. If finances were short, Dan would phone up a 'large foreign club' who just happened to be in town playing a friendly, and arrange for them to play an extra game. The ground would be packed to the rafters, Palace would snatch an unlikely late draw, and the wages could be paid for another six months.

Somehow, against all the odds, Dan got Palace to Wembley in 1984 (playing, not watching), but for once the gate receipts couldn't assist in making both ends meet. The first law of comic writing had to be obeyed and, seeing a brighter future ahead, Dan moved on. Durrell's Palace bit the dust a year later, having hovered on the brink since they first arrived in the comic. Dan, however, had been noticed as a result of his triumphs with Palace (and also, presumably, his lucky habit of arranging hugely profitable friendlies with just one phone call) and the big time was calling.

It always felt bizarre that, in his earlier years, Roy had been kidnapped by people for no other reason than their desire to play a friendly against the Rovers. Dan Wayne was able to achieve something very similar using nothing more menacing than a telephone – and not even one of the magical red ones.

Dan's new employers, Wolverdon, were a top flight side, and 'Wayne's Wolves' could have been a tale of uninterrupted glory. Inevitably, there was a downside, though, and, true to form, we soon discovered that Wolverdon were virtually bankrupt. Dan, it seemed, brought his own dark clouds, just in case the silver linings ever threatened to break through. Thereafter, a chain of events began that must have left even an eternal optimist like him shaking his head in disbelief. It was a good job Joe Croke didn't follow him to Wolverdon, as he could only have been one refrain of 'I told you it would all go wrong' away from getting throttled.

Wayne brought some of his old players along with him and, predictably enough, they took the step up from non-league to top division football in their stride. Then he prepared his side for the third round of the FA Cup; three wins later and he was preparing them for the sixth round. A glorious day to remember saw them through to the semi-final, and by then the writing was on the wall. Propelled to Wembley, Wolverdon went all the way, and in Dan Wayne's first season of top-flight management, he won the FA Cup. As a reward, they scrapped the storyline, presumably because it was felt it had gone as far as it could. You could probably hear

Joe Croke chuckling away to himself for miles around, the miserable old sod.

Equally low-key, and permanently battling against the powers that be, was Tommy Barnes. Tommy was so troubled that his story was actually titled 'Tommy's Troubles'. Built along the same unprepossessing lines as Billy Dane, football was Tommy's life. Unfortunately, this was not a view shared by Crowhurst School, which prided itself on its rugby-playing tradition and history. Had Tommy been educated anywhere else, his life would have been more straightforward, but *Roy of the Rovers* would also have been without an endearing story about a schoolboy with troubles.

In order for the drama to be played out in full then, Tommy had to go to Crowhurst and, once again, the first rule of comic scriptwriting ensured not only that he did, but that the head boy and his 'henchman' took a dislike to young Tommy which bordered on the pathological. For Waller and Swate, the gruesome twosome who sought to ruin Tommy's life, the sight of him playing football, holding a football, bouncing a football or indeed looking as if he was possibly thinking about football, was enough to bring murderous thoughts to the surface. Their world was oval shaped and involved kicking the ball over the bar and as such they stood as a metaphor for all that was evil in the world, which in hindsight was perhaps a touch unfair.

Tommy and his erstwhile companion Ginger Collins campaigned to persuade the headmaster to allow them to form a football team and, after much effort and numerous run-ins with Waller and Swate, he agreed that they could, on condition that Tommy managed also to gain a place in the rugby team. The logic of this decision was unclear but it did fit the general theme of the story, which was that anything rugby related was illogical and the next best thing to evil.

Tommy managed to get into the team, of course, which seemed to result in a constant round of trying to finish a 'rugger' match in time to scoot off and start a football one. Along the way Waller and Swate would throw him a succession of hospital passes, both literal and metaphorical, but Tommy would come out on top time after time. It would be wrong to say he emerged unscathed, though. Tommy Barnes ended up about as scathed as it was possible to get without being mortally wounded, but in the spirit of comic characters everywhere, as soon as the illustrator's eraser had rubbed away the bruises, he was as good as new.

The story was important in many ways. Not only did it regularly fare well in the feedback from the readers, thus making it a long-term favourite, but it allowed one of the magazine's more senior figures to show his versatility, as Vosper explains:

> If you look, though, you can see the talents of the writers in making different stories feel different in very marked ways. People might have thought that one sort of writer tended to produce one sort of story, but if you look at Fred Baker, he produced this lovely, comic, light-hearted storyline in the shape of Hamish and Mouse each week, and then he had Tommy's Troubles, which was all about a boy overcoming odds, with bullying and hardship and all that sort of stuff thrown in.

Sadly, on 4 June 2008, Fred Baker passed away. He had lived a long life, and his work will never be forgotten by any of the millions of children who read it. Thanks to Baker, both Hamish and Billy Dane came to life, as well as Skid Solo in *Tiger* and a host of other characters. Many of the people who have enjoyed his work over the years probably don't even realise it – such is the life of a comic book scriptwriter – but a part of Fred Baker lives on after him, and will do for years to come, in a million different, yet vivid childhood memories.

Returning to Tommy and his troubles, eventually he and his side finally found a ground when they persuaded the local council to allow them to have a bunch of unused grass tennis courts, large enough to form a football pitch. In 21st century Britain, the idea of councils having tennis courts of any sort is increasingly novel, let alone just happening to have a spare expanse of grass ones to give away, but these were more innocent times.

Tony Russell is about the same age as the others in this chapter who have recalled their various favourites and, just like them, puts forward a compelling case for why his chosen strip was superior to the others.

> Tommy was about more than football because he was always getting such a raw deal in life, and nobody ever wanted to give him a fair hearing. It wasn't as if he was a tearaway or some kind of troublemaker, either. He just wanted to run a football team, and this seemed to really upset the world he lived in.
>
> I tried to start up a team at the same time as Tommy's story was running – I must have been about twelve. It never got off the ground – we had no kit, no money, no idea of how to join a league or anything like that. We never got offered a pitch, either. Thinking back, though, I reckon I was happier at things going wrong, and making me feel more like Tommy, than I would have been had they gone right. I don't think I really wanted to run a football team, to be honest. I wanted to live out one of the comic strips, and when my team failed to get off the ground, I could convince myself I was having the same troubles as Tommy. Actually, it was just that I wasn't very good at organising things.

As a nation, we might have stood on the brink of the miners' strike, the privatisation of the railways and the 'greed is good' era, but in the pages of *Roy of the Rovers*, there was always a spare football pitch to be given away when the occasion required. Which is just one more reason why, as a ten-year-old, when two newspapers and two comics came thumping through the letterbox once a week the brightly coloured offerings, packed to the rafters with intrigue and optimism, were so much more enticing than the grey pages of the papers.

But, of course, this was an illusion. Proof that your comic book heroes (or in this case villains) weren't necessarily as memorable to everyone else as they were to you, comes little more clearly than admission from their creator, Ian Vosper, that he can scarcely remember them.

Oh my God, what an extraordinary memory! Waller and Swate! They were like the two prefects who wanted Tommy to play rugger the whole time. I know it might have seemed like a slightly old-fashioned view of the world, but of course, you've also got to remember how old the scriptwriters were back then. Fred Baker, who wrote it, must have been in his fifties already, and that was back in the mid-1970s. You were talking about people from a different era.

Tommy was a little scruffy individual – he was an unlucky little chap, almost a fifties character, always on his uppers, one way or another. But we had no end of people like that.

Look at Mike's Mini Men – Mike had a perfectly sized garden shed, just ready to take a table football table, and so did all the rest of his friends. That's the beauty of cartoon storylines like that, you can just make them fit as neatly as you want, and so of course, that's exactly what we did.

That story developed because we had a lunchtime table football league running at IPC. I remember there was a chap in the art department called Ted Healy, and he sat on the table once and dented it, and thereafter the ball would always run down into the dent and you couldn't play out of it, and it became known as the 'Healy Slope'.

'Mike's Mini Men' was indeed another stalwart, and another example of not letting reality intrude on a comic storyline. Everyone in the story, which revolved around a table football league run by Mike Dailey, did indeed have a vast, empty, clean and unused shed at the end of their garden, in which to set up their matches. Indeed, some of them were so large, with copious spectator access around the perimeter, that had Tommy Barnes made a bid, a sympathetic council official would doubtless have ensured that Barnes United had an indoor training area to go along with their bastardised tennis courts.

Barrie Tomlinson has equally fond memories of the table football adventures of Mike Dailey and his friends.

I remember Mike's Mini Men, not just because it was a popular storyline, and I was a bit surprised at that, although very pleasantly so, but because we had quite a nice little tie-in going on with Subbuteo. Again, it was no more than taking a good look around at the world our readers lived in, seeing what entertained them, and what they liked to do, and acting on it. Loads of them played table football, Subbuteo was the most popular version, and so the story was matched to the demand.

It sounds very simple, but once again it is. Sometimes people make things more complicated than they have to be, just so they'll look clever, and the idea suffers because of it. We just kept our ears open, and acted on what the readers told us. Subbuteo produced a Melchester side, complete with a number nine who had blond hair, and the link between the comic, the story, the readers and the subject was complete. It really couldn't have been any simpler.

Keeping it simple remains the basic premise of most of Tomlinson's editorial decisions, few of which have ever been shown to be wrong. There are many reasons for Roy's longevity, not least of which the power of the central storyline and the public desire to read ever more about the adventures of a muscular, blond-haired striker.

For a man, though, who as we reflected earlier, loved teamwork and refused to believe anyone was bigger than the game (and a host of other clichés, besides) the strength of his supporting cast played as large a part in Roy's success as anything. Whether it be the comic antics of the two duos, Hamish and Mouse, and Johnny and Viktor, Billy and his magical boots, Tommy hurtling down the wing to escape from the world's first known example of rugby hooligans or Mike and his endless supply of sheds, the team around Roy was an impressive one.

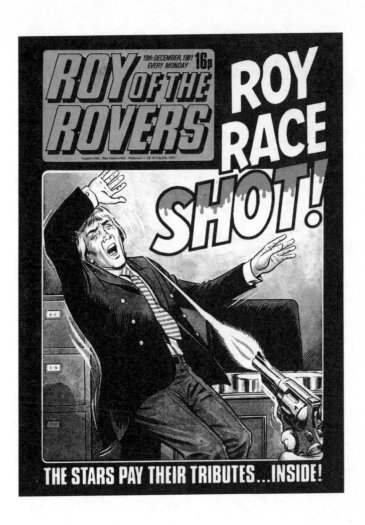

CHAPTER NINE

THE PUPPETEERS

'I can remember when Billy got to the end of the football season, and I didn't know what was going to happen. Then they found an old pair of cricket boots, just like the ones he wore to play football in! As a nine-year-old, I thought that was genius. Part of me still does . . .!'

Mark Church

Barrie Tomlinson doesn't try to hide his delight at having done a job he has enjoyed so much, for so many years. When the subject turns to comics, his enthusiasm is immediately clear, and his successor was plainly made from a very similar mould. Ian Vosper lives in Portsmouth these days, a stone's throw from the sea, a short stroll from his favourite football club, and is sufficiently animated when talking about his days at the helm of *Roy of the Rovers* to make you wish everyone could be so lucky in their career choices. When the chance to join the comic first came along, it wasn't so much that he'd had to prepare for the interview, as that he'd seemingly spent most of his life waiting for the opportunity to arise.

> Even when they first asked me to come on board and work on the comic, back in 1976, I knew all about it, because I'd been a reader since I was a kid, and obviously I'd been lucky enough to work with Barrie before, so I knew him well. The history wasn't something I had to look up or study, because I'd lived through it. That, at least, was absolute manna from heaven as far as I was concerned. There couldn't be a better job than being asked to edit *Roy of the Rovers*.

Originally introduced to the world of comics through his work on *Scorcher*, where 'Danny and the Dazzlers', Roy's forerunner to a certain extent, had once been housed, Vosper almost drifted straight back out of it, before Tomlinson first remembered, then set about recruiting him.

> I'd gone away – I'd left *Scorcher* and gone to this little

publication, connected to the Football Association, strangely enough, a drop-in-the-ocean publishing house, based above Hampstead tube station, and totally different from IPC, which was absolutely vast. I got a call one day, just asking if I'd like to come back on *Roy of the Rovers* and work as a sub-editor. It was just meant to be, so off I went.

From his very earliest days at the comic, Vosper was under no illusions as to the place in British life Roy and his side held. It was, on one view, little more than just a collection of illustrated stories, and yet to a greater extent – perhaps more so than *The Beano* – it had become a British cultural reference point. It was a huge honour, and he doesn't try to hide the fact, to edit the comic, but with that came responsibilities.

It was like dealing with a real person, in a way. The people who lived around me heard as much about Roy as they did about any of my distant relatives, because that was the nature of the working relationship. Because of that, and because, if he was real to me, he was an awful lot more real to a lot of people, we did have a responsibility with the way in which we portrayed him, and the things we decided he was going to do.

There was no alcohol, no affairs, no nothing like that, and we also had a responsibility to keep the dialogue right in the stories. We were very proper about dialogue – take, for example, 'em for 'them'. We just wouldn't do that. We tried to encourage the grammar aspect – we didn't split infinitives. Many of those standards, stretching right back to the Fifties, were worth keeping. There are certain characteristics of Roy, which will always survive from generation to generation.

And yet the comic was nearly named as something else. Tomlinson had always seen the promise in Roy, even when it was just a footballing storyline in *Tiger*, but recalls that while the popularity was never doubted, the name, for a while, caused definite concerns.

The powers that be were quite taken aback at first, because it [*Roy of the Rovers*] had, in their opinion, just far too long a name. We were living in an age of *Scorcher, Eagle, Tiger, Lion* and things like that, and they just thought the idea of calling a comic *Roy of the Rovers* was asking for trouble.

Then one of them suddenly said, 'Hang on though, what about *News of the World*?'

From that moment, when they could see how a four-word title could be successful, there were no more queries about the name. I don't know how many people know that, but the comic was allowed to exist under its own name simply because the *News of the World* had already gone out there and shown how a longer title could still be competitive.

One of Roy's great ironies then turns out to have happened before his comic even drew breath, as a newspaper which went on to depend in large part on the misbehaviour of footballers, guaranteed the birth of a comic about a footballer blessed with impeccable discipline. It wasn't a decision anyone would live to regret.

Given its standing in the game, the comic was able to ask favours of people, and make requests nobody else would have considered. As important as anything else, though, was both the innocence of the time and the way football was then run. The automatic response of 'How much?' to every question had yet to find its way into the national game, and that, coupled with the affection with which people felt towards the publication, made life a lot simpler for its editor. Vosper explains:

We used to do 'sign please' which was a feature where we had autographed photos of players across a whole page. We just used to send them a piece of card, with a picture and a pen, a self-addressed envelope and a fiver, and ask them to sign it. We even used to let them keep the pen!

Only one player ever refused to sign for us, and I think he came from Leeds, but there you go. When it came to pictures being taken with Roy himself, it was even simpler. Absolutely everyone, footballer or not, wanted to stand beside that cut-out and smile as the camera flashed away – Eric Morecambe, Mike Yarwood, Rod Hull – you name them, really, and we had them. Roger DeCourcey and Nookie Bear were really keen. They absolutely jumped at the chance to be in *Roy of the Rovers* alongside the great man.

I think someone in the art department made that cut-out, and it was literally just a blown-up picture of Roy, stuck onto a piece of hardboard and cut to shape, but it featured in more pictures, with more people than anyone could have believed!

At the time, Morecambe and Wise were bringing in almost 20 million viewers for their Christmas shows, and while Rod Hull might not have occupied quite such an exalted position as Eric and Ernie, he was certainly a huge star of the time.

Vosper's biggest coup, in footballing terms at least, came in the wake of the most talked about story Roy ever endured (and almost didn't). The plot began with a shadowy figure, reaching out with a pistol, and shooting our hero. While a nation waited to see if he would recover, life with the Rovers had to go on. Someone had to hold the managerial reins and make sure things went smoothly until Roy regained consciousness, then fitness, then goalscoring form. Out of this disaster, Vosper thought, with some imagination, the comic could emerge stronger than ever before.

I went for Sir Alf [Ramsey]. Well, why not aim right for the top? I went off to meet him at his bungalow, and offered him £50 to do it, and I took an Instamatic camera, and I took pictures of him in his garden – profile, mugshots, three-quarter views – all for the illustrator, and then I took him for lunch to his local pub, and he was absolutely fine.

Now, if that had been Danny of the Dazzlers he wouldn't have agreed, but because Roy of the Rovers was a name that meant something to people across all generations, there wasn't the slightest problem.

There are many tales associated with Roy of the Rovers which beg comparisons between the footballing worlds of then and now, and the gap is usually huge and unflattering, but none illustrates it as clearly as this one. For the price of £50 plus a pub lunch, the only manager ever to bring the World Cup back to English shores, or in Sir Alf's case, to stop it leaving them, was happy to be caricatured in a children's comic. Ramsey was retired from football by then, and kept himself at a distance from the game, but his agreement to go along with Vosper's idea would doubtless have caused raised eyebrows among many.

The reasons for his agreement are hinted at in Vosper's answer, but deserve highlighting, if only to place the standing of the comic in its proper context. If we put aside for one moment the possibilities of any England manager since Sir Bobby Robson doing something similar for anything other than an extortionate fee, why would Sir Alf agree to feature? The money he received was little more than a gesture, and the pub lunch an irrelevance, but he knew he could trust the comic to portray him accurately, without trying to ridicule him, and he knew that, whilst it was clearly a gimmick, it was a gimmick in the appropriate spirit. Such things, one suspects, mattered to Sir Alf Ramsey.

During his time at the comic, it is the episode that, one suspects, fills Tomlinson with the most pride. If *Roy of the Rovers* needed a seal of approval, Sir Alf delivered it in impressive, caricatured style. Tomlinson recounts the episode with every bit as much relish as Vosper, as well as placing into perspective some of the other, less likely 'signings'.

> There was a sense of affection for the comic, so that when we needed a favour, it was easy to get it. Imagine getting an England manager to do that these days? Even a former one? Certain things happened that could only have happened to Roy of the Rovers.
>
> We had two of Spandau Ballet sign for Melchester Rovers and play in midfield! That was a coup! They were nice lads, and in the music business they could have just about anything they wanted. They could only play football at the highest level, though, if they did it in the pages of our magazine, so they signed for Melchester.

It was an intriguing signing, to say the least, but it came at a time when the comic was perhaps slowly moving away from the aims it had been set by Frank S. Pepper so many years earlier. Pepper had set out to create a character who achieved fantastic things, but did so in a way that was essentially believable. With the introduction to the Rovers' midfield of two members of a New Romantic band, signed in a 'deal' which contained no financial rewards, and was built almost entirely around the publicity each side would receive, it would be hard to argue those dreams were being followed too closely.

If there were issues to be resolved among the editorial depart-ment concerning the selection of pop stars in midfield, there were problems of a different kind for David Sque and the art department.

> It was a bloody nightmare for me . . . so much drawing! I remember one, I think it was a cover, which featured the whole band with their instruments and everything. I met the lead singer, Tony Hadley, in the end. He worked at IPC before the band took off, it turned out, on *Love* magazine, with an old mate of mine. They were nice, ordinary blokes, but they were very big at the time. I had to draw them all, but it was only the two of them who played.
>
> Apparently they used to go out and get the comic every Saturday morning, hangovers, whatever. They loved it – absolutely loved it.

As claims go, it's a dubious one, but equally a lovely image. There may have been the odd occasion when one or the other of the footballing Spandaus popped into a newsagent's and collected the comic alongside a morning paper and a packet of fags, but somehow, the thought of them getting up and heading automatically down to the corner shop for their copy of *Roy of the Rovers* seems a little far-fetched.

Both Tomlinson and Vosper frequently refer to the standards of the comic and the way it presented itself. While they were in command, for many years there remained a commitment not only to move the new stories forward, but to keep checking back, ensuring it was never allowed to drift too far from its roots. Many of its rivals were attempting to make their name by following trends, but Tomlinson understood the value of remaining apart from anything so transitory:

'We concentrated on keeping a steady course, doing the sort of things we felt Roy would do, regardless of everyone else. It's wrong to say we ignored the rest of the world, far from it, because we were aware that the attraction of Roy came from his refusal to bow to the pressures of whatever else everyone else was doing.'

If it was remarkable that Sir Alf arrived at Melchester at all then, it was made even more so by the circumstances that put Roy temporarily out of commission. The biggest storyline the comic had ever run, by Tomlinson's own, cheerful admission, had little to do with football, yet ended up attracting one of its biggest names.

I remember when Roy was shot, and there was a queue of suspects building up. It's fascinating to look back at it now and see how it was done, and how we went beyond our normal boundaries. We ended up with Sir Alf as manager, and the Rovers trying to win by a new British record in order that the crowd noise, when carried through the radio placed next to his bed, would wake Roy up. All a bit ridiculous, perhaps, but a lot of fun, too.

And all because people wanted to believe in a footballer who had never existed, other than in the imagination, or on paper, having been put there by an artist who most of the time had no interest in the game. Choosing to believe in such things, and opting to regress to childhood every time we read the comic, were a small price to pay to enter the world we did. And besides, we had worked out the secrets – we knew the inside stories, the ones the writers had spent years assembling about each player, and were going to release to the readers a drip at a time. Didn't we?

According to Vosper, no, we didn't: 'Everyone seemed to think they knew something about one of the players that nobody else

did, and they all believed the world we created was far wider than
it actually was. In truth, almost everything that wasn't directly
mentioned in the comic existed only in the individual's
imagination. We certainly didn't have time to build an elaborate
back story for every player.'

It's a myth Tomlinson is equally happy to debunk, as a small
piece of childhood mystique comes crashing to the ground.

'Everyone who read the comic has their own ideas about every
character, and every single one of them thinks we revealed more
than we actually did. They filled in the blanks for themselves most
of the time, and I don't think they even realised it. People always
do that with comics, but they did it a lot more with Roy, just
because it was around for so long.'

And yet, the imagination expended on the stories was essential,
because deep down we all knew that's all they were. Stories based
around an imaginary character, dreamt up and put on paper. Or, in
some case, a six-foot high piece of plywood, as Vosper remembers
fondly:

Life on Roy was fun. I still remember my first interview –
Peter Marinello. I was so nervous, but off I went, with my
large, cardboard cut-out, and we just got on with it. You
wouldn't have any idea of quite how many doors that cut-out
opens. Honestly, it's unbelievable. We went to see Charlie
Nicholas on the day he signed for Arsenal.

I had this little 2CV, and I drove up to Highbury with the
life-sized cut-out of Roy sticking out of the sun-roof, and
everyone was thrilled to see us. We took pictures on the
pitch, and after we went back to Charlie's flat, and he just
loved it, he was great.

We all knew that Charlie had a history with long-legged blondes,
but which of us knew that the one he took back to his flat the day
after he came to Arsenal was a better striker than he was? The
whole thing is such a good story it really has to be a one-off. Apart
from, in true Roy of the Rovers style, the other occasions when
similar adventures took place. Arriving at Highbury with a
cardboard cut-out of a cartoon footballer was one thing, but if you

really wanted to cause a stir in the game, and Vosper clearly did, sights had to be set slightly higher.

> We once went to see George Best at Wembley Stadium. I think he was injured, or maybe it was just a long time before kick off. Can you imagine, though, the fun and games of getting off at Wembley Park tube station on a match day with a life-sized cut-out of Roy of the Rovers? It was packed, that train, but both me and Roy got a seat . . .
> We got a picture of these two prize winners, both holding their copies of the comic, with the cut out of Roy behind them with George Best with his arm around all of them.

Vosper's habit of referring to his cardboard cut-out as a real person is one of the more endearing aspects of talking to him, but it comes purely out of habit, and also as a result of the way Tomlinson had gone about putting together the stories and coming up with the ideas. Without stopping to consciously address the matter, Vosper cheerfully agrees with his old boss about the public's habit of adding details to a story that simply don't belong there.

> We knew from the correspondence we got that people were hugely interested in the characters, to an extraordinary degree, and that they took the storylines desperately seriously. We had lots of letters querying tactical errors people felt had been made, and even the occasional refereeing mistake. We didn't get overburdened with letters inquiring about the background stories of individual characters, though, because people thought they already knew them.
> Almost everyone who read the comic, I suspect, had a slightly different team in their head, because almost everyone had given slightly different attributes to the individual members of the side – details that, as a writer, you'd never have time to expand upon.
> In reality, the players were like blank canvases – we gave them very bland and limited back stories, otherwise the whole thing would have got terrifically complicated. We had to make up for that by giving these really over the top traits

to four or five of them, and hoping that the overall impression was one of a side packed full of personalities and characters. That was as far as we planned it, though, and how much of that has stuck in the back of people's minds is something that always amazes me.

That the readership added to the limited descriptions of some of the players is hardly surprising. Given our age at the time, the inviting and exciting nature of Roy's world, and the desire to enter into it as fully as possible, it would have been strange had we not. Where imagination was not required, obviously, was the question of Roy's appearance. How he was styled was a matter of discussion between Sque and Vosper, and for the editor, there were certain principles to observe.

There were a few style points which probably developed, rather than being set down in stone. Roy might get muddy, but he tended not to get bloodied, regardless of where he stuck his head. Lofty Peak, the centre half, would be the one to end up with blood all over him, but Roy didn't. I'm not quite sure why, but I guess we maybe felt it wouldn't look quite right on the front cover if Roy was bleeding – which of course added to the impact when we had him shot.

There have been a few different versions of Roy of the Rovers over the years, from different styles of kit to different styles of drawing, but to most people he'll always be remembered the way he was drawn when they first saw him. I don't know, perhaps he's a bit like Dr Who in that regard. I will only recognise the strip I put him in – the red with the yellow stripe down the side of the chest. I wouldn't recognise the others, because you get used to seeing him a certain way. Roy was drawn, in the time I was there, a certain way, and never deviated from that. The descriptions we gave were so strict and so precise there was very little scope for changing it around, anyway.

But while Vosper was setting down the reasons why Roy looked exactly as he did, for his artist, working away from the office, the description, no matter how detailed, still offered scope for imagination. The Roy he settled on, and the one who will forever be associated with the 1980s, came, as Sque admits, from some unexpected roots.

There were several factors behind Roy's appearance, but it came down to an amalgam of four things. Firstly, he looked as he always had, but was slowly transmogrifying to my style. Secondly, there was a little bit of Kenny Dalglish in there, who was the striker of the moment in the real world. Thirdly, there was my own haircut, because that was the style back then, so I used that, and fourthly, there was a little bit of Cliff Richard in there. In fact, Roy's nose was Cliff's nose, because I was a fan.

And there, from the mouth of the artist who drew him, is possibly the most startling revelation yet about Roy Race – that he had Cliff Richard's nose. After a moment's consideration, though, it isn't such an unlikely match. Roy's record was unblemished by scandal or tantrum, and he wasn't averse to delivering the occasional moral lecture. He did, of course, go and marry Penny, while Cliff and Sue Barker never quite made it up the aisle, but it seems unfair to lay the blame for that at David Sque's door.

Sque's version of events must be taken as the definitive one – he was the man, after all, who actually drew the character. It might come as something of a surprise to his former editor, however, who was under the impression that the star of his show was gently transforming into someone else entirely. Then again, given Vosper's love for Portsmouth Football Club, that is both unsurprising, and entirely forgivable.

A fair bit of Roy may well have been based on Alan Biley, the legendary Portsmouth striker, because they had the identical haircut. We used to sponsor Biley's kit, actually. It cost us something like £50 a season, and in the back of the programme, there would be a picture of Alan Biley, and next to it they'd explain that he was sponsored by Roy of the Rovers. We arranged a presentation down here, before a game between Portsmouth and Oxford, who were managed by Jim Smith, because Biley had scored 50 goals in 100 games, or some amazing strike-rate.

Anyway, this game was just before Christmas, and Pompey were 1–0 down, when a bloke dressed as Santa Claus ran onto the pitch, and stopped the game for a couple of minutes. The referee added on the time, in those days it was at his discretion because there were no boards that went up to tell the crowd how long, and Biley scored twice for Portsmouth, in the 91st and 93rd minute to win them the game.

Jim Smith went absolutely mad, and while he was losing his temper, the chairman of Portsmouth went and presented the trophy to Alan Biley. Well, the publicity we got as a result of those two, late goals was unbelievable. It was a Roy of the Rovers finish, and that got us into every match report of every national paper. Wonderful stuff.

Of course, Smith's anger had doubtless been brewing since 1986, when his Oxford side celebrated their first season in the top flight by winning the League Cup, only for the nation's young boys to insist that it was Melchester who had earned the silverware, despite having Bob Wilson and Emlyn Hughes in their side. Such over-sights among the young can cause a manager terrible angst.

The ability of Roy to be whoever the reader wanted him to be is never better highlighted than by Sque and Vosper, both of whom seem, understandably, convinced that their version of Roy's back-ground was the right one. The truth is that he was precisely as Sque described him – 'an amalgam' – yet of even more characters than the artist thought. A small part of Roy was unique to each individual reader, in that he took on whichever personality we each felt fitted him best. If Melchester was wherever we imagined it to be, so Roy was, for all his character and adventures, a blank canvas onto whom we projected whichever fine details we chose.

We enjoyed the illusion of him being a real person, and we thought we knew everything about him, but in reality we knew very little. Most of what we carried in our minds was created not by writers and artists, but by our own imaginations. While writers and artists put in the basic outlines, we filled in the areas that were otherwise left blank.

And, given the way Roy was presented to us, the players we used in order to fill those missing aspects were all perfectly behaved and very successful. It was no good trying to fill in the missing bits of our personal Roy Race by using the characteristics of a hard man or a troublemaker, because that wasn't what Roy was about. Neither was there much point in focusing on a well-behaved but hopelessly unsuccessful player, because that would have been equally wide of the mark. Roy had to be faultless, both in terms of behaviour and talent. It made for a potent combination, as Vosper acknowledges.

'Nowadays they would call us a brand. Roy had a clean-cut image, he didn't drink, he didn't have affairs, so there was never a problem with him causing difficulties for anyone because of his behaviour. Penny ran off to Crete once – that got us four columns in the *Guardian*, but I think that was about the extent of any negative publicity Roy ever gained.'

Far from generating negative publicity, it seems Roy's influence spread wider than anyone could have imagined. Polite, softly-spoken and as law-abiding as anyone you could ever meet, Vosper is not exactly a habitual criminal in need of policemen turning a regular blind-eye. As he recalls, however, sometimes Roy's influence stretched a very long way indeed.

I remember when we were doing the column with Gary Lineker, in the late 1980s, and I was driving over to his house in St John's Wood in this ancient Alfa Romeo I used to have. I pulled around someone, and suddenly heard a police siren. He wanted to see my licence, and as he took my details he asked me what I was doing there. I explained I was going to see Lineker and that I was a journalist. He asked who for, and so I told him it was *Roy of the Rovers*.

'Oh,' he said. 'Billy's Boots still in it, are they?'

So we had a quick chat, and after five minutes he just said, 'Ah yes, happy days they were. Now, just be bloody careful in future, eh?' and he sent me off on my way.

Between the two of them, Vosper and Tomlinson were in charge of *Roy of the Rovers* through the very highest points of its existence, and arguably as successful a time, in terms of publicity and sales combined, as any comic ever enjoyed. Along with the satisfaction of the successes, though, there is a palpable sense of regret at the way in which, towards the end of Vosper's time in charge, the comic industry began to fade away as a whole.

Roy of the Rovers may have been the highest profile title to suffer a downturn in fortunes, but it was not alone. If other, competing interests were dragging readers away from it, they were also taking them from all manner of other titles. The industry in general was facing difficult times. For Vosper, it seems akin to a craftsman looking back at a trade which people no longer wish to enter; hearing him describe the care and precision taken over each issue, it is hard, even for someone who never worked in the industry, not to share his sentiments.

It's a dying art now, making cartoon strips, because there's less of it being done than there ever used to, so people will never appreciate just how much work went into it. Certainly, though, underpinning all the technical tricks was the good, old-fashioned discipline of writing down every single scene description as carefully and in as detailed a fashion as you possibly could.

Continuity doesn't just go frame by frame, though, it runs week by week and making sure the style is immediately accessible and familiar to people is absolutely crucial. Every week you've got between sixteen and seventeen frames to tell that story – or in Roy's case, between twenty-three or twenty-four – and so it's a disciplined environment and a very specific skill, because there isn't a lot of latitude to play with. If you look at something like 'Scorer', which Barrie does in the *Mirror*, you can't spend any time looking back at all, because otherwise you'll never move the story forwards.

And hardest of all is the knowledge that doing things well, adopting the very highest of standards, and using the best people available, wasn't enough to keep things afloat. When we come to look at the moment when *Roy of the Rovers* reached the peak, before beginning a slow descent, it is hard to place any of the blame on the people who brought it to its position of popularity in the first place. The more Vosper explains the mechanics behind the publication, the clearer it becomes just how much attention to detail was involved.

> When we subbed a script, we made sure we gave the artist every tiny little piece of information that we could, particularly if the artist was working on it from abroad. We wanted them to know where things were happening on the pitch – and precisely where they were happening on the pitch, not vaguely. If someone received the ball having been passed back to him from over the halfway line, we couldn't have him suddenly standing in the opposition penalty area. That would have been unprofessional and, to be honest, unacceptable. You need standards to stay around as long as we did.

Putting the stories together, it seems, was as much about exhibiting extraordinary discipline and powers of organisation as it was displaying imagination and flair. The process in the office had to run on rails if they were to avoid the entire operation juddering to a halt, as storylines began to clash and inconsistencies began to creep in. Vosper, as all editors are to a degree, resembled the con-ductor of an orchestra, trying to bring everything together at the same time, to produce as impressive a cumulative effect as possible.

The stories certainly developed in a measured way, but rarely, to our junior viewpoints, predictably so. Or at least not so predictably that it actually troubled us. Besides, throwing in a few mid-season goal-less draws, just to be unpredictable, would hardly have whetted our appetites for more. When it came to a toss up between predictability and glory, we'd take glory every time. It was a comic after all, and Vosper knew how to keep the tales churning out.

We were working on about five or six issues at once, so we were about a month and a half ahead of the game as far as organising the plotlines was concerned.

Every now and again we'd change something, sure, but by and large these guys were experienced scriptwriters – they'd been doing it for donkey's years, and they knew exactly what they were doing, so it was never a case of looking over their shoulder the whole time to make sure things were being done properly.

We'd meet up for example, though, myself and Tom Tully, who wrote Roy of the Rovers, and Fred Baker, who wrote Hamish and Mouse, and this would happen fairly regularly. We'd all mull over who was going to be bought, who was going to become a new character, who was going to be sold, so who was leaving, and in a sense I left it to their expertise. I gave them a bit of guidance, sure, but it was a bit like making a film – after a certain point, it's up to the actors how that character takes off, with a little guidance along the way.

You also need other pieces of assistance, it seems. Take, for example, the league table.

We had a really good sub-editor called Ray Harrison, who used to keep an eye on things like fixtures and results, to make sure we were getting them right. Ray and others were in charge of all of that, and you'd be amazed how much detail they had to go into. FA Cup dates had to dovetail, European dates had to fit in and, domestically, teams we'd said the Rovers had already played and who they had still to play arrived in the story in the right order. A reader, somewhere, would notice if any of this was wrong. They always did.

The best way round this was to have the whole league played out on paper each week, that way we were guaranteed to be consistent. We kept the table right using 'League Ladders' from *Shoot*, which was produced just down the corridor.

At this moment in time, any children of the Seventies reading will be luxuriating in nostalgia's warm glow at the mention of League

Ladders. They were made from one, large piece of cardboard with a series of slits cut into it, one for each place in the league, into which a small, cardboard tab was inserted, printed with the name and colours of the team it represented. In years to come they would make them out of plastic, which was slightly more durable, but their first incarnation saw them punched from cardboard, and fraying at the corners after about a fortnight.

They refused to stop at just doing the top flight of football, either and, crazed with the power of temporary cardboard football league tables, produced one for each of the four English divisions, plus two in Scotland. The end result was that more than 120 pieces of swiftly crumbling cardboard were held in place, just, by being wedged into a cardboard sheet. This, in my experience, was then stuck to a bedroom wall, fridge door or wherever else seemed sensible at the time, although as a 12-year-old, my version of sensible may not have accorded with my parents'. Moving it, once it had been in place for more than a fortnight, was impossible, as it would crumble like ancient parchment, depositing hundreds of pieces of coloured cardboard onto the floor.

It also acted as a magnet for every shoulder, careless arm, elbow, bag or back which walked past. The merest brush would see clubs tumbling out of contention, like a particularly brutal year in the third round of the FA Cup. It was a toy of its time, and if we were smitten with our comic before, discovering that the engine room that kept it running was powered by League Ladders does little to divert our affection.

In their own way, Tomlinson and Vosper are quite a duo. When they had command, and Roy followed a steady course doing what he had always done – doing plausible things with implausible frequency – the comic prospered. While Tomlinson is the man with the extraordinary track record all over the industry, however, we should be careful not to underestimate the achievements of his successor. There's a lot to admire in Ian Vosper, and lots to learn, especially given the way he had to watch much of his good work achieved in his career undone by the actions of others who failed to listen to his advice. He could remain bitter about it, but he seems to be able to put it down to experience, and look back with sadness for what was lost, rather than anger at the way it went. Besides, he works at his beloved Portsmouth FC now, thus confirming his ability to move from dream job to dream job.

Alongside Tomlinson, though, and with the talents of a host of others, he created something very special indeed. When the baton was first handed to him, few people could possibly have imagined the aplomb with which he would seize the chance, and the single-mindedness with which he would apply himself to the task ahead. However carelessly people pulled apart his dream, the memories he created will remain firmly out of their reach.

The sales and the prestige represent only one small part of Tomlinson and Vosper's achievements with *Roy of the Rovers*. True, they sold many more copies than anyone would have imagined, and they left a lasting mark on the pop culture of this country, but where they really triumphed remains locked deep in the memories of all who read the comic while they were in charge. They left us with stories that saw us through the most impressionable years of our lives.

And, as Tomlinson explains, their creation opened some formidable doors. Having photographs taken with a cut-out was impressive, but compared to his parting shot, delivered almost as an afterthought, it was still nothing to write home about. People may yet try to copy some of Tomlinson's more imaginative marketing ideas, and maybe, just maybe, someone might pull one of them off with half as much charm and style. Some of the things he managed, though, will never, ever happen again.

I remember we once had the entire Manchester United squad, all stood in formation, on benches, as if for a team photograph, except that we took a picture of each and every one of them with a copy of *Roy of the Rovers* in their hands, as if they couldn't take their eyes off it long enough to allow the photographer to take a picture.

Imagine how much you'd need to spend to get footballers to do that these days, and as for how much it would cost to get the whole Manchester United squad at once?

You just would never be able to do it – it just couldn't be done. We did it, though, because we were *Roy of the Rovers*.'

CHAPTER TEN

ENDGAME

'I'm a bit young to have read the comic, to be honest, and I feel like I missed out on something. I do remember the pineapple flavour chews, though – they were very good. Imagine being so famous as a comic character that they name sweets after you? That's the ultimate children's compliment!'

Andy Rowley

Depending on your age, chronicling the first three years of the 1990s means either recalling the finest years of a comic, cruelly cut down in its prime, or looking at the last gasps of a much-loved publication that, for the time being, had simply run out of energy and ideas. In order to ensure completeness, it would be wrong not to applaud Roy's tenacity in making sure Andy Maclaren fitted into the Melchester way of doing things, and also the dramatic flouncing out of director Charlie Sutton, who took umbrage at being proved wrong by the manager when it came to assessing the abilities of the new signing.

Sutton fitted into a long line of characters who arrived in Roy's life, caused him all manner of difficulties, looked for a while as if they were going to gain the upper hand, and then found the tables turned, common sense returning to everyone, and Roy emerging from the situation more popular than ever before. Had he thought to check his history, boastful, pushy old Charlie would never have crossed swords with Roy, who ended up marking him down as just one more doubter to be proved wrong. He had, after all, been in the professional game for almost thirty-five years at this point, and his international career was just starting to bloom.

All the baddies in the world crossing swords with Roy couldn't stop the comic's heyday from waning in the end, however, although Vosper identifies one moment and one particular action as being as important as anything else. Once the ownership of *Roy of the Rovers* changed hands – from IPC to Fleetway, an arm of Mirror Group – he believes, despite having initially appeared to be in as robust health as ever, its fate was as good as sealed.

On the surface, you wouldn't have thought there was

anything wrong, because the comic was something everyone wanted to be associated with. We occupied a unique place in people's affections. We used to have a Centre Forward of the Year lunch, and the year Paul Mariner won it we held it in a large, Central London hotel. Sir Alf turned up to that – a World Cup-winning manager just strolling around at a Roy of the Rovers lunch! It was a great time.

Behind the scenes, though, it was a period when things started to go awry, in my view. Things changed, economies were forced onto us – for example, the paper quality went down markedly, and all that was simply to save money, which is a bit of a sad reason to change things, given its history.

The cuts were being made in preparation for, and eventually as a result of, a takeover, which seemed, again to the outsider, to be a positive move. Ideally, we would have had IPC stay there in charge for ever, but only because we were used to seeing their logo and name on the back of the comic. When Robert Maxwell became interested, though, even the youngest and most innocent of us could understand that it was a big step. We saw Maxwell on the television, and we understood his importance. He was a big, blustering man, who talked to lots of important people and smoked cigars, and we could see how and why he had become so famous. With him in charge, Roy and his side could go from strength to strength for years to come.

And while we might have been young and innocent, there were a lot of people who were older and more experienced who fell for much the same line of patter. And as we now know, and as a lot of his former employees can painfully testify, what Robert Maxwell promised could be very different from what he delivered. Initially, though, hopes were high, and Vosper paints a glorious picture of life working on a comic, which, thankfully for those of us amused by such things, sounds just like life working on a comic should.

In the Maxwell era, we shared an office in IPC towers with *Eagle*, and we had *Battle* down the corridor along with *2000AD*. It was wall-to-wall comics – there were *Whizzer and Chips* just down the way, and then us and the other sporting/war type comics, and then down a bit there was *Shoot* and the other football titles.

Then, elsewhere, there were the female magazines, *Women's Realm* and the like, but they were a lot more grown up – a lot more serious. Where we were was like a big party some days. There were lots of practical jokes, itching powder and that sort of stuff, and there were always people flicking those paper cone things that made a huge 'crack' sound when they were done in the right way. It was a very particular sort of atmosphere. You couldn't move for whoopee cushions.

Any job which invites the retrospective comment 'You couldn't move for whoopee cushions' is, one would think, doing very well at keeping in touch with the feelings of its young readers. Behind the laughs, however, it was a major operation. Vosper continues:

When I got there it was a huge department because before web offset, in the days of overlays, there were loads of people, painting the strips red or blue, then doing balloon lettering corrections, and we had people who could just change one particular frame if they needed to, but that was rare, because the interpretation was particularly good. The sheets were never done as the same size as they appeared on the page, they were twice as big and then shrunk down, which made it easier to make corrections. All of these techniques, though, helped to make it look the way it did, and that appearance was very distinctive.

The thing was, and this gives an idea of the scale of magazine buying at the time, *Roy of the Rovers* was a bit of a minnow compared to some of the other titles on offer at IPC. We were big-ish in the youth group, but probably still fell behind *Shoot*, but compared to things like *Woman's Weekly*, which were doing a million copies a week, we were nothing to write home about.

Eventually, and inevitably, things came to a head. There was an inevitability that, surrounded by larger publications, the accountant's eye would not pass over *Roy of the Rovers* for long, and when it did, the man in charge would waste no time before indulging in some brutal pruning. Vosper, as editor, saw it all at first hand.

It was a hard time – circulation was going down, Maxwell had taken over, and a lot of us were asked to work from home. We left without contracts, but just a lot of promises, which was a crazy thing to do, and against this background the costs were being cut everywhere. My house became the office, effectively, and I had people coming around at 10 p.m. to help set out pages. The cost to family life was enormous. It was a mad time.

It's funny actually; children's perception of things is entertaining in hindsight. They thought that because we had a PO Box number there was this huge operation going on to produce this comic, but it was far from the truth. It didn't stop me getting lots of letters from teachers and people like that, asking if their groups could come round and have a look at our offices!

They might have been a little disappointed had they turned up, because it wasn't quite as sleek, modern and glamorous as they'd envisaged it. I had a sub come in two or three days a week, and thankfully there were people like Ray Harrison helping to keep things running, sorting out the readers' votes and the suchlike, but there were still hordes of other people who had to come in and sort out the artwork, so it did get very crowded.

For a long time, my house was the *Roy of the Rovers* office.

It's a stark statement, and a very sad one. The most famous footballing comic of them all, which entered the language and retains a place in the popular culture of this country, ended up being produced in the back room of the editor. *Roy of the Rovers* deserved better than to be reduced by a thieving owner's greed, to being created in surroundings akin to a fledgeling fanzine.

And yet what struck as fatal a blow as anything Maxwell managed was the game itself, and the way it changed its sense of priorities and generosity. Vosper, during the course of a day of conversation and memories, cites two stories not directly connected with each other, but which illustrate just how badly *Roy of the Rovers* was hurt by the change in the culture of football. When things were good, as he explained, they were very good:

> Getting hold of players used to be very easy, but I can't imagine it's still like that. In fact, I don't suppose we could do it any more – it would be impossible. We'd have to go through agents the whole time, and nothing would get done because everyone would want paying for every single little thing, every step of the way. The goodwill's all gone from the game, and that's very sad.
>
> When we dealt with Lineker, he used to write out in longhand, on sheets of airmail paper, while he was flying between wherever he was at the time, and then he'd either send it in himself or get his wife to send it in on his behalf. He had a proper agent, though, and he used to tell us not to bother him, but just talk to Gary directly. He understood the value of someone like Gary being associated with something like *Roy of the Rovers*. We worked very well with each other.

And then, at the other end of the spectrum, was a conversation with someone who viewed things very differently. To this day, Vosper sighs as he tells the story. It is, after all, one which seems even sadder when you know how things eventually turn out. One solitary story, perhaps, represents the turning of a tide.

> I remember towards the end of my time there, having to call an agent because I needed to ask a question to a player he represented – just one single question. So I called the agent and asked the question, and he said, 'How much?'
>
> 'But we're a comic!' I said to him. 'It's one question, just to fill out a feature.'
>
> 'No pay,' he said, 'no effin' way,' and put the phone down. And I remember sitting there, with the receiver in my hand, thinking to myself, 'Is this the way it's all going to go?'

It was just about the last straw for Vosper. With the cutbacks and the indignities, and now with the greed which was starting to surround the game, one suspects he might even regret staying for as long as he did. But despite all the problems, there is no disputing that he absolutely loved the job, and knew the chances of getting anything else that engaged him quite so much were few and far between. After fourteen years at *Roy of the Rovers*, twelve of them as editor, Vosper was finally beaten down by the cutbacks and changes, and, it seems, aware that the best years were now behind Roy, the Rovers and their beloved comic.

> I was very, very sad to leave, there's no point in denying it. My last editorial meeting I was verging on weeping. I'd been there a long time, so it was always going to be a wrench. It's a moving-on process, though, isn't it? I went to work elsewhere, then I got the best job in the world, editing football programmes for the FA. I did Euro 96, the lot, and it was very different from Roy, which is probably just what I needed. Roy, I once said to someone, was great fun, but it was like having your favourite meal every day.

It must have taken a huge amount of dissatisfaction for Vosper to leave the helm of a comic he had edited for longer than anyone else. And yet, as the world moved on, and Maxwell's cuts bit ever harder, things were just not the same as they had been. As he readily admits, the climate for selling comics was getting harder all the time, and technology was always doing its best to drag potential readers off in new directions.

> Kids just stopped reading as much as they used to – it stopped being something that kids did. When we started there was *Look and Learn*, umpteen kids' comics, and as well as *Eagle* and *Tiger*, there were a host of war comics and numerous competing titles. In the girls market there were literally dozens of titles, from typical teenage stuff to younger titles and with just about every base you can imagine covered by a title somewhere or another.
>
> Computer games came along, and that was really the big

factor. It was the Super Mario era, and before that the ZX Spectrum. People just popped them on, played a tape or put in a disc, and suddenly a game was transporting them away into another world, in the way *Roy of the Rovers* had once done. How many kids do you see playing in the park with a ball any more? For that matter, how many kids do you see playing in the street with a ball any more? None – not even if it's a back street.

The storylines of the preceding months are easier to understand once the circumstances in which they were written are explained. With the promises of a new management being shown, one by one, to be worthless, and with the pressures of working from home (having been dispatched from the office in order to cut costs) the need to find a storyline that might capture the attention sooner rather than later must have been overwhelming. Roy may have held his audience for as long as he did because of a patience and continuity when it came to conveying his adventures, but under the new management, it was clear that results were expected sooner rather than later, and shocks were prized over subtlety. Within weeks of Vosper departing, we discovered just how far-fetched things were set to become.

By April 1990, we should have been excited by the prospect of Rovers, with Race and Maclaren forming a mighty attacking threat, playing in yet another cup final, but we were distracted. Shortly before the game, Melchester announced that Radio One DJ Simon Mayo was to become their honorary vice-president. Suddenly we reappraised Martin Kemp and Steve Norman, and decided they weren't the absurd signings we'd first assumed. Daft, yes, but not, any more, the daftest. By comparison, Geoff Boycott was a reasonable choice and Sir Alf was completely obvious. Any moment soon, Rod Hull and Emu would be playing in central defence, and the lunacy would be complete. The obsession with celebrity was turning readers against the comic like never before in its history.

We loved Roy of the Rovers because it had stayed true to the idea Reg Eves first had, which Derek Birnage refined, Frank S. Pepper developed and Joe Colquhoun made real. It was meant to be, within boundaries, realistic, and when realism was temporarily suspended, it was supposed to be football-related. A simple creed, but for three decades it had managed to be exactly that, prospering as a result. Suddenly, rather than going onto *Celebrity Squares*, people were signing for Melchester Rovers, and the players all looked as if they'd spent the summer eating steroids and lifting weights. Everything seemed to be changing, and much of it seemed to be changing just for the sake of it.

Inevitably, Melchester won the trophy, which was Roy's eighth FA Cup, with a late goal from Andy Maclaren, and he lifted the trophy looking as proud as ever, wearing his Panini-sponsored shirt. The journey from a global sportswear brand to a sticker-book maker should have been further warning that all was not well. At the start of the season, Bruno Johnson, months after winning the FA Cup, decided to retire from football and return to university to finish his music degree. What with half of Spandau Ballet having just left, and with a DJ on the board, he probably would have maintained closer contact with his music if he'd stayed playing football.

Roy's battle against the hooligans continued, as Melchester prepared to return to Europe, with the ban on British clubs having been observed by a fictional, comic book side every bit as completely as it was by the real ones. At the end of the final game before Rovers headed off to Belgium to play their first European tie for five years, Roy addressed the Melchester fans over the public address system.

'So, if anyone has got any ideas about causing trouble . . . be warned! I'll find out who you are . . . and I will get you banned from football grounds for the rest of your life. People who treasure our national game don't want you. I don't want you.'

Which suggested, with his powers of detection, that had Melchester police left him to find the person who shot him all those years earlier, the crime might have been solved a lot sooner. Melchester won their first-round tie, winning 3-0 at home to overturn a first-leg defeat, but the comic seemed rather rudderless. The reasons were not hard to pinpoint.

Vosper was probably better off not having to witness at first hand the way things were going with *Roy of the Rovers*. David Hunt, who had edited *Eagle* and the Gary Lineker-inspired *Hot-Shot!*, arrived as editor, and set about trying to build the readership back to the levels it had once reached. There were, the thinking went, two ways of doing this. Either return to the way the comic ran in the 1970s, ditch the pop stars and coach accidents, and be true to the original idea, or up the ante and have a fresh disaster every week in a bid to compete with the more lurid titles, television programmes and video games which now made up boys' entertainment options. We knew which was the preferred choice.

On the way home from a cup game, in January 1991, Rovers were involved in a coach crash (again) and as a result, in addition to serious injuries to several other members of the squad, Blackie spent months in hospital. Once more, Roy had to rebuild the Rovers. Our doubts weren't so much triggered by the fact the crash had happened, or that the squad needed to be rebuilt, but that it happened so soon after the last coach crash the side had suffered.

We accepted recycled storylines because, to a degree, they had always been a part of Roy of the Rovers and, given the demands of producing weekly stories about one footballer and his colleagues, that was hard to get annoyed about. Suddenly, though, they were turning up so quickly, one after the other, that it felt like only a matter of months ago that the last incident of its type happened. We didn't mind that, after forty years, not every tale was truly unique, but repeating them while their first incarnation was still fresh in our minds was a little hard to take.

Roy pieced together a side of youth team players, who got Melchester through the next round, and then replaced them with the returning senior members of the squad, who promptly got them knocked out in the next. Even for Roy, the game still occasionally threw up something of a surprise, it seemed. They made it through to the semi-finals of the Cup Winners' Cup, only to go out to Dinamo Vlaznia, the snappily named but ultimately underwhelming Albanian side.

Once more, though, there was no sign of a sponsor. Panini had proved easier to remove than their stickers, which, if we were to examine our childhood bedrooms closely enough, would still be adhered to a surface somewhere, sticking more stubbornly than the tiles on the Space Shuttle. In their place came Fleetway, who published the comic. Putting an advert for an in-house service in a magazine is always a sign of a space-filler, but running a 'house ad' on the front of the Melchester shirts was perhaps taking things to a new level.

Roy Jnr had, by this time, descended from the tree house for long enough to prove to be a decent player, and was signed up by the Rovers to play alongside Blackie's son, Mark. Of course, they both had to operate under nicknames, hence they were known from then on as Rocky and Cracker. They would have sounded as if they belonged in a comic, even if they didn't. What both of them playing for the side did to combat claims of nepotism is unrecorded.

All such claims would have been rendered pointless had Roy accepted an offer to go and coach the American national side, but despite a contract which could have brought him almost $10m over its five-year duration, he felt unable to leave Melchester, and turned it down. It was yet another indicator of his longevity – not so long ago, or so it felt, he had discussed with Charlie Carter how the £50,000 the music business looked as if it might bring him would set him up for life. Suddenly, a figure not far removed from one hundred times that was not enough of a temptation to lure him from his club.

As another season ticked over, so another shirt sponsor rolled into town, as Sega replaced Fleetway. This was an intriguing move, given the threat that video games seemed to pose to the comic, but there was no denying that it was an impressive name to capture. Whether or not it was too late to change the comic's fortunes, we waited to see.

What immediately sprang to mind, as the 1991–92 season opened, was that a little bit of personal spite had appeared in the stories for the first time, which had never before been anywhere in evidence. Roy had scored 421 goals in his career to date, although as he was now thirty-five years old, the strike rate seemed, if anything, to be far lower than we remembered it. Besides, at least 400 of those 421 had been scored in the last three minutes of major finals or league title deciders.

His goalscoring feats had put him within fifteen or so of the all-time record holder, Dennis 'Chippy' Croker. Croker was now a TV pundit, and was known for using the phrase 'It's a silly ole sport, ennit?' He had thinning hair and a moustache, and was a thinly-veiled caricature of the former Tottenham and England striker, Jimmy Greaves. By now a real-life TV pundit, Greaves had battled alcoholism and managed to end his career before the huge money paid to modern players entered the game. Despite this, he remained entertaining and generous, and never let slip a moment of bitterness. He may have felt frustrated at the way life had turned out, but he was grateful for what he had, aware things could have been worse and, vast as they were, he never harked on about his own talents as a player.

Chippy was nicknamed well. He hated the plaudits handed out to Roy, seemed to believe that the game of football had been getting less attractive since the day he retired, and cut an insincere, carping figure. He was the opposite of Greaves, and it was, we felt even back then, an unfair and unkind representation of the man Chippy was clearly supposed to be. These days, it could have ended up in the libel courts. It was one of the less attractive storylines the comic ever ran, and given their proclivity for kidnap and car crashes, the competition for that particular title is fierce.

Having grown used to the way the writers could twist a tale all the way to the very end of the season, it came as no surprise to see that, by the last day of the campaign, Rovers needed to beat Kingsbay to win the title, Roy needed one more goal to beat Chippy's record, or that Roy had signed Chippy's son Matthew to play for the Rovers. He had also signed Mervyn Wallace's son, but by now we were accustomed to the idea that the Mel Park crèche had a side entrance that led directly into the home dressing room.

In the course of the season Chippy had bet £10,000 that Roy wouldn't replace him in the record books, which Roy matched with the inevitable proviso that the money would go to charity. Having just lost out on the best part of $10m, it wasn't a bet he was desperately keen to lose.

Roy, of course, scored in the last minute, latching onto a deflection from Matthew Croker, and claiming the record, the league title and £10,000 for the richest 'local youth club' in the world. As they trotted around parading the trophy, joined in their celebrations by Chippy, who added two-facedness to his already impressive list of character traits, little did we know that it would be the last time Roy Race, as a player, would ever delight in such a scene.

The 1992–93 season was far from happy, right from the start. Rovers had 'TSB' on their shirts, making the transition seamlessly from gaming to banking, and Roy, as he did from time to time, was falling out with a chairman who, as they did from time to time, was trying to win a battle of wills with his manager. Sir Jeremy Sinclair was an autocratic sort, who wanted things done his way, and only his way. The two of them fell out over player behaviour, which was an unlikely ground on which to be able to attack Roy, with his puritan approach to discipline and personnel. Eventually, in October, it became too much for Roy.

For the purposes of the comic, and in a bid to appear contemporary, Roy was interviewed by Sky Sports, who had just entered the world of football, floating the fledgeling Premier League on a tide of money that would change it for ever. Especially keen in recent years to chase a trend, the nation's oldest, most traditional footballer was giving 'interviews' to its newest, least traditional broadcaster. Richard Keys wore a yellow blazer, for reasons best known to the artist, Michael White, and didn't have nearly hairy enough hands; while Andy Gray, who had more hairs and fewer chins than the modern incarnation, adopted the knowing nod which has served him so well whenever trapped in camera shot as pre-match questions are being directed to the person sitting next to him. It was to them that Roy decided to announce that he was stepping down as manager. Both of them wore slightly vacant, wide-eyed expressions of surprise as Roy explained that he now wished only to play for the club, not manage it.

The directors tried to change his mind, but the toys were too far from the pram, and Roy was not being moved to change his mind. Roy wanted Mervyn Wallace to succeed him, but the board favoured Ralph Gordon, who Roy plainly felt was all image and no substance. He had won nothing in his ten years at Melboro, so perhaps the lack of substance was understandable. Gordon was said to be popular with players, and the choice of the man in the street. In many ways, with his inability to win the really important football matches yet considerable expertise at currying public favour, he became a blueprint for several managers over the next few years, right the way up to international level.

By December, Ralph, who we feared might be all image and no substance, had secured his new job and, under his style of play, Rovers were going through some erratic times. They scored plenty of goals, but conceded far too many while doing so, and despite the players urging him to listen to Roy, the new manager refused to change his ways. Eventually, in March 1993, the revolt happened. During a game against Redstoke, the Rovers played the way Roy used to encourage, and won 4-0. Ralph Gordon went mad and stormed to Sir Jeremy's office to demand Roy's sacking. It was, in the world of Roy of the Rovers, akin to his King Canute moment; it ended, predictably, with Gordon storming off and resigning, and Roy reinstated.

The players, led by Rocky, were in celebratory mood but, ever the professional, Roy realised that, if he was to be manager again, he had work to do. As he had sat in the dressing room, Charlie Madden, the chief scout, had told him about a young player called Darren Lewis, who played in the Bexley Homes League, and was worth a look. What's more, Lewis was playing that night, so if Roy took his helicopter he could get there to watch the match.

'He's going to crash that helicopter . . .' we said to ourselves, with the certainty of readers who had seen this sort of thing flagged up before. If the thing got into the air safely, there was no way it was getting back to earth in the same happy state – that much we knew for sure.

And, not for the first time, but probably for the last, we were right. We didn't even know he had a helicopter until the caption decided to inform us that 'Roy, who held a private pilot's licence, had been looking forward to the trip'. How could he have been? He didn't know he was going until an hour ago! When did he get this licence? Why weren't we told he was getting it? How can you drop these bombshells on us? It was all headed one way, and it wasn't a promising one, either.

It was, we feared, the last Racey's Rocket we'd ever see, when it ploughed out of the sky in a ball of flames. As the crowds gathered outside Melchester General, they chanted Roy's name, and waved a sea of red and yellow scarves. One child squirmed his way to the front, where he was held back by a policeman, dressed like an extra from *Dixon of Dock Green*. It was 1992, and policemen didn't dress like that any more, but he was a sympathetic one and as such the artist obviously decided he had to look old-fashioned. It's hard to clasp a terrified and grieving youngster warmly to a stab vest, after all. As the family gathered, the fan could take no more.

'He's not going to die, is he, Rocky? Promise me!!!' the youngster implored.

Rocky paused on the hospital steps, before delivering a response that wasn't exactly designed to fill us with optimism for hopes of Roy's recovery.

'I'll promise you one thing! Whatever happens, the name of Roy Race will be around for a long time to come! Rocky is just my nickname! I'm a Melchester player, and I wear the number nine shirt, just like Dad! Don't ever forget that . . .!'

It was intriguing. Instead of a message of hope and confidence in the ability of the medical team, Rocky, whose father had only just plunged out of the sky, was telling everyone not to worry, because he was there and, after all, he was the future. He didn't tell us to stop going on about Roy, and talk about himself instead, but he might as well have done. If we'd been in the Melchester police, we'd have had him arrested there and then.

We weren't depressed about the plunge our hero had taken, because for the vast majority of people it was all over already. What surprised us though wasn't so much the decline of something that had seemed such a solid part of childhood, but the lemming-like surge our favourite comic had suddenly made towards the edge of the cliff. From the moment pop stars and DJs started turning up at our club, the comic equivalent of an assisted suicide was being played out in front of our disbelieving (and disapproving) eyes.

We would eventually wait for six long months to find out if Roy had survived, much of it amid an information blackout, wondering what was going on, because our comic had suddenly disappeared. The last issue, which had arrived on our doorsteps in March 1993, was the one in which he plummeted to the ground and, as if to provide us with a hint, the front cover was completely black, save for a small, oval picture of Roy in the centre. It was there, having begun to set up potentially the most exciting storyline of its entire existence, and then suddenly it was gone. How had it all come to this? Even Barrie Tomlinson finds it difficult to understand.

I do look back, still, and there is a part of me which to this day can't work out quite how things all went so wrong as to leave a comic that had been bought by so many people going out of business, or at least shutting down. It just seems incredible that it could have hit such highs and then reached such depths, but there are reasons, to be fair to the people in charge, why it went so badly wrong.

What I think ultimately hurt the comic was that computers came along, and suddenly children weren't doing the things they always had. Roy was based on quite a romantic idea – the idea of going over the park, playing football, and living out the lives of your heroes. It was about kids who played in the street with a battered old ball, and every time one of them scored, in his head he was Roy Race.

Suddenly, computers came along and they weren't going out and getting muddy knees any more, though. Football became a thing you played on the television screen, using your computer, rather than something you played in the park. Once they lost interest in football, they lost interest in *Roy of the Rovers*, because it was a comic about real football, not football the way it appeared on a computer screen.

Nobody who talks to him would accuse Tomlinson of self-serving reasons for his approach. His regret at the turn things took is all too clear, but his concerns stretch beyond the simple matter of the closure of a comic. He is not, after all, a man who achieved what he did without a shrewd appreciation of the bigger picture.

One of the other changes that people didn't seem to appreciate was that, as the readership became more sophisticated, and everyone seemed to be growing up a bit more quickly, they wanted stories that were more realistic. They started to rebel against stories that were far-fetched, which was odd, because comic stories are, by nature, far-fetched. When they stop smiling along with the jokes, though, and get annoyed by them, it's a problem.

You couldn't do the kidnap stories now, because people would start to protest. Back when we ran it, people just accepted that it was only a comic strip, there was no offence intended, and it wasn't supposed to be taken too seriously.

And he's absolutely right. When we were younger and the world was a more innocent place, the comic wasn't something to which we attached huge importance, outside of the immediate requirement of entertaining us. We didn't want huge meaning to be interwoven through every story and, apart from Roy's determination to remind us each week of the importance of fair play and maintaining decent standards, we didn't want social responsibility to arrive as a side order to our football. Yet, as Tomlinson explains, despite keeping things as simple as they did, the figures, and the successes of *Roy of the Rovers*, speaks for itself.

In terms of scale, comics were a different world back then. We were selling 450,000 copies of *Roy of the Rovers* each week at its absolute peak, and when you take into consideration the 'pass on' readership – the extra people who read each copy without buying it – then you could very easily assume, and you'd be fairly accurate, that we were getting about a million readers a week. That's a lot, by any standards.

Ian Vosper, reviewing his own career, reaches a very similar conclusion.

'I was working on *Scorcher* when it closed down, and we were still doing 125,000 copies a week, which by today's standards is a staggering number. *Shoot* used to sell something phenomenal, but the last I heard, I think it might have become a monthly and it's down to 40,000. I suppose the market has just reached saturation point now, because there are so many of them.'

In June 2008 *Shoot* closed, too, selling a little over 35,000 copies a month by the end – another era coming to an undignified close. Things have changed so much in the modern era that a return to that sort of volume seems highly unlikely, not to say impossible. It's certainly difficult to imagine it happening at the present time, although, with typical foresight, Tomlinson is unwilling to write off the chances of such a return ever happening.

> At the moment, nobody's ever going to come close to that sort of figure again. Just not even close, but it's always dangerous to say that something's never going to happen again, because when you do, it's got a strange habit of turning around and doing exactly that. It's difficult to see it happening, though, I admit.
>
> Roy stood for something, and after I left, and when the more extreme storylines started coming in, it did seem very sad that some of the new marketing ideas people came up with were so much more extreme and less imaginative than the ones we'd had. I mean, having Roy lose his foot in a helicopter crash! It's guaranteed to bring in a few headlines, I know, but you can hardly repeat the trick, can you? Once it's gone, it's gone, and how did anyone ever think that they were going to rebuild the comic from there?

Ah, yes, the missing foot. We were coming to that. Or, as it would be more accurate to say, we finally got round to that some six months later, in September 1993, when, after the chopper first crashed its way into the ground, we found out what had happened. Roy had come back from many injuries in his time, but even with the hugely over-muscled frame he had developed over recent years, a complete recovery from an amputated foot seemed unlikely.

Roy of the Rovers, we were being told, in no uncertain terms, had reached the end of its life, at least in the current format, and, as if to underline the point, our hero had his foot cut off. Having discovered this in September, we then waited until October for further news – not because of another unscheduled delay, but because our fix of Roy of the Rovers would, from now on, arrive monthly, not weekly. Having maimed the lead character, and left the readership a nice, six-month gap to go off and find other things to read, it was returning with a central character who could no longer play football, and then only monthly, rather than weekly. Had the publishers tried to sabotage it, they could hardly have done a better job.

Roy moved to Italy to manage AC Monza, where, bereft of ideas that might earn them a few headlines, a bit of attention and a few extra readers, they killed off Penny in a car crash. Poor Penny never really had much luck, but this was harsh, by any standards. Thousands of young boys thought she was a villainous figure, dedicated to stopping Roy playing football and trying to make his life difficult. She left impressionable minds deeply suspicious of women, who existed only, we decided, to curtail our fun. And then, with one, final ironic twist, by the time we grew old enough to know better, they killed her off.

During this time, Rocky stayed and played for Melchester, reverting once more to the 'two storylines at once' tactic they had adopted when Roy made his brief move to Walford. As Vosper remembered, this had been difficult to keep up with at the time, as a weekly. How they thought it was going to work as a monthly we were never quite sure, but when it finally ground to a halt, after less than two years, we greeted the decision with as much relief as sadness. Roy should, like all champions, have gone out at the top, in his pomp and with his glories still around him. He was fictional, after all, it wasn't that hard to arrange.

Instead they messed around with celebrities, merged and separated storylines with confusing speed and, despite the fact he kept winning games until the end, managed to somehow wear thin the affection we felt for Roy. One dramatic twist too many had exposed the fact that the writers had lost their touch and, having been messed around already, the audience was in unforgiving mood. That particular aspect of its downfall was all the sadder for being avoidable. It is a point Vosper recognises all too well.

Roy was all about good timing. He came to attention first of all in the 1950s when there was no television to distract from him, and people read for pleasure. Things change, though, and there's less innocence now. These days kids don't want to be kids for a split second longer than they have to. As soon as they've got a chance, they want to be adults, and that means doing without things like comic book stories, which is a shame.

There was also a greater familiarity with footballers back then. They were heroes, the same way they ever have been, but they were never untouchable, because that's not the way the world developed. These days they're very remote from real life, some of them, and the nature of the hero worship has changed.

Vosper is absolutely right about this, and it remains one of the major reasons why the game has changed so fundamentally. As a child, I could stand by the players' entrance at Charlton and collect autographs as the players strolled in before the game and trudged out after it (we weren't a very successful team – too relaxed before kick off, too depressed after it). These days, stewards escort the players from their cars and walk them through a cordoned-off area of car park, before ushering them through gates, away from view, lest they be forced to sign the autograph book of a youngster whose ticket helped to pay their wages.

If quizzed, they occasionally explain that they fear the autograph will appear on Internet auction sites, largely because this is a reason they've heard parroted by some of the world's most famous players. The irony, of course, is that some of our players wouldn't attract a bid on those sites if they put themselves up for auction, let alone their autographs, but it has become the accepted thing to be too important to sign, and this is a convenient excuse. Footballers, as Vosper says, have in many cases grown away from the fans, and the game has a different, less inclusive feel as a result. What is the point of having heroes who don't want you anywhere near them?

It would be lovely, and somehow strangely life-affirming, to discover that there was still a market for a *Roy of the Rovers* comic in the modern world, but I fear that times have moved on too far.

It would have to exist as a 'standalone' title, and not be lumped in with something else, featuring in another publication as a gimmick. Having broken free from *Tiger*, the story now, surely, either exists on its own two feet (or one, if we're being tasteless and pedantic) or not at all.

For the sake of completeness, it should be recorded that Roy spent four years managing the Rovers through thick and thin (and by that time it was more thin than thick) inside the covers of *Match of the Day* magazine. He won a further FA Cup as a manager, but it was a poor impression of the comic in its pomp – akin to watching a tribute band and claiming to have seen the original. The Roy who appeared in *Match of the Day* bore little relation to the one who was first spotted by Alf Leeds, and nobody was going to convince us that he did. As 'Trigger' from *Only Fools and Horses* once recounted: 'I've had the same broom for fifteen years. It's only had eight new heads and nine new handles.'

Roy of the Rovers had been so special because it had avoided the vagaries of fashion and trend, and stuck to what it did best. It lives on through a splendid series of books, where selections of his adventures are grouped together and reproduced between hard-back, A4 covers and also through an affectionate and wonderful official website, but a celebrated past is no substitute for a promising future.

Vosper is right to observe that football is a very different game in the modern era, and Tomlinson is absolutely correct when he reflects that Roy's success was down to remaining true to an idea, and yet neither think a comeback is likely. It would be lovely to be able to construct an argument against their slightly pessimistic viewpoint – lovely, but impossible. Football has made its bed, plumped up with unevenly distributed piles of cash, and it must lie on it. Aside from a thunderous shot and a never-say-die attitude, Roy needed two things for his adventures to find a welcoming home: a degree of humour and a large slice of irony. The mood of the day provided ample portions of both, despite the relative poverty of the game.

Once upon a time, we understood that there were certain aspects of football which could exist only in comics and dreams, so we bought the comics, dreamed the dreams and never felt short-changed. These days, marketing men tell us that television can make the dreams real, and money can ensure events on the pitch can be just as colourful and dynamic as ever they were in the pages of our comic heroes.

Roy always kept his end of the bargain, though, because fiction has a happy habit of turning out exactly the way the writer wishes it. No matter how many promises they make, and how slick their production becomes, whether the televised game of the 21st century can live up to the same promise remains to be seen. Somehow I doubt it.

Somewhere on a dusty shelf of comic book heaven, Roy is sitting, along with Alf Leeds, who plucked him from obscurity half a century ago, and looking to see who, if anyone, might arrive to take his place. They may have a very long wait.

INDEX

Rawson, Harvey 154, 157
Real Santana 159–60
Reeves, 'Bomber' 67
Revie, Don 18, 127, 129–30
Richard, Cliff 211
Richards, Rob 156
Robson, Bobby 167
Rogan, Rockfist 23
Rooney, Wayne 59
Rover 21
Rowley, Andy 220
Roy of the Rovers (comic) 7–8, 9, 11, 74, 76–7, 83, 89, 90, 119–22, 201–2, 214, 221–7
Roy of the Rovers *see* Race, Roy
Rush, Ian 141
Russell, Tony 195–6
Rythoven Olympic 93–4

'Safest Hands in Soccer, The' 190–1
San Angino 47
Sandilands, Phil 16
Schiaffino, Julio 183, 186, 187
Schonved 53
Scorcher 201–2
Seaford Athletic 93
Seegrun, Johan 128, 129
Shackelton, Len 17
Sharp, Larry 106
Sheffield Wednesday 20
Shermall United 50–2
Shevnik Sparta 67–8
Shoot 236–7
Sinatra, Frank 22
Sinclair, Jeremy 232
Sleeford Town 109
Smith, Jim 212
Smith, Paul 72
Smith, Ted 37, 38, 43
Soon, Pak 166
Southampton 112
Spangler, Sammy 108–9
Sque, David 80–4, 101, 165, 210, 211, 212
Stalzburg 54
Stambridge City 142–4, 166
Standard Liege 94
Standard Wasserdram 94–6
Stenning, Andrew 50, 51
Stevens, Pete 42
Stewart, Gordon 189–91
Stewart, Rick 191

Stokes, Dick 37
Storme, Tony 101–2, 105
Styles, Andy 166
Sutton, Charlie 170, 221

Thomas, Clive 140
Thompson, Andrew 107
Tiger 7, 9, 10, 11, 20–1, 22, 35, 73, 74, 75, 81, 83, 89, 119
Tomlinson, Alan 59, 64
Tomlinson, Barrie 74–80, 81–5, 120–1, 147, 178, 187, 197–8, 201–18, 235–6, 237
'Tommy's Troubles' 194–7
Tottenham Hotspur 52–3, 100
Trevillion, Paul 101
Trudgeon, Jumbo ('Lordy') 62–3, 105, 108
Tupper, Alf 21
Tynecaster 163

Victor 10, 21
Vigors, Lance 50–1
Villar, Carlos 159, 160
Viollet, Dennis 50
Vosper, Ian 63–4, 147–8, 152, 153, 156, 177, 183, 187, 188, 195, 196–7, 201–18, 221–7, 236–7, 238–9, 240

Walford Rovers 153–4, 157
Wallace, Mervyn 102, 103, 119, 123–4, 132–3, 134, 143, 149, 150, 233
Watford 18, 158
Wayne, Dan 192–4
West, Terry 96
Westbury Town 135
Wharton, Arthur 152–3
White, Chalkie 68, 100, 102
White, Michael 165, 181
Wilson, Bob 161
Wilton, Hal 20
Wizard 21
Wolverhampton Wanderers 56
Woodburn Spartan 93
Woods, Tiger 101
Wright, Billy 22, 56

Young, Christopher 59

Zalmo 142
Zaragosa 132